THE
VOIC.
for LIFE
GUIDE TO
MUSICIANSHIP

A complete resource for the teaching and assessment of aural awareness and sight-reading in the Voice for Life *scheme*

CONTENTS

THE VOICE FOR LIFE GUIDE TO MUSICIANSHIP

Project editor: Tim Ruffer
Written by Anthony Marks and Chris Fay

Voice for Life was developed by Leah Perona-Wright in consultation with experienced practitioners from across the UK and beyond. These include: Gordon Appleton, Colin Baldy, Roger Brice, Chris Broughton, Lesley Cooper, June Cox, Colin Davey, Paul Ellis, Peter Futcher, Susan Gardner, Ameral Gunson, John Harper, Esther Jones, Sally Leeming, Hilary Llystyn Jones, Sue Moore, David Ogden, Keith Roberts, Sheila Robertson, Ben Saunders, John Wardle, Alistair Warwick, Geoff Weaver and Jenevora Williams.
We are grateful for their contributions.

Design and layout: Anthony Marks
Music origination: David Iliff
Editorial assistance: Julian Elloway

Much of the music in this book comes from a variety of RSCM publications. We are very grateful to the composers whose work we have used. The preparatory exercises were composed by Chris Fay.

Printed in Great Britain by Halstan Group Limited

ISBN 978-0-85402-216-8

THE ROYAL SCHOOL OF CHURCH MUSIC
19 The Close, Salisbury, Wiltshire, SP1 2EB
Tel: +44 (0)1722 424848   Fax: +44 (0)1722 424849
E-mail: education@rscm.com Website: www.rscm.com
Registered charity no. 312828

Distributed exclusively in North America by GIA Publications, Inc.
7404 S. Mason Ave., Chicago, IL 60638
Toll free: 800 442 1358   Website: www.giamusic.com

If you have used the *Voice for Life* scheme for a while, you will know that it is about much more than teaching people to sing, important as that is. It uses singing as the core activity in a range of contexts to develop well-rounded choral musicians. As they work through the modules and levels, singers acquire vocal technique, music theory and history, and an understanding of church music – as well social, organizational and pastoral skills.

At the heart of *Voice for Life* is a requirement to sing both by ear and from notation, and a requirement to understand what is being sung. The activities in the workbooks ask students to sing, to listen, to read, to identify, to reproduce music; in short they emphasize good musicianship. At each level, the acquisition of musicianship and related skills is systematically assessed by means of targets.

Developing a 'good ear' is essential for any musician, but it takes years of practice and experience. Cultivating aural awareness will help singers to read music more easily – especially if they are singing a harmony part – and will help develop musical memory and all-round musicianship. Aural and theory combine to help musicians understand the notes and details on the score in front of them – and to realize them in performance. Progress takes time and, above all, regular practice.

Another essential skill for musicians is an ability to sight-read. It provides access to a world of repertoire that would otherwise be hidden. Choirs will learn new pieces much more quickly if their members can read the music from notation. Valuable rehearsal time will be saved which can then be used to improve the choral blend, intonation, ensemble, phrasing and delivery of text and meaning. Yet, for a number of reasons, vocal and instrumental teachers alike often neglect to develop sight-reading skills. In a choral context, it is often brushed aside because of a perceived lack of time in rehearsal.

The *Voice for Life Guide to Musicianship* is intended to help you – whether you are a choir trainer or director, a conductor or a singing teacher – to develop in your singers the fundamental musicianship skills of aural awareness and sight-reading. It will help you to prepare your singers for the *Voice for Life* aural and sight-reading assessments at White, Light Blue, Dark Blue, Red and Yellow levels, and the three RSCM Awards (Bronze, Silver and Gold).

Enjoy *Voice for Life*!

Andrew Reid
Director, RSCM

Icons   The icons in this book mean:

 Important information

 Something to think about

 More information in the singer's workbook

 A listening activity

 A singing activity

 A clapping activity

 Refer to the singer's copy

The aural tests at White, Light Blue, Dark Blue, Red and Yellow levels
For the 'colour' levels of *Voice for Life*, as a choir trainer you will probably run the tests yourself in order to fill in the target boxes in the workbooks. You can do this as formally or informally as you wish, according to how you work with your singers.

At the lower levels, if you incorporate aural training into general choir practice, you can assess singers for many of the targets without their even being aware that a test is taking place. This is suitable if you run an informal scheme or have singers who are intimidated by formal testing. However you may prefer to test your singers (when you feel they are ready) at an appointed time. This certainly gives a sense of occasion, and is good preparation for the RSCM award exams. At the higher levels, testing is more formal anyway – it is harder to do it surreptitiously.

Whichever approach you take, singers need to be familiar with the structure of each test and what is expected of them. Each test corresponds directly to one of the Module B targets listed at the back of each workbook ('The singer has read and understood the music theory in Module B and can ...'). Refer singers to these to make sure that they understand what is being assessed.

There is no formal script for the tests, but with practice singers should get used to their structure (for example how many bars of pulse you will clap; when you will sound the tonic and key chord; and so on). The material for each test at each level contains:

- details of what is being tested (technical requirements, scope and limits)

- some specimen tests (if appropriate) to show the format and required level

- some hints to help you prepare your singers

- details of how to deliver the test and assess its outcomes

- test materials to use for the actual target assessments (these are indicated by a vertical double line in the margin, as shown on the left)

Aural tests as part of the RSCM awards
The RSCM awards are externally examined and moderated. Visit **www.rscm.com** to consult the syllabus. Each award tests what has been learned at the previous *Voice for Life* 'colour' level. The Bronze and Silver award sections of this book contain:

- details of what is being tested (technical requirements, scope and limits)

- some specimen tests (if appropriate) to show the format and required level

- hints to help you prepare your singers

- detailed information about what happens in the exam so that during preparation you can replicate the tests as closely as possible

'Colour' targets are tested over time, as often as needed, by a familiar choir trainer in a familiar place. Award exams, on the other hand, are special events that may place candidates under pressure. While some individual award aural tests may appear slightly less taxing than their 'colour' equivalents, taken as a whole the exams are an independent, holistic measure of the skills that have been acquired to that point.

There are no separate aural tests for the Gold award (see page 186 for more information about the Gold award exam).

The sight-reading tests at Light Blue, Dark Blue, Red and Yellow levels
There are no sight-reading tests at White level. From Light Blue onwards, the sight-reading targets (listed at the back of each workbook) gradually increase in complexity.

Sight-reading needs a more formal approach than aural tests. Again, singers need to know what to expect. In most cases choir trainers are required to select a test passage suitable for the range of the individual singer. This book contains sample tests, preparatory passages, and test materials. Extra downloadable resources (see below) are available to give to singers when preparing or testing them.

The material for each sight-reading test at each level contains:

- details of what is being tested (technical requirements, scope and limits)
- some example tests (if appropriate) to show the format and required level
- some hints to help you prepare your singers
- details of how to deliver the test and assess its outcomes
- assessment materials, indicated by a vertical double line in the margin, as shown on the left (do not share these with singers before their tests)

Sight-reading tests as part of the RSCM awards
The RSCM awards are externally examined and moderated. Visit **www.rscm.com** to consult the syllabus. Each award tests what has been learned at the previous *Voice for Life* 'colour' level. In the Bronze, Silver and Gold award sections of this book, you will find the following sight-reading materials:

- details of what will be tested (technical requirements, scope and limits)
- some specimen tests
- hints to help you prepare your singers
- detailed information about what happens in the exam so that during preparation you can replicate the tests as closely as possible

'Colour' targets are tested over time, as often as needed, by a familiar choir trainer in a familiar place. Award exams, on the other hand, are special events that may place candidates under pressure. While some individual award sight-reading tests may appear slightly less taxing than their 'colour' equivalents, taken as a whole the exams are an independent, holistic measure of the skills that have been acquired to that point.

The downloadable singer's copies
From Light Blue level onwards, you will need to show singers a separate copy for the sight-reading tests (and some aural tests). At **www.rscm.com/musicianship** you will find downloadable documents for each level and each award. These contain all the materials singers need for the tests themselves and for any preparatory exercises. The icon on the left directs you to these copies. Tests are grouped according to their page numbers in this book. For full information about how to use this resource, see page 200.

It is advisable to print only the pages your singers need for specific tests. There is no restriction on the number of pages you may print from these documents.

WHITE LEVEL

Introduction

The aural tests at White level are concerned with the fundamental elements of music training – pitch and pulse. There are five simple tests:

a) to match the pitch of a note played on the piano (within an appropriate range)

b) to sing five notes that move up and down by step (at an appropriate pitch) after hearing them on the piano

c) to identify which of two notes is higher or lower in pitch

d) to sing back a simple one-bar melody within a five-note range

e) to clap the pulse of a familiar song or hymn

The exercises in Module A of the White workbook (pages 10–12) will prepare singers technically for these tests, and familiarize them with the types of sounds they are expected to reproduce. The theory activities in Module B (pages 14–22) will supply the vocabulary and concepts singers need to understand what is being asked of them.

Preparing for the tests

To a certain extent, singing any music develops listening skills. Singing scales, clapping rhythms and pitching notes will all feature at beginner level, and are useful preparation for the levels to come. To help singers get used to the idea of reproducing what they hear, regularly ask them to sing things back to you – try to listen and (within reason) correct mistakes.

Some beginners – primary age singers in particular – find it difficult to pitch notes from a piano because their ears hear some of the piano's overtones more loudly than is normal. This then confuses them as to the real pitch of a note. If you suspect this is happening, try asking the singer to respond to whistled or sung notes instead of the piano. This will nearly always be more successful and more encouraging! Patient training of the ear to recognize the true pitch of a note will be needed.

Delivering the tests

Some young singers may be intimidated by tests, others motivated by them. At White level it isn't necessary to test formally unless you feel it would be useful. As you work with individual singers you will be able to tell whether they are able to achieve each of the targets listed above. Formal details of the tests are unnecessary, but here are a few hints:

• Whether or not the notes you are playing are to be reproduced by the singer, always choose pitches close to the singer's own range.

• Do not hurry the tests. Play everything at a leisurely pace, repeating if necessary.

• For test (c), ask 'Which note is lower?' or 'Which note is higher?' before playing two different pitches; pause briefly; then play them again. Then wait for the answer.

Test (d) can contain as few as three notes. Sound the key chord and the tonic before starting. The melody to be reproduced should:

- always be in a major key

- always start and end on the tonic

- be one bar in length

- contain simple note values

 For test (e) choose a song or hymn that you know is familiar to the singer. Select something with a simple time signature and a medium-to-fast tempo. For this test, a singer should be able to begin clapping fairly soon after you start playing, and hold the pulse clearly and confidently throughout.

 Sight-reading at White level
There are no formal sight-reading tests at White level. However, some useful preparatory work for the next levels can be done at this stage, particularly in the context of showing singers what music notation looks like. This activity also links to the final three Module B targets at White level, which concern the ability to identify and understand elements of written notation.

Try to produce actual music for your singers to look at. Avoid the temptation simply to give them the words and teach the music by ear. This method may be cheaper (and in the short term, easier), but it does not allow singers to see the shapes the notes make around the words they are singing. It also encourages the worst practice (often called 'note-bashing') where singers will parrot back what they hear played or sung to them without reflection.

 It is likely that you will use scales and arpeggios as warm-ups, and to test and improve the tone and range of your singers. These patterns are basic elements in music and crucial to the reading of it, so show your choir the notation for them and similar exercises. (Make a sheet of them in various keys, or write them on a board.) Encourage your choir to follow the music as they sing. Simple tasks like following the notes with a finger are a first step towards reading music. They reinforce the connections between how the music sounds and how it looks when written down.

 Bear in mind too that although singers are not expected to read music at White level, they will learn to identify certain notational features (time signatures, notes of different lengths, barlines, repeats, rudimentary dynamics, bar numbers and so on). The Module B targets (see page 34 of the White level workbook) test familiarity with these, requiring singers to: find their place in a score using bar numbers; identify their voice part in a score; and identify common musical symbols, note values and dynamics (listed on page 35 of the workbook). From time to time, when singers are looking at printed music, you could ask them to identify some of these items.

Finally, try to incorporate aspects of sight-reading into choir rehearsals when learning new music, rather than having your singers simply copy the piano. In this way, choirs come to view sight-reading as an integral part of learning music and not just an exam exercise.

LIGHT BLUE LEVEL

Introduction
The four aural tests at Light Blue level assess singers' ability to: reproduce simple melodies and rhythms after hearing them; sing a major scale after hearing its key chord and tonic; and tap the beat and identify the metre of a short extract.

The 'Tone and range' section of Module A in the Light Blue workbook (page 9) will prepare singers technically for these tests, and familiarize them with the types of sounds they are expected to reproduce. The theory activities in Module B supply the vocabulary and concepts singers need to understand what is being asked of them.

Light Blue aural test (a)
To sing back a simple melody. The key chord and tonic (starting note) will first be sounded and the pulse indicated. The melody will be played twice. The melody will:

- always be in a major key

- always begin and end on the tonic

- always be two bars long

- always be in 2/4 or 3/4

- contain mainly stepwise movement up and down from (and either side of) the tonic, but also leaps of a third

- contain only (undotted) crotchets and quavers

Here are some sample tests. Use the criteria above to create more of your own for practice purposes. For the test itself, use the passages on page 13.

Preparing for the test
This test develops memory and pitching. Play the phrases at an appropriate pitch and expect accurate tuning and rhythm in response. Preparatory work might include accurate pitching of a few notes from a phrase, or you could devise simpler phrases and slowly increase the complexity until the test level is reached.

It can help if you encourage singers to respond immediately with no break in the pulse. Suggest they tap the pulse as you play, and continue tapping as they sing. Or encourage them to hum along as you play, before breaking out into a more focused sound for their response.

Delivering the test

Use one of the tests below that suits your singer's range: you may need to play tests an octave lower for tenors and basses. If you want to use a particular test that may be beyond the range of a singer, it is acceptable to transpose it into another key.

Sound the key chord first, and then the tonic. Sound two bars of the pulse by tapping with one hand. Then play the melody twice. After this, indicate that the singer should respond.

Assess the accuracy of the response. Listen for accurate reproduction of pitches and rhythms, and a sense of security and confidence. If you are unsure about the result, test the singer with a second passage.

Light Blue level: aural test (a)

Light Blue aural test (b)
To clap back the rhythm of a simple melody. The pulse will first be indicated and the passage played twice. The melody will:

- be in a major key

- end on the tonic

- be two bars long

- be in 2/4, 3/4 or 4/4

- contain crotchets, quavers and minims, and may contain the occasional dotted crotchet/quaver pattern

Passages for this test may contain elements (such as simple dotted rhythms and certain intervals) which are beyond the scope of the formal theory of Module B, as sometimes at this level singers will be required to clap features of music that they may not yet be able to name, sing or describe.

Here are some sample tests. Use the criteria above to create more of your own for practice purposes. For the test itself, use the passages on page 15.

Preparing for the test
This test develops musical memory and rhythmic response. Preparatory work might include asking singers to clap one-bar rhythms, or even shorter patterns, to a pulse. Expect accurate and immediate responses, with no hurrying. Encourage singers to tap the pulse as you play and as they respond, with no break between the two.

There are plenty of other ways to develop rhythmic facility in your singers. These include clapping games (where, to a pulse, singers copy a short rhythm that you clap to them, or share rhythms in pairs); clapping the rhythm of words to a pulse (write some rhythmic phrases on the board); and gesture games where singers move in time to a pulse. Some music teachers give entire lessons to a pulse (provided electronically) so that everything takes place in rhythm.

Delivering the test

Tap two bars of the pulse with one hand. Then, maintaining the pulse, play the passage twice, leaving two bars of pulse between each playing. After this, indicate that the singer should respond and continue to keep the pulse. Assess the accuracy of the response. Listen for accurate reproduction of the rhythm and a sense of security and confidence.

Light Blue level: aural test (b)

01

02

03

04

05

06

07

08

09

10

Light Blue aural test (c)
To sing, unaccompanied, a major scale (ascending and descending) of one octave. The key chord and tonic note will first be sounded. Singers may use any syllable that feels comfortable. The scale should be sung at a pace which enables the singer to get up and down in one breath.

The chords below indicate the suitable ranges for singers at this level.

Soprano

Alto

Tenor

For newly changed tenor voices, begin no higher than E

Bass

Preparing for the test
Designed to develop good intonation, this is perhaps the hardest test at this level. Singers will be familiar with scales from warm-up exercises, but may be challenged when asked to sing them alone and in tune. Until intonation is secure, preparatory work might include singing up and down the first five notes of the scale, or down from the upper tonic to the fifth below and back up.

Encourage singers to keep the tonic note in their head as they sing. They may find it useful to sing the notes of the scale to the numbers 1 to 8 (ascending) and 8 to 1 (descending). There is more about this on pages 25–27 of the Light Blue workbook.

Delivering the test
Once the singer knows what is expected, simply sound the chord and the key note. To achieve this target, singers should respond with a good tone, and with sensible breathing to support the top notes.

Light Blue aural test (d)

To tap or clap the pulse of a passage of music and state whether it is in 2 or 3 time. The passage will be played twice. On the second playing the singer should tap the pulse, stressing where the strong beat falls, then state whether the music is in 2 or 3 time. The music will:

- be in 2 or 3 time

- last about eight bars (long enough for the singer to identify the pulse)

- be of a tempo and style where the pulse is clear and easy to identify

Preparing for the test

This test develops listening and rhythm skills. To help your singers practise, any music with an apparent beat in simple 2 or 3 time is appropriate, at any tempo. (Bear in mind though that inexperienced singers may have problems identifying the beat if the music is very fast or very slow.)

When playing, lightly stress the first beat of each bar. Make the pulse clear but play musically without overemphasis. At first, simply ask singers to clap along (as they did for test (e) at White level). Then ask them to identify the stressed beats and count 'One' (or clap more loudly) on each of these. They can then work out how many beats there are between each stressed beat, and thus whether the music is in 2 or 3 time.

If a singer has continued difficulty with this activity, it may not be a problem of hearing but one of comprehension. Check that he or she understands pulses, beats and time signatures. Refer to pages 19–21 of the Light Blue workbook.

Delivering the test

Once the singer knows what is expected, simply play the music twice. (The passages for this test are shown below and overleaf.) To achieve this target, singers should respond by clapping the beats clearly, emphasizing the first beat of each bar. After clapping, they should state whether there are two or three beats in a bar.

Light Blue level: aural test (d)

`01`

Lively

Introduction

The two sight-reading tests at Light Blue level assess singers' ability to clap and sing simple rhythms and melodies from notation. The notational elements tested will be familiar to singers who have worked on the theory section of Module B, and the tests are well within the limits of the concepts introduced there.

Light Blue sight-reading test (a)

To clap a rhythm from sight, or sing it on one note (on any vowel). The rhythm will:

- be in 2/4, 3/4, 4/4 or 2/2

- contain a maximum of four bars

- feature (undotted) minims, crotchets and quavers without rests

Here are some sample tests. Use the criteria above to create more of your own for practice purposes. For the test itself, use the passages on page 22.

Preparing for the test

Rhythm is as much a part of sight-reading as pitch – if not more so, as rhythm is central to the crucial ability to keep going even after making errors. Rhythmic security is the all-important first element of sight-reading and should be practised separately from pitch, at least to begin with. This is why there are separate rhythm-reading tests at Light Blue and Dark Blue levels.

The ability to recognize time signatures and reproduce rhythms by ear – as tested in aural tests (b) and (d) – is vital to rhythm reading. When teaching rhythm recognition, use rhythms that are consistent with the music theory introduced at Light Blue level: the simple time signatures of 2/4, 3/4, 4/4, 2/2, and note values of quavers, crotchets, minims and semibreves. (There is more about this on page 21.)

Check that your singers understand the idea of pulses, beats and time signatures, and also that they can recognize and identify the necessary notational elements. (Refer to Module B and the reference section of the Light Blue workbook if necessary.)

On the next page, you will find some detailed procedures for practising rhythm reading with your singers.

Practising rhythm reading

Here is an example of how to approach a rhythm-reading exercise with your singers, using passage 05 on the previous page.

1) Choose an exercise and show it to your singers

Write this example on a board or use print-outs from the downloadable singer's copy. Let them study it for a while. (It might be useful to ask them to identify notational elements of the music – refer to pages 42–43 of the workbook if necessary.)

2) Establish the pulse

Clap or use a metronome, and then ask singers to count each 4/4 beat aloud in time to the pulse.

3) Count the pulse, clap the rhythm

While counting aloud, singers should clap the rhythm (in the example below, everything except the beats shown in brackets needs a clap). When they are confident, ask them to stop counting aloud, but to keep clapping while they 'think' the beats.

Additional activities for rhythm reading

Divide the singers into two groups. Ask one group to count the pulse while the other claps the rhythm. Then swap the groups over. Once singers are secure, suggest that they *clap* the pulse and *sing* the rhythm on one note. Can they move smoothly between this and the procedure described in (3) above?

Further examples

Below are examples of suitable rhythms for this level in 3/4 and 2/2, which you can use in the same way. You can also make up your own rhythms. Hymn books or collections of traditional songs are useful resources for simple rhythms, too.

Possible pitfalls

Some singers will be confused by the concept of 2/2 time, and why it is different from 4/4. This is perhaps the most awkward problem with rhythm at this level. It is necessary to address this here because, while the aural tests at this level do not require singers to make a formal distinction between these two time signatures, the sight-reading tests require familiarity with both.

Recognizing the difference between 2/2 and 4/4 is usually a case of thinking about speed and accent. A lot of music in 2/2 time is fast – and to avoid writing lots of short note values, composers choose duple rather than quadruple metre. In this example, we have the same tune written in both metres, sounding the same:

In the first example, it is possible to hear the music in 4/4 (if you simply change the time signature in your head), but the beat is rather too fast. The music may be heard and visualized as the second example, but some of the accents are in the wrong place.

When playing passages for recognition, choir trainers should always give a good accent on the first beat of the bar – and for tests to determine music in 2/2 time, choose music of a suitable speed. When trying to recognize the time signature, singers should always start by identifying where the first beats of the bars are, and then count between those accents.

At this level it is unreasonable to expect singers to differentiate between 2/2 and 2/4. What should be developed here is the ability to differentiate between duple and quadruple metre; and hence the ability, when sight-reading, to think of 2/2 as duple time.

Light Blue level: sight-reading test (a)

Delivering the test

For the test itself, choose one of the passages below.

Establish whether the singer plans to clap or sing the test. Hand over the singer's copy and indicate which passage is to be attempted. Allow up to 30 seconds of preparation time. If the singer has not begun to clap or sing at the end of this, prompt him or her to begin. Listen for rhythmic security, a steady pulse and the ability to keep going regardless of minor slips. (It is better to perform the test from start to finish with a few imperfections than to deliver the first bar perfectly and then stop.)

It is acceptable to allow the singer a second attempt. If you remain unsure as to whether the target has been achieved, test a second passage.

Light Blue level: sight-reading test (a)

Light Blue sight-reading test (b)
To sing a simple stepwise melody from sight on any vowel, or (at the singer's choice) using the set words. The key chord and tonic will be sounded. The singer will then be given 30 seconds to look through the music. The key chord and tonic will be sounded again before the test is attempted. The test will:

- be in 2/4, 3/4, 4/4 or 2/2

- contain a maximum of four bars

- move by step covering a range of no more than a fifth, ascending or descending from the tonic, in C, F or G major

- feature (undotted) minims, crotchets and quavers without rests

Sample tests are shown below, and there are more in the preparatory material that begins on page 25. For practice purposes, use the criteria above to find or create more tests of your own. For the actual test, use the passages that start on page 28.

In this test, the singer is accompanied. You should use the piano accompaniment provided but in a 'supporting' way. As you need to assess the singer's own ability to establish the pulse and sing the rhythm, within reason you should follow the vocal part rather than providing too firm a pulse yourself.

Preparing for the test
Singers will need careful preparation to complete the pitch test confidently and successfully. Only move on to the pitch exercises when rhythm is secure.

 At this level, the major scale forms the basis of the tests. Singers should already be familiar with this. However, before you begin preparation for sight-reading pitches, it may be helpful to revise briefly the Light Blue theory for the major scale, the concept of the key note or tonic, and key signatures. (See pages 25–29 of the workbook.) Here are some suggestions about how to present pitch exercises.

1) Choose an exercise and show it to your singers
The example below has a range of just three notes. Again, write it on a board or provide paper copies. (You may want to use only the treble or only the bass clef as appropriate.) Allow singers a while to study it. It might be useful to ask them to identify notational elements related to pitch.

 ### 2) Establish the pulse and the rhythm
Before attempting the melody, singers should clap the rhythm. This is an extension of the skills acquired for sight-reading test (a).

3) Establish the key note
Sing or play the tonic chord and key note. Encourage singers to examine the music for steps up, steps down and repeated notes.

 ### 4) Establish the three notes to be sung
Play the preparatory bar below, then encourage singers to sing the notes to *nah* or *la*, keeping the pulse (by clapping a foot or toe) and following the pitches with a finger. You can help by accompanying on the keyboard.

 Encourage singers to spot where the melody returns to a note they have already sung, like the Ds in the penultimate bar above. A firm grasp of the key note will help the impression that the music is 'returning home' at the end. Identifying and using such anchors is an important part of sight-reading. (There is useful information about the psychology of sight-reading on pages 100–101.)

At this stage, singers may sing with a weak, nervous tone as they lack confidence. However, make sure they can sing the previous exercise with a good tone before you proceed to the one below, which has slightly more melodic movement. Follow the procedure on the previous page.

 Additional activities
There are a number of games you can play with exercises like this. For instance the notes marked with an asterisk (below) could be left unaccompanied. This builds confidence as singers start to pitch notes at sight without the support of the piano.

 Once singers are very secure, you could play the example again, this time altering one note. See if singers can spot which note has changed. This shouldn't be too much of a challenge, and more able students may be able to sing or name the new note.

Expanding the range
Once singers can cope with simple examples like the ones above, extend the range to a 4th and, finally, a 5th.

Bear in mind that some examples will *fall* from the key note, and it is important to practise these too:

More hints and tips for singers
Once rhythm and pitch reading are fairly secure, singers will be ready to attempt the sample tests that begin on page 23. (There is a further preparatory test below.) When working on these, encourage singers to use their preparation time constructively. For each passage, they should:

- clap the rhythm before attempting the pitches

- say the words (having worked out the rhythm)

- decide whether the pattern rises or falls from the key note

- sing the 5 notes ascending or descending from the key note

- look for steps and repeated notes

- look for places where the melody returns to the key note

- follow the melody with a finger. This aids security.

- keep going at all costs even if they think they have made a mistake. It is *always* better to complete the test than to stop in the middle.

Some hints and tips for you
Here are a few things to bear in mind when monitoring your singers' progress.

- Do not expect 100% accuracy on the first attempt – always give the singer a second chance to sing the test.

- Encourage a good tone, supported by good breathing. Make sure singers don't forget technique in their attempt to read!

- The keyboard accompaniment supports the melody throughout. Singers may be put off by the odd harmony note (such as the E in the penultimate chord in the test below, which some singers may try to sing!). Persuade them to sing their part independently, without simply copying what they hear the piano play.

Here is another preparatory test.

Light Blue level: sight-reading test (b)

Delivering the test

Select a test with a range which is suitable for the singer. Hand over the singer's copy and indicate which passage is to be attempted. Sound the key chord and tonic. Allow 30 seconds for preparation. At the end of this, sound the key chord and tonic a second time, then accompany the singer's attempt at the test. Listen out for security of rhythm and pitch, and the ability to keep going regardless of minor slips.

It is acceptable to allow the singer a second attempt. If you remain unsure as to whether the target has been achieved, test a second passage.

Light Blue level: sight-reading test (b)

01 Unhurried

02 Brightly

Light Blue level: sight-reading test (b) *cont.*

03

With energy

Hearts and voi – ces raised ____ in song.

Hearts and voi – ces raised ____ in song.

04

Lively

Ri – ding o – ver hill and vale we sing a mer – ry song.

Ri – ding o – ver hill and vale we sing a mer – ry song.

05

Gently

Leaves come fal – ling down, red, gold, yel – low, brown.

Leaves come fal – ling down, red, gold, yel – low, brown.

Light Blue level: sight-reading test (b) *cont.*

06

Joyfully

Praise to the ho – liest in the height.

Praise to the ho – liest in the height.

07

Steady

Je – sus is Lord of heav'n and earth.

Je – sus is Lord of heav'n and earth.

08

With vigour

Let's raise our glas – ses and drink with cheer.

Let's raise our glas – ses and drink with cheer.

Light Blue level: sight-reading test (b) *cont.*

09

Gently flowing

Win – try wea – ther, i – cy cold, the wind be – gins to blow.

Win – try wea – ther, i – cy cold, the wind be – gins to blow.

10

With a gentle lilt

Sing to the Lord with all of your heart.

Sing to the Lord with all of your heart.

DARK BLUE LEVEL

Introduction
The six aural tests at Dark Blue level assess singers' ability to: reproduce simple melodies and rhythms; distinguish between major and minor chords; identify the key of a piece of music from its two opening bars, and name and sing the starting note in their own part; sing a specified interval above a note played by the examiner; and tap the beat and identify the time signature of a short extract.

 The 'Tone and range' exercises in Module A of the Dark Blue workbook (pages 9–10) will prepare singers technically for these tests, and familiarize them with the types of sounds they are expected to reproduce. The theory activities in Module B supply the vocabulary and concepts singers need to understand what is being asked.

 Dark Blue aural test (a)
To sing back a simple melody. The key chord and tonic will first be sounded and the pulse indicated. The melody will be played twice. The melody will:

- be in a major or minor key

- begin or end on the tonic (but not necessarily both)

- be up to four bars long

- be in 2/4, 3/4 or 4/4

- contain stepwise movement, and also leaps of a third, fourth and fifth (usually as elements of the tonic triad)

- contain a variety of note values which may include minims, crotchets, quavers and semiquavers. Dotted notes may be used.

Here are some sample tests. Use the criteria above to create more of your own for practice purposes. For the test itself, use the passages on page 36.

Preparing for the test

This test further develops musical memory and accurate pitching. Play the tests at an appropriate pitch and expect accurate tuning and rhythm in response. Preparatory work could include the accurate pitching of one, two or three notes from a phrase, or you could devise simpler phrases and gradually increase the complexity until the test level is reached.

At this level, the range of notes and size of jumps is increased; and minor keys are introduced. For some singers, these things may cause insecurity of pitch. You can help this by isolating problem notes and intervals for repetition, and also by encouraging the singer to hear and sing individual pitches in relation to the tonic. You can also suggest that singers hum along with the test as you play it, then break out into a more focused sound for their response.

As the passages are likely to be longer or rhythmically more complex than at Light Blue level, singers may benefit from keeping the pulse throughout when practising this test. Encourage an immediate response with no break in the pulse, or suggest that singers tap the pulse as you play, and continue tapping while they are singing.

Dotted rhythms will cause problems for some singers, since they can make the beat difficult to follow. Begin with a simple example, like the one below, where the movement is very straightforward:

Counting the beat aloud with the music playing will identify where the dotted note is. Ask singers to identify which beats it is between. Then move on to counting the beat, adding the word 'and' where indicated. Finally, clap the rhythm back (perhaps while counting the beat), taking care not to clap at the beginning of beat two in the second bar.

Delivering the test

Use one of the tests below that suits your singer's range: you may need to play tests an octave lower for tenors and basses. If you want to use a particular test that may be beyond the range of a singer, it is acceptable to transpose it into another key.

Sound the key chord first, and then the tonic. Sound two bars of the pulse by tapping with one hand. Then play the melody twice. After this, indicate that the singer should respond.

Assess the accuracy of the response. Listen for accurate reproduction of pitches and rhythms, and a sense of security and confidence. If you are unsure about the result, test the singer with a second passage.

Dark Blue level: aural test (a)

01
02
03
04
05
06
07
08
09
10

Dark Blue aural test (b)
To clap back the rhythm of a melody. The pulse will first be indicated and the passage played twice. The melody will:

- be in a major or minor key

- begin or end on the tonic (but not necessarily both)

- always be in 2/4, 3/4 or 4/4, and up to four bars long

- contain a variety of note values which may include minims, crotchets, quavers and semiquavers. Dotted notes may be used, including dotted quaver/semiquaver patterns.

- perhaps contain one or two simple ties or syncopations

Passages for this test may contain elements which are beyond the scope of the formal theory of Module B, as sometimes at this level singers will be required to clap features of music that they may not yet be able to name, read, sing or describe.

Here are some sample tests. Use the criteria above to create more of your own for practice purposes. For the test itself, use the passages on page 38.

Preparing for the test
This test develops musical memory and rhythmic response. Preparatory work might include asking singers to clap one-bar rhythms, or even shorter patterns, to a pulse. Expect accurate and immediate responses, with no hurrying. Encourage singers to tap the pulse as you play and as they respond, with no break between the two.

There are plenty of other ways to develop rhythmic facility in your singers. For example, can they clap or tap the pulse of more complex music as it is being played? Dotted or syncopated rhythms may cause a loss of steadiness at first. Another exercise is to take a couple of names (their own and yours might do) and chant a very metrical rhythm to them, such as:

Chris-to-pher Co-lum-bus,   An-drew Lloyd Web-ber.

Dark Blue level: aural test (b)

(i) **Delivering the test**
Sound two bars of the pulse by tapping with one hand. Then, maintaining the pulse, play the passage twice. After this, indicate that the singer should respond.

Assess the accuracy of the response. Listen for accurate reproduction of the rhythm and a sense of security and confidence.

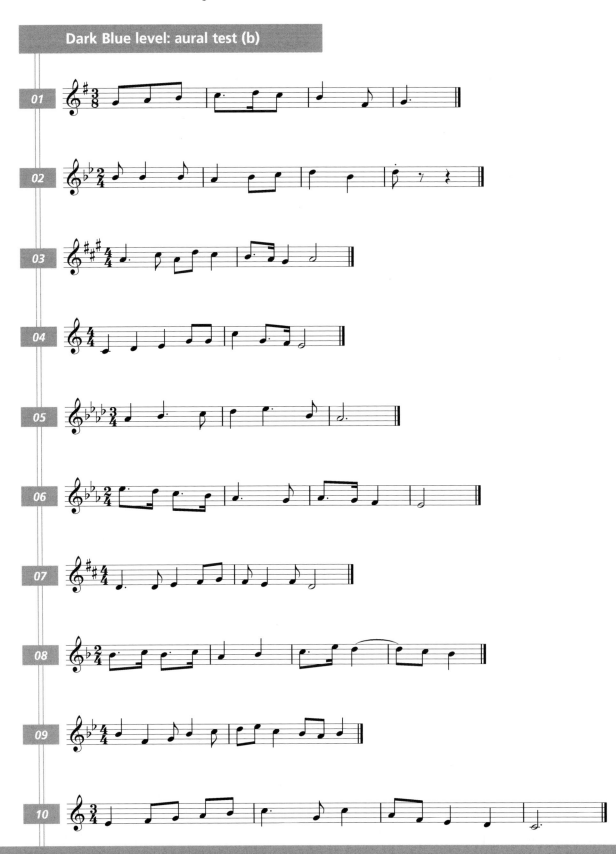

Dark Blue level: aural test (b)

Dark Blue aural test (c)

To listen to a triad played twice by the examiner and identify it as major or minor. The triad will be played in root, closed position, in a register appropriate for the singer's voice. (Examples of suitable chords are given below in treble and bass clefs.)

 Preparing for the test

For those who find this difficult, it is important to understand that it is the middle note of the chord that makes the difference. Play a triad and encourage singers to sing the individual pitches of it. This may enable them to hear the difference between the major and minor third. (It will also help with sight-reading and with aural test (e) on page 44.)

Singers might like to be shown how to play, say, a C major and C minor chord on the keyboard and to hear and feel the difference. In addition, play a minor chord and demonstrate how 'Greensleeves' would naturally follow on from it. Then play a major chord and do the same with 'Oh when the saints'.

Delivering the test

Inform the singer that you are going to play a chord twice, and that they are to tell you whether it is major or minor. Expect a prompt response. You may want to test more than one triad to check that the student's answering is secure.

  Dark Blue aural test (d)

To look at two bars of music and identify its key. Singers should then name the pitch of the first note in their part, and, on hearing the tonic chord, sing this note. The test passage will:

- be in a major key of up to three sharps or flats

- begin on a tonic chord (so the singer will always be required to sing a note from the tonic triad)

 Here are some sample tests. Use the criteria above to find or create your own examples. For the test itself, use the passages on page 41.

 01

02

Soprano / Alto / Tenor / Bass

Fa – ther, hear the prayer we __ of – fer,

Key: F major

Soprano: A
Alto: F
Tenor: C
Bass: F

03

Soprano / Alto / Tenor / Bass

Judge e – ter – nal, throned in splen – dour

Key: A major

Soprano: A
Alto: E
Tenor: C sharp
Bass: A

04

Soprano / Alto / Tenor / Bass

As with __ glad-ness men of old

Key: G major

Soprano: G
Alto: D
Tenor: B
Bass: G

Preparing for the test

Test (d) makes a clear link between theory and performance, and will only be successfully passed when the theory at this level is thoroughly learned. Singers need to know the names of the major key signatures of up to three sharps or flats. Pages 23, 24 and 46 of the Dark Blue workbook will help with this.

Delivering the test

If for any reason you are unfamiliar with the singer you are testing, ask which part he or she sings in choir, as this affects the second answer. Select one of the test passages below, find it in the singer's copy and give that copy to the singer. Allow a brief time for consideration (half a minute or so should be sufficient). At the end of this, prompt the singer to name the key and starting note if he or she has not already done so.

If the answer is correct, play the tonic chord at a suitable register and ask the singer to sing his or her starting note. Check for accuracy. Note that while some singers at this level may manage to name the note correctly, they may still struggle to pitch it within the triad.

 Dark Blue level: aural test (d)

01

Key: G major

Soprano: G
Alto: G
Tenor: B
Bass: G

02

Key: B flat major

Soprano: F
Alto: D
Tenor: B flat
Bass: B flat

03

Key: E flat major

Soprano: E flat
Alto: B flat
Tenor: G
Bass: E flat

04

Key: C major

Soprano: E
Alto: G
Tenor: C
Bass: C

05

Key: D major

Soprano: A
Alto: F
Tenor: A
Bass: D

Dark Blue level: aural test (d) *cont.*

06

Key: F major

Soprano: A
Alto: F
Tenor: C
Bass: F

07

Key: A major

Soprano: A
Alto: E
Tenor: C sharp
Bass: A

08

Key: C major

Soprano: C
Alto: E
Tenor: G
Bass: C

Dark Blue aural test (e)
To sing, above a given note played on the piano, the interval of a major or minor third, perfect fourth or perfect fifth.

Preparing for the test
Test (e) is directly linked to the sight-reading tests and theory for this level. The theory section of the workbook has advice on how to pitch intervals (from page 17). Singers need to take their time at first, but should be encouraged to make a quick response to pass the test. The usual approach is either to sing up from the given note to the required interval as shown, or to remember tunes which begin with certain intervals. In addition to the fourth and fifth which are given on page 19 of the workbook, major and minor thirds can be identified by:

- minor third: *Greensleeves*
- major third: *While shepherds watched their flocks by night*

Choir trainers will, of course, have their own ideas.

Here are the intervals in question at this level – all beginning on the note C. This is a good starting point for familiarisation with the sound of the intervals.

Delivering the test
Tell the student the interval required, then play and hold the first note. The singer should be able to pitch the bracketed note (to a confident *lah*) quite quickly. Some singers may wish to *quietly* sing or hum up the scale from the given note before giving the answer, and this is fine. You should allow a second attempt if the singer is unsure – and test another interval if you wish to.

Dark Blue aural test (f)
To tap or clap the pulse of a passage of music in 2, 3 or 4 time. The singer should be able to tap the beat and stress where the strong beat falls. They should then state whether the music is in 2, 3 or 4 time.

Test (f) follows on from test (d) at Light Blue level. Here, however, music in 4 time has been added; and the beat may be disguised slightly by syncopations and tied notes. Singers need to identify the stronger beats of the bar to pass this test.

Preparing for the test
The advice on pages 17, 19 and 21 may be useful here. You can help singers to prepare for this test by playing suitable passages on the piano or using recordings. (Recordings help to attune the ear differently as the students cannot rely on the physical clues you involuntarily supply when playing.) You should still aim to use passages with a clear pulse and reasonably identifiable time signature.

At this level, music in 4 time has been added. Some students will find it difficult to distinguish between 2 time and 4 time. To overcome this, make sure the strong beats (ie the first beat of each bar) are clearly delineated. Then establish how many beats there are between each count of '1'.

If the problem persists, it will be to do with the speed of the pulse and the way the singer perceives the music (see page 21). For example, the first test below could be mistaken as being in 4 time, but the beat would be uncomfortably fast!

Dark Blue level: aural test (f)

Introduction
The two sight-reading tests at Dark Blue level assess singers' ability to clap and sing rhythms and melodies from notation. The notational elements tested will be familiar to singers who have worked on the theory section of Dark Blue level Module B.

Dark Blue sight-reading test (a)
To clap a rhythm from sight. The rhythm will:

- be in 2/4, 3/4, 4/4 or 2/2

- contain a maximum of four bars

- feature minims, crotchets, quavers (in pairs or groups of four) and semiquavers (in pairs or groups of four)

- may also include dotted crotchet/quaver patterns

Here are some sample tests. Use the criteria above to create more of your own for practice purposes. For the test itself, use the passages on page 48.

Preparing for the test
Rhythmic security is crucial to successful sight-reading: it is still useful at Dark Blue level to practise and test it separately from pitch. The preparatory advice on pages 19–21 remains relevant here, but the singer is expected to know more time signatures and note values at Dark Blue level, as outlined in the bullet points above.

By this level singers should understand the idea of pulses, beats and time signatures. If you suspect that this is not the case, refer them to Module B and the reference section of the Light Blue workbook.

You should continue to encourage singers to count the beat and clap the rhythm (see page 20). Below you can see the 'counted' versions of the first two exercises above.

Delivering the test

For the test itself, choose one of the passages below.

Establish whether the singer plans to clap or sing the test. Hand over the singer's copy and indicate which passage is to be attempted. Allow up to 30 seconds of preparation time. If the singer has not begun to clap or sing at the end of this, prompt him or her to begin. Listen for rhythmic security, a steady pulse and the ability to keep going regardless of minor slips. (It is better to perform the test from start to finish with a few imperfections than to deliver the first bar perfectly and then stop.)

It is acceptable to allow the singer a second attempt. If you remain unsure as to whether the target has been achieved, test a second passage.

Dark Blue level: sight-reading test (a)

Dark Blue sight-reading test (b)

To sing a short melody from sight on any vowel, or (at the singer's choice) using the set words. The key chord and starting note will be sounded. The singer will then be given 15 seconds to look through the music. The key chord and starting note will be sounded again before the test is attempted. The test will:

- be sung to a piano accompaniment

- be in 2/4, 3/4, 4/4 or 2/2

- be in any key up to and including three sharps or flats

- be up to eight bars long (not necessarily starting on the first beat)

- cover a range of up to an octave

- begin or end on the tonic (but not necessarily both)

- move by step, or by intervals of a third, fourth or fifth

- include semibreves, minims, crotchets, quavers and possibly their equivalent rests; dotted crotchet/quaver patterns may occur

- include simple dynamic markings to be reproduced when singing

For an idea of the level of complexity, look at the actual test passages that begin on page 57. Use the criteria above to find or create more tests of your own for practice. The information below about preparing singers for this test also contains suitable sample passages and advice about how to use them.

Preparing for the test

This test is quite a step up from its Light Blue equivalent, and careful preparation will be needed to instil confidence. The learning of the theory for this level goes hand in hand with the sight-reading tests: a thorough knowledge of key signatures, tonic triads, intervals, dynamics and dotted rhythms is essential for the successful reading of the music. All these topics are covered in Module B of the Dark Blue workbook.

The singer has 15 seconds of preparation time. The key chord and starting note are sounded before and after this. There is no piano introduction. This absence of lead-in tests singers' ability to use notation to set a suitable pulse and tempo. It also means that singers must be able to retain the starting note (normally one from the tonic chord, but not necessarily the tonic) before they start to sing.

Don't insist on 15 seconds of preparation time at first: this is an aspiration. Instead, encourage plenty of sight-reading in an unhurried, supportive manner so that it becomes a normal part of music-making. Only when your singers are comfortable should you start to reduce the preparation time as you move towards assessment for the level. (For further ideas about sight-reading training, see page 100.)

As sight-reading tasks become more complex, singers need to acquire – before starting to sing – an 'aural image' of the test passage. Robust knowledge of notation and theory is vital. To sing at sight accurately and confidently, singers must be comfortable with certain concepts – particularly, at this level, triads and intervals. On the next page there is some advice about how to integrate these into sight-reading practice so they become part of the singer's aural imagination.

The tonic triad
At Dark Blue level, singers should already be familiar with the sound of a triad. and with the idea of triads based on the first note of the scale. (At this stage the term 'tonic' is not explicitly used in the workbook, though singers may well have encountered it, or the term 'root'.) As the tests at this level are based firmly on the tonic triad, consolidation during practice will help students considerably.

Begin by playing some triads and encouraging singers to sing them back to you in a pattern of your choosing. It can help to reinforce the intervallic concept of the triad if you ask students to sing the degree number of the scale for each note – for example '1, 3, 5' (from lowest note to highest) or '1, 3, 5, 3, 1' (from lowest note to highest and back again). See page 17 of the workbook for more about this. Singing to note-names is also helpful.

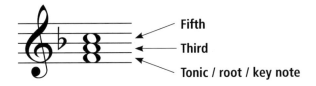

When singers are comfortable with this, encourage them to sing upwards to the key note above the triad, and then down to the fifth degree below the key note. (Make sure that these notes are within range.) Once again, note names or scale numbers may help.

At this level, test (b) will be in any key, major or minor, up to three sharps or three flats – 14 triads in all. These are shown opposite. Singers need to be able to recognize these triads in notated music (this is covered in the workbook); name the notes in each one; and visualize how the triad is written down when they hear it without the notation. Theory work will reinforce this.

Try the following exercise with your singers using each of the triads on the opposite page:

- Play a triad and name it, or write it on the board and ask singers to identify it.

- Ask singers to name the three notes.

- Ask singers to sing the tonic, third and fifth (or by letter name) in any order. (If you have shown it as notation, play the key note to help pitching.)

- Ask singers to sing the tonic above the triad and the fifth degree below the tonic, if these notes are within their range.

(i) Here are the 14 triads that singers need to know for sight-reading test (b). Encourage singers to sing, hear and feel the difference between major and minor triads.

C major   C minor   D major   D minor   E flat major   E minor   F major

F sharp minor   G major   G minor   A major   A minor   B flat major   B minor

(i) **Singing intervals: thirds**

The requirement to sing intervals of more than one step may cause problems for some singers at first, so it is important to build confidence gently. Begin with the interval of a **third**. Singers should be familiar with the sound of the third by now, as they will have encountered it in the triad.

Play this passage for your singers and ask them to sing it back to you. It is basically built on the sound of a triad, but includes a couple of steps too. To reinforce the difference, ask singers to identify which intervals are steps and which are jumps.)

Ah

If singers find this difficult, try the exercise below, which is entirely stepwise. Repeat this passage several times with your singers, gradually reducing the volume of the notes in brackets until the thirds remain exposed. Encourage singers to 'think' the notes in brackets but not sing them aloud.

Ah

(i) The following exercise is also useful for pitching thirds. Over time, try it with your singers in all the major keys shown opposite. Then proceed to the minor keys and encourage them to listen to the difference.

Nah nah nah *etc.*

Singing intervals: fourths and fifths
Young or inexperienced singers may confuse fourths and fifths. Mis-pitching can often lead to the music going completely off–track, so good preparation is needed.

Firstly, note that both intervals are included in the arpeggio of the extended triad shown on page 50. So the sound of these intervals should be familiar, but singers also need to know what they look like in notation. The theory in the Dark Blue workbook will help interval recognition, while aural work will help pitching.

There is a tendency to think of intervals rising, whereas in sight-reading they are just as likely to fall. Both instances need to be secure, and aural tests should reinforce this – as should the exercises below.

At this level, the most likely occurrence of the fourth interval will be the dominant leading upwards to the tonic, often at the beginning of the test on an upbeat. The most likely occurrence of the fifth will be as a leap from the tonic – or where the interval leads on to the dominant. In all instances, if the dominant and tonic are firmly held in the mind, there should be few problems.

This exercise will help the recognition and pitching of fourths:

And this one will help the recognition and pitching of fifths:

A note about accompaniments

Once your singers are secure with triads and intervals, use the tests on the following pages to prepare them for sight-reading test (b). In the preparatory passages and the test itself, singers will need to sing to a piano accompaniment, so here are a few points to help them with this.

At this level, the accompaniment acts as a harmonic, not melodic, support. Some melody notes will be supported by the piano (often the first note, for example), but the accompaniment will not contain the complete melody. Some singers may find this hard at first for various reasons.

Singers may gravitate to whichever note is uppermost in the piano, regardless of what the notation asks them to sing. Of course there is no substitute for a well-developed aural imagination and the ability to identify and reproduce notes – but lack of confidence may cause singers to follow what they hear, not what they see. You can encourage the necessary independence in stages.

At first, accompany singers as they sing familiar hymns or folk tunes. Gradually remove the melody from your accompaniment, playing instead supporting chords, notes from the alto, tenor and bass parts, or even a descant. You can make this into a game – how tenaciously can singers hold the melody while you try to divert them from it by playing other notes?

You can then do this with less familiar music, as long as the melodies are straightforward. Ask singers to read short passages which you play at the same time as a single line on the piano. Once they are comfortable with this, make the accompaniment deviate from the melody bit by bit, while they retain the written pitches. You can also play a chordal accompaniment but drop out at random places: this will encourage singers to become self-supporting of their own line.

It is also a good idea to prepare for these tests by asking singers to attempt parts of the test passage unaccompanied. This will encourage them to focus on the melody and intervals. When the piano part is added later, it can act as intended – as a support, not a lead.

Some preparatory tests

On the following pages you will find some exercises to help your singers prepare for this test, together with ideas to help successful completion. The actual test passages begin on page 57.

Start with this preparatory test, and use the hints below.

 The singer should be able to:

- name the key, and the three notes of the tonic chord

- find the notes of the tonic chord in the music

- after hearing the tonic chord, sing the notes F, A and C

- recognize instances of the interval of a third. In the example above, these are all from the tonic chord. As a starting point for singing the entire melody, the singer could be asked to sing the notes on the words *had*, *a*, *fleece* and *was*.

- clap the dotted crotchet/quaver rhythm before singing the melody

- keep the tonic (the starting note in this instance) firmly in the head

- establish a 3/4 moderato pulse and start to sing independently

Do not expect 100% accuracy on a first attempt; always allow a second chance. Encourage the singer to keep going at all costs, and to sing with a good tone supported by good breathing.

Bear in mind too that the words are optional: singers may prefer to sing on any appropriate vowel, or to 'la'.

The following test is longer and a bit harder, but the same preparation points apply.

The singer should be able to:

- name the key and the notes of the tonic chord, and find these anchor notes in the music
- after hearing the tonic chord and key note, sing the notes G, B, and D, followed by the lower D
- sing the first two notes
- sing the last three notes, realizing that the music returns to the tonic
- sing the notes to the words 'from Peru'
- find where the melody and the top note of the piano part coincide.
- clap the rhythm
- remember to sing with a good tone, supported by sensible breathing

So, there is quite a lot you can do to prepare for a test like this. Of course this is too much to fit into the preparation time, but careful preparation instils good practice. As this music is based firmly around the tonic triad, the theory work for this level will have been worthwhile. The next passage is rather more difficult:

The singer should be able to:

- name the key and the notes of the tonic chord, and find these anchor notes in the music

- after hearing the tonic chord and key note, sing the notes D, F, and A

- sing the last three notes, pitching the leading note well

- sing the notes to *dark despair*

- hold the melody independently of the accompaniment, which often moves in contrary motion

- control the breath and volume well during the closing *diminuendo*

Delivering the test
The test passages begin below. Find the relevant passage in the downloadable singer's copy; establish which clef the singer requires and hand the copy over. Sound the key chord and starting note; allow the singer 15 seconds to review the music, then sound the key chord and starting note again. When the singer begins, accompany sensitively and let him or her establish the pulse and tempo.

Listen for accurate rhythm and pitching, and good breath control. A good student will also observe the dynamics.

 Dark Blue level: sight-reading test (b)

Dark Blue level: sight-reading test (b) *cont.*

Dark Blue level: sight-reading test (b) *cont.*

buy my ro – ses, ru – – by red.

buy my ro – ses, ru – – by red.

Allegretto

mf

A ship sailed down the Thames to

mf

A ship sailed down the Thames to

mf

sea, down the Thames to sea.

sea, down the Thames to sea.

Dark Blue level: sight-reading test (b) *cont.*

05

Hush – – a – bye my lit – – tle

Hush – – a – bye my lit – – tle

one, _____ O hush – – a – by.

one, _____ O hush – – a – by.

06

Je – sus is Sa – viour, Lord and _____ King,

Je – sus is Sa – viour, Lord and _____ King,

Dark Blue level: sight-reading test (b) *cont.*

Hal – le – lu – jah, let us sing.

Hal – le – lu – jah, let us sing.

Lento

I love the sun it shines___ on

I love the sun it shines___ on

me, bring – ing with it warmth and light.

me, bring – ing with it warmth and light.

Dark Blue level: sight-reading test (b) *cont.*

08

Andante

mf

Join with us, Oh join with

Join with us, Oh join with

us, and sing a new song glad - ly.

us, and sing a new song glad - ly.

09

Adagio

p   *mp*   *mf*

Christ has died, Christ is ri - sen Christ will come a - gain.

p   *mp*   *mf*

Christ has died, Christ is ri - sen Christ will come a - gain.

p   *mp*   *mf*

Dark Blue level: sight-reading test (b)

BRONZE AWARD

The material in this section reflects the order and titles of the tests in the award exam itself. For more details see the syllabus for the RSCM singing awards, which is downloadable from **www.rscm.com** free of charge.

Singing at first and second sight: introduction
Section B1 of the Bronze award exam contains three linked sight-reading tests: (a), (b) and (c). These assess singers' ability to clap and sing rhythms and melodies from notation. They require much the same skills as those required for Dark Blue level, though the format is slightly different. The theory and notational elements tested will be familiar to singers who have completed Dark Blue Module B.

How to use this section of the book
In the exam, the three sight-reading tests are delivered in sequence from a single page of music which the examiner hands to the candidate. The aim of this section is to help you prepare students for each individual test first, then to enable you to conduct a mock exam with candidates – when you feel they are ready – which imitates the exam procedure as closely as possible. See page 74 for the mock exam.

You are advised to begin by reading the Awards syllabus, which can be downloaded from **www.rscm.com** free of charge. Then, if you are unfamiliar with the Awards exams, read as far as page 73 *before* you start to use this section with students. This will enable you to use the sample exercises (and any other material you select or devise yourself) in lessons. It isn't necessary to teach all the tests at once, but it is necessary to understand how they fit together before you start working on each one.

Bronze award section B1, test (a): sing a pattern of four notes
Candidates are required to sing (from a copy which the examiner will provide), in free time and using a single breath, a pattern of four notes starting with the tonic. Candidates may choose to sing from treble or bass clef (the copy provided offers both options). The examiner will first name and sound the key chord and starting (tonic) note. Candidates are allowed two attempts at the test. The notes to be sung:

- will be in D, F, G or A major
- will be pitched in the range low C to upper C#
- may include the first five notes of the scale (tonic to dominant) as well as the lower dominant and submediant
- will contain no interval greater than a perfect fourth

Here are some sample tests. You can also use the criteria above to create more of your own for practice purposes. On the opposite page ('The test itself') you will find the words that the examiner will use when delivering the test.

Preparing for the test
Candidates who have achieved Dark Blue level should find this well within their capabilities. However this test is unaccompanied, so singers will need to be confident in retaining the tonic after hearing it played, and must also judge intervals with care.

It may help when practising to use note names, sol-fa or the degree numbers of the scale (see pages 17–19 of the Dark Blue workbook). If a singer has difficulty with a particular interval, sing or play it a few times for imitation. (It may also be a good idea to have the singer name the intervals too.)

What the examiner is listening for
Full marks will be given for a faultless first attempt in which the four notes are sung in one breath, perfectly pitched, with regular lengths. A second attempt will always be offered unless the first is absolutely faultless. Marks will be deducted for:

- insecurity of pitching or intonation

- irregularity of pace, breathing or rhythm

- hesitation or lack of confidence

- technical problems or lack of consistency

When proposing a second attempt, the examiner will not explain what the faults were in the first. Marks will be gained if during the second attempt a candidate noticeably corrects or improves errors made in the first.

The test itself
The text spoken by the examiner is shown below in *italic* type, and the instructions to the examiner are shown [in square brackets]. To practise with your singers, use this in conjunction with the tests shown opposite (which are also available in the downloadable singer's copy).

Have a look at tests A on this page of the leaflet. [Offer the candidate leaflet, open at page 1.] *If you'd prefer to see these tests in bass clef, please turn over the page.* [Say this to all candidates.]

First, I'd like you to sing the group of four notes you can see, in free time and a single breath, using any vowel or sol-fa.

Here is the chord of G major: [Play the key chord.]

and your first note, G. [Play the tonic.]

[If bass clef is chosen, play both of these an octave lower.]

Take a few moments to prepare, and begin as soon as you are ready.

Thank you. Let's have a second attempt. [The second attempt at each item must always be offered unless the first attempt at it was faultless.] *Here is the key chord again* [play] *and your first note* [play].

Bronze award section B1, test (b): clap a rhythm
From a copy provided by the examiner, candidates are required to clap, tap or sing on one note, in strict time, a rhythm pattern of notes and rests. The candidate sets the tempo and is asked to count two bars of the pulse aloud before starting. The rhythm:

- will be in 2/4 or 3/4

- will contain 8–10 crotchet beats

- will begin on the first beat of the bar

- may include crotchets and quavers (including dotted patterns, minims and (in 3/4 time) a dotted minim, as well as crotchet and quaver rests

Here are some sample tests. You can use the criteria above to create more of your own for practice purposes. Opposite, you will find the words that the examiner will use when delivering them. Once your student is familiar with all three sight-reading tests and therefore ready for a mock exam, proceed to page 74.

Because these are useful for training purposes, two 4/4 examples are included below. Note however that in the exam itself the tests will only be in 2/4 or 3/4.

Preparing for the test

Singers who have achieved the sight-reading targets at Dark Blue level should have little difficulty with this test. They should already be familiar with the concepts and sound of dotted notes, but familiarity with the notation for this particular figure may need checking.

Singers may find the external exam situation places them under pressure. Emphasize the importance of security of pulse – this is the single most effective way of ensuring confidence with the rhythm patterns. Encourage your students to count two introductory bars of the pulse before starting to clap, tap or sing; this is a good exercise in pulse stability as it provides a context for the rhythm.

What the examiner is listening for

Full marks will be awarded for a faultless first attempt in which the rhythm is perfectly articulated with a solid, confident sense of pulse. A second attempt will always be offered unless the first is absolutely faultless. Marks will be deducted for:

- insecurity of rhythm or pulse
- irregularity of pace or rhythm
- hesitation or lack of confidence
- an inconsistent pulse (speeding up or slowing down)

When proposing a second attempt, the examiner will not explain what the faults were in the first. Marks will be gained if during the second attempt a candidate noticeably corrects or improves errors made in the first.

The test itself

Below, the text spoken by the examiner is shown in *italic* type, and the instructions to the examiner are shown [in square brackets]. To practise with your singers, use this in conjunction with the tests shown on the left (which are also available in the downloadable singer's copy).

Now, the rhythm pattern. I'd like you to clap or tap in strict time the notes in this pattern. Set your own tempo, and count out loud two bars of the pulse as introduction. Begin as soon as you are ready. [The candidate may ask to sing the pattern, on one note.]

Thank you. Let's have a second attempt. [The second attempt at each item must always be offered unless the first attempt at it was faultless.]

Bronze award section B1, test (c): sing two phrases
Candidates are required to sing two melodic phrases at sight, to an accompaniment provided by the examiner. (The accompaniment is shown in the candidate's copy.) The phrases will contain melodic and rhythmic elements – together with the key and time signatures – already encountered in tests (a) and (b).

The examiner will play and name the key chord, then sound the first note of the test passage. After 15 seconds' preparation time, the key chord and starting note will be sounded again before the candidate starts to sing. A second attempt will be allowed. The melody:

- will be in 2/4 or 3/4, up to six bars in length, starting on the first beat of the bar
- will be in D, F, G or A major, with no modulation
- will be in the same key as test (a) and the same time signature as test (b), and feature the same pitches and rhythmic patterns
- will not necessarily begin on the tonic
- will be mainly stepwise but may include leaps up to a perfect fifth.
- will include some simple dynamic markings

Additional information:

- The top note of the accompaniment will double the melody in three helpful places.
- The candidate sets the tempo, which the examiner will follow when playing the accompaniment.
- The phrases may be separated by a rest or rests.
- The candidate may choose to sing the test unaccompanied, but must request this during the 15 seconds of preparation time.

Here are some sample tests. You can also use the criteria above to create more of your own for practice purposes. On page 73, you will find the words that the examiner will use when delivering them. Once your student is familiar with all three sight-reading tests and therefore ready for a mock exam, proceed to page 74.

Preparing for the test

Singers who have successfully completed the Dark Blue sight-reading targets will find little technical difficulty here. But remember that the external exam situation may be unfamiliar and a source of some anxiety. It is important to alleviate this by making sure singers are adequately prepared.

Students may feel that 15 seconds of preparation time is brief, but it is in fact long enough to clap and sing the entire passage before starting; encourage singers to do this. Advise them to look for triad shapes and awkward intervals, and also to identify where anchors appear in the music – most usefully, the notes of the tonic chord. It is important that candidates are used to singing what they see, not what they hear. (The accompaniment will differ from the sung part.) Once again, the best route to this skill is regular practice.

If your student is stronger in certain aspects of this test than others, suggest they concentrate for the first attempt on their strong point and refine any weaknesses at the second attempt. For example singers who pitch securely and easily but find rhythm reading harder should be encouraged to get the notes right at the first attempt and refine the rhythm at the second. Good rhythm readers may want to work the other way round, concentrating on pitch afterwards.

Here is a preparatory example, with a few pointers to pass on to the candidate:

- Look for notes of the tonic triad in the music. Keep these notes firmly in mind when preparing and when singing. (In the example above, these are marked with asterisks.)

- During the preparation time, sing or clap the rhythm out loud.

- Before you start, establish the pulse you have chosen (maybe inaudibly by tapping a finger or toe)

- Try to keep going at all costs. If you make a mistake do not stop, or you will lose the accompaniment!

- Sing with a good, confident tone, supported by good breathing.

- Sing what you read in the music, not what you hear in the accompaniment. Don't get distracted if the accompaniment sounds different from what you are singing.

What the examiner is listening for

Full marks will be given for a faultless first attempt in which both phrases are perfectly articulated, with a solid, confident sense of pitch and pulse; the examiner will also listen for details like accurate interpretation of any dynamics, good breath control and appropriate shaping of phrases.

Marks will be deducted for:

- insecurity of pitch, rhythm or pulse
- irregularity of pace or rhythm
- hesitation or lack of confidence
- inconsistency of pace or tone

When proposing a second attempt, the examiner will not explain what the faults were in the first. Marks will be gained if during the second attempt a candidate noticeably corrects or improves errors made in the first.

The test itself

Below, the text spoken by the examiner is shown in *italic* type, and the instructions to the examiner are shown [in square brackets]. To practise with your singers, use this in conjunction with the tests that begin on page 70 (which are also available in the downloadable singer's copy).

Finally, the third test you can see on this page. I'd like you to sing me these two phrases, using any vowel or sol-fa, whilst I play the accompaniment. You will set your own tempo.

Here is the key chord of G major ... and your first note, G. [Play these exactly as before.]

Take a few moments to prepare, and you may sing out loud if you wish.
[Allow a pause of 15 seconds. During this time, the candidate may ask to sing the test unaccompanied.]

Here is the key chord again [play] *and your first note* [play, leave a short pause]. *Please begin now ...* [Accompany sensitively, allowing the candidate to set and control the tempo, but gently encouraging momentum.]

Thank you. Let's have a second attempt. Here is the key chord again [play] *and your first note* [play].

[The second attempt at each item must always be offered unless the first attempt at it was faultless.]

A mock exam

Once your student is familiar with the individual sight-reading tests (a), (b) and (c) which make up section B1, you can perform a mock exam using the materials in the downloadable singer's copy for this section of the book.

There are four sets of tests in all, one set per page, in the same format as they appear in the exam booklet. It is advisable to print out only what the student needs for the practice tests at any given time. Each set is available in treble and bass clef versions. In the exam, the examiner will select a page from a leaflet to hand to the candidate, offering the choice of treble clef on one side and bass clef on the other; in the context of this book, it may be easier for you to establish which clef your candidate would prefer and print just that page. But make students aware that in the exam itself they will be offered a choice.

The entire script and instructions used by the examiner are shown below. Once again, the text spoken by the examiner is shown in *italic* type, and the instructions are shown [in square brackets].

A note about sight-reading in exams

Singers taking the Bronze award for the first time may not have experienced a music exam before and may be anxious about it. The best solution is to make sure they are as well prepared as possible. The exam will seem less intimidating if candidates know what to expect: the order of sections; what happens in each part; what the examiner will do and say. It also helps to know about the practical aspects of the exam: where to go; what happens on arrival; how long it will last and so on. All this information will be available from the exam centre.

Sight-reading in exams is often a cause of student anxiety. This may be because, by its very nature, it is the part which is least easy to anticipate. Candidates may feel, with some justification, that they aren't *meant* to know what to expect in advance. But of course the criteria are clearly stated in the syllabus, and familiarity with these will definitely help.

At this level, the sight-reading tests only examine certain key and time signatures, rhythms and intervals. Reminding candidates of what they will and won't encounter can alleviate stress. For example, if singers know that the tests will be in D, F, G or A major, they also know that they don't have to worry about other key signatures. You may need to tell your students this frequently. (It may help to practice several sight-reading exercises in the same key in one lesson; and then several in another key in the next one. In this way it is possible to cover all the possibilities – and to tell candidates that you have done this.)

Tests A

Have a look at Tests A, on this page of the leaflet. [Offer the candidate the appropriate treble or bass clef section of the downloadable copy.] *First, I'd like you to sing the group of four notes you can see, in free time and a single breath, using any vowel or sol-fa.*

Here is the chord of G major: *and your first note, G:*

[If bass clef is chosen, play both of these an octave lower.]

Take a few moments to prepare, and begin as soon as you are ready.

Thank you. Let's have a second attempt. [The second attempt at each item must always be offered unless the first attempt at it was faultless.]

Now, the rhythm pattern. I'd like you to clap or tap in strict time the notes in this pattern. Set your own tempo, and count out loud two bars of the pulse as introduction. Begin as soon as you are ready. [The candidate may ask to sing the pattern on one note.]

Thank you. Let's have a second attempt. Please begin. [The second attempt at each item must always be offered unless the first attempt at it was faultless.]

Finally, the third test you can see on this page. I'd like you to sing me these two phrases, using any vowel or sol-fa, whilst I play the accompaniment. You will set your own tempo. Here is the key chord of G major ... and your first note, G. [Play these exactly as before.] *Take a few moments to prepare, and you may sing out loud if you wish.* [Allow a pause of 15 seconds. During this time, the candidate may ask to sing the test unaccompanied.]

Here is the key chord again [play] *and your first note* [play, leave a short pause]. *Please begin now ...* [Accompany sensitively, allowing the candidate to set and control the tempo, but gently encouraging momentum.] *Thank you. Let's have a second attempt. Here is the key chord again* [play] *and your first note* [play]. [The second attempt at each item must always be offered unless the first attempt at it was faultless.]

Tests B

Have a look at Tests B, on this page of the leaflet. [Offer the candidate the appropriate treble or bass clef section of the downloadable copy.] *First, I'd like you to sing the group of four notes you can see, in free time and a single breath, using any vowel or sol-fa.*

Here is the chord of D major: *and your first note, F sharp:*

[If bass clef is chosen, play both of these an octave lower.]

Take a few moments to prepare, and begin as soon as you are ready.

Thank you. Let's have a second attempt. [The second attempt at each item must always be offered unless the first attempt at it was faultless.]

Now, the rhythm pattern. I'd like you to clap or tap in strict time the notes in this pattern. Set your own tempo, and count out loud two bars of the pulse as introduction. Begin as soon as you are ready. [The candidate may ask to sing the pattern on one note.]

Thank you. Let's have a second attempt. Please begin. [The second attempt at each item must always be offered unless the first attempt at it was faultless.]

Finally, the third test you can see on this page. I'd like you to sing me these two phrases, using any vowel or sol-fa, whilst I play the accompaniment. You will set your own tempo. Here is the key chord of D major ... and your first note, F#. [Play these exactly as before.] *Take a few moments to prepare, and you may sing out loud if you wish.* [Allow a pause of 15 seconds. During this time, the candidate may ask to sing the test unaccompanied.]

Here is the key chord again [play] *and your first note* [play, leave a short pause]. *Please begin now ...* [Accompany sensitively, allowing the candidate to set and control the tempo, but gently encouraging momentum.] *Thank you. Let's have a second attempt. Here is the key chord again* [play] *and your first note* [play]. [The second attempt at each item must always be offered unless the first attempt at it was faultless.]

Tests C

Have a look at Tests C, on this page of the leaflet. [Offer the candidate the appropriate treble or bass clef section of the downloadable copy.] *First, I'd like you to sing the group of four notes you can see, in free time and a single breath, using any vowel or sol-fa.*

Here is the chord of F major: *and your first note, F:*

[If bass clef is chosen, play both of these an octave lower.]

Take a few moments to prepare, and begin as soon as you are ready.

Thank you. Let's have a second attempt. [The second attempt at each item must always be offered unless the first attempt at it was faultless.]

Now, the rhythm pattern. I'd like you to clap or tap in strict time the notes in this pattern. Set your own tempo, and count out loud two bars of the pulse as introduction. Begin as soon as you are ready. [The candidate may ask to sing the pattern on one note.]

Thank you. Let's have a second attempt. Please begin. [The second attempt at each item must always be offered unless the first attempt at it was faultless.]

Finally, the third test you can see on this page. I'd like you to sing me these two phrases, using any vowel or sol-fa, whilst I play the accompaniment. You will set your own tempo. Here is the key chord of F major ... and your first note, F. [Play these exactly as before.] *Take a few moments to prepare, and you may sing out loud if you wish.* [Allow a pause of 15 seconds. During this time, the candidate may ask to sing the test unaccompanied.]

Here is the key chord again [play] *and your first note* [play, leave a short pause]. *Please begin now ...* [Accompany sensitively, allowing the candidate to set and control the tempo, but gently encouraging momentum.] *Thank you. Let's have a second attempt. Here is the key chord again* [play] *and your first note* [play]. [The second attempt at each item must always be offered unless the first attempt at it was faultless.]

Tests D

Have a look at Tests D, on this page of the leaflet. [Offer the candidate the appropriate treble or bass clef section of the downloadable copy.] *First, I'd like you to sing the group of four notes you can see, in free time and a single breath, using any vowel or sol-fa.*

Here is the chord of A major: *and your first note, A:*

[If bass clef is chosen, play both of these an octave lower.]

Take a few moments to prepare, and begin as soon as you are ready.

Thank you. Let's have a second attempt. [The second attempt at each item must always be offered unless the first attempt at it was faultless.]

Now, the rhythm pattern. I'd like you to clap or tap in strict time the notes in this pattern. Set your own tempo, and count out loud two bars of the pulse as introduction. Begin as soon as you are ready. [The candidate may ask to sing the pattern on one note.]

Thank you. Let's have a second attempt. Please begin. [The second attempt at each item must always be offered unless the first attempt at it was faultless.]

Finally, the third test you can see on this page. I'd like you to sing me these two phrases, using any vowel or sol-fa, whilst I play the accompaniment. You will set your own tempo. Here is the key chord of A major ... and your first note, A. [Play these exactly as before.] *Take a few moments to prepare, and you may sing out loud if you wish.* [Allow a pause of 15 seconds. During this time, the candidate may ask to sing the test unaccompanied.]

Here is the key chord again [play] *and your first note* [play, leave a short pause]. *Please begin now ...* [Accompany sensitively, allowing the candidate to set and control the tempo, but gently encouraging momentum.] *Thank you. Let's have a second attempt. Here is the key chord again* [play] *and your first note* [play]. [The second attempt at each item must always be offered unless the first attempt at it was faultless.]

Aural exercises: introduction
The aural exercises for the Bronze award require the same skills and knowledge as the tests for Dark Blue level, but these are examined slightly differently. There are three tests, which assess candidates' ability to: reproduce short rhythms and melodies after hearing them (by clapping or singing); and identify and reproduce the intervals learned at Dark Blue level (major and minor third, perfect fourth and perfect fifth).

If candidates have completed the Dark Blue workbook, they should have all the necessary knowledge to complete the tests at Bronze Level.

Bronze award section B2, test (a): clap a rhythm
Candidates are required to clap the rhythm of a melody. The examiner will indicated the pulse and play the passage twice. The passage will:

- be in 2/4, 3/4 or 6/8

- be two bars long

- begin on the first beat of the bar

- contain a variety of note values, including minims, crotchets, quavers and semiquavers (dotted notes may be used, including dotted quaver/semiquaver patterns)

Passages for this test may contain elements which are beyond the scope of the formal theory of Dark Blue Module B, as sometimes at this level singers will be required to clap features of music that they may not yet be able to name, read, sing or describe.

Here are some sample tests. Use the criteria above to create more of your own for practice purposes. On the next page you will find more practice tests and the words that the external examiner will use when delivering them. This will help you to familiarize your singers with the format of the test before the exam itself.

Say: 1, 2, 3, 1, 2, 3   *Say:* Again …

Say: 1, 2, 1, 2   *Say:* Again …

Say: 1, 2, 1, 2   *Say:* Again …

Say: 1, 2, 3, 1, 2, 3   *Say:* Again …

Preparing for the test

Singers who have successfully achieved Dark Blue level aural test (b) (see page 37) should have little difficulty with this. Once again, encourage singers to feel the pulse either by clapping along (at first) or tapping a toe.

The test itself

Below, the text spoken by the examiner is shown in *italic* type. This will enable you to conduct a mock test with your singer before the exam.

Please clap or tap, in strict time, this rhythm pattern. I will play it to you twice.

Now, I will count out loud two bars of the pulse, as introduction to the first playing.

01

Say: 1, 2, 3, 1, 2, 3   *Say:* Again ...

02

Say: 1, 2, 1, 2   *Say:* Again ...

03

Say: 1, 2, 1, 2   *Say:* Again ...

04

Say: 1, 2, 3, 1, 2, 3   *Say:* Again ...

05

Say: 1, 2, 1, 2   *Say:* Again ...

06

Say: 1, 2, 1, 2   *Say:* Again ...

07

Say: 1, 2, 3, 1, 2, 3   *Say:* Again ...

Bronze award section B2, test (b): echo test (singing)
Candidates are required to sing (as an echo and in strict time) three simple two-bar phrases; each is heard only once. The key chord and the tonic will be sounded, and the pulse indicated, before the passage begins. The melody will:

- be in a major or minor key

- not necessarily begin or end on the tonic

- be in 2/4, 3/4 or 6/8

- contain stepwise movement, and also leaps of a third, fourth and fifth (not always as elements of the tonic triad)

- contain a variety of note values which may include minims crotchets, quavers and semiquavers. Dotted notes may be used.

Here are some sample tests. The first one shows you the 'mechanics' of the test: what the examiner plays and when the candidate is expected to sing. Below it and over the page are more examples which follow the same format. If you feel it necessary, transpose any of these examples into a key more suitable for your singers.

Use the criteria above to create more of your own for practice purposes. On page 83 you will find more practice tests and the words that the external examiner will use when delivering them. This will help your singers familiarize themselves with the format of the test before the exam itself.

Preparing for the test
This test should be straightforward for singers who have achieved Dark Blue level, but the format is new and may need work. The requirement to echo passages in rhythm demands an instant response, with less time for reflection and consideration. Some singers may feel pressurized by this. The best preparation is practice.

Help singers by encouraging them to 'harness' the pulse: if they can keep time, it will aid rhythmic accuracy. This is more than half the battle when it comes to the echoes. If singers falter, complete the whole passage before revisiting problem pitches, intervals or rhythms. This way maintains both the pulse and the singer's confidence.

Listening for anchor pitches can be useful too. Candidates who focus on the first and last notes of each phrase, and maybe an important note in the middle, will sing with more confidence and shape – even if they may not manage to reproduce all the pitches at first. The most useful anchor pitches are the tonic and dominant, but bear in mind that these may not always begin and end the test passages. Any 'strong' pitch on a strong beat can serve as an anchor.

The test itself
Below, the text spoken by the examiner is shown in *italic* type. This will enable you to conduct a mock test with your singer before the exam.

Next, the singing echo exercise. Will you sing back to me, as echoes, each of the three phrases I will play you? Here is the key chord. This is your first note. And ready now, two bars of the pulse.

[Choose a tempo helpful to the candidate, and indicate it by counting aloud two bars of the pulse as an introduction. Play the whole example an octave lower, or another transposition, if necessary to suit the candidate's range.]

Bronze award aural test: intervals
The examiner plays a key note which the candidate is asked to sing; this note is then re-sounded together with a note a minor third, major third, perfect fourth or perfect fifth above it. The candidate is asked to sing the upper note. The interval is then played again, after which the candidate is asked to name the interval. Two or three examples will be given, within the candidate's vocal range.

Preparing for the test
This should pose few problems for singers who have passed test (e) at Dark Blue level, but here singers are asked to sing both notes of the interval and to name it. This needs familiarity with the sound and 'feel' of intervals in the voice, which will be achieved by regular practice and study of theory. (The intervals in this test are covered in Module B of the Dark Blue workbook, and shown here beginning on the note C.)

It is vital to be able to hear and sing the higher of two notes played together. This could be practised with with any interval. Once this is secure, move on to identifying intervals by singing from the lower note to the upper – either filling in the notes between, or by stepping – using the methods practised earlier (see page 44).

The test itself
Below, the examiner's script is shown in *italic* type and the instructions in [brackets]. These will enable you to conduct a mock test with your singer before the exam.

Finally, I should like you to sing and name me some intervals. I might play you a major or minor third, or a perfect fourth or fifth. Sing me this key note [Play a note in the lower part of the candidate's range] *and listen to this interval.* [Play the two notes, simultaneously; sustain for a thoughtful length of time.] *Now, sing me the higher note.*

Listen again to the interval, and please name it. [Play the two notes again, simultaneously.]

Now, a second one: [and maybe a third; use the same script but different key notes. A third example is not necessary if the first two responses are prompt and faultless.]

Use any of the examples below, transposed if necessary to suit the candidate's range.

Section B3: technical questions
In section B3, the examiner refers the candidate back to the anthem or song that he or she sang in section A3 of the exam. Using the music for this piece as a starting point, the examiner will test the candidate's familiarity with aspects of notation and theory by asking questions about such things as:

- notes in the treble or bass clef (the examiner will use the same clef as the candidate chose in test B1)

- time values of notes (including dotted patterns)

- time signatures (in simple time, with crotchet or minim pulse)

- key signatures (major and minor, up to three sharps or flats)

- dynamic markings

- performance instructions

Preparing for the test
Candidates who have successfully completed modules B and C of Dark Blue level will have sufficient technical knowledge to answer these questions. The performance instructions on page 28 of the workbook and the reference section on pages 44–46 are important reading in this context. The questions about performance instructions, for example, are drawn from those in the Light Blue and Dark Blue workbooks.

It is not possible here to provide sample questions about all the pieces on the syllabus list. Make sure your candidate is prepared for the sort of questions that might be asked about his or her chosen song or anthem. All the pieces in section A3 are available in the *RSCM Bronze Collection*, books 1 and 2; and each one has training notes that you should consult by way of preparation. You should also ensure (by testing) that your candidate knows the following details of the piece:

- the names of all the pitches in the chosen clef or part (including sharp or flat names as dictated by key signature or accidentals)

- the time signature of the piece, and what it means (the number of beats in a bar and what type of beats they are); and also the meaning of other time signatures (2/4, 3/4, 4/4 and 2/2)

- the names of all the note values (British or American terms) and their durations (including ties and dotted patterns)

- the tonality of the piece (major or minor) and the relevance of the key signature to that tonality (candidates should be familiar with key signatures of up to three sharps or three flats)

- the meaning of all performance directions in the piece, including tempo markings (and tempo changes); dynamics (and dynamic changes); repeat marks; and marks of articulation

- the meaning and use of all the words and symbols on page 28 of the Dark Blue workbook

Test candidates' knowledge of the chosen piece by frequently asking questions about these different elements of the music; and test wider knowledge by asking similar questions about other music too.

RED LEVEL

Introduction
The five aural tests at Red level assess singers' ability to: sing melodies (in a variety of keys and time signatures) after hearing them played; sing a one-octave arpeggio, major or minor, ascending and descending, after hearing the key chord and key note; to identify, name, and sing keys and notes in extracts of printed music; to sing any major, minor or perfect interval up to and including the octave; and to mark the pulse and identify the time signature of a short passage played by the examiner.

 The 'Tone and range' exercises in Module A of the Red workbook (pages 11–14) will prepare singers technically for these tests. The theory activities in Module B (pages 17–29) will supply the vocabulary and concepts singers need to understand what is being asked of them. All the necessary keys and key signatures are covered there too.

  Red aural test (a)
To sing back a melody which is played in two two-bar sections. The key chord and tonic will first be sounded and the pulse indicated. The first section will be played twice; after the second playing, the singer should echo it. The second section will then be played twice, after which the singer should echo it. The melody will:

- be in a major or minor key

- not necessarily begin or end on the tonic

- be in 2/4, 3/4, 4/4 or 6/8

- contain stepwise movement, and also leaps of a third, fourth and fifth (not always as elements of the tonic triad)

- contain a variety of note values which may include minims, crotchets, quavers and semiquavers. Dotted notes may be used.

Here are some sample tests. Use the criteria above to create more of your own for practice purposes. For the test itself, use the passages on pages 89–90.

Preparing for the test

This test further develops musical memory and accurate pitching. Play the tests at a pitch which is appropriate for the singer. Expect accurate tuning and rhythm in response. Preparatory work could include the accurate pitching of one, two or three notes from a phrase, or you could devise simpler phrases and gradually increase the complexity until the test level is reached.

At this level, the range of notes and size of jumps is increased and rhythms are more complex. Rhythmic insecurity may lead to problems of pitch, so at first it may help if singers reproduce the rhythm alone, either by clapping or singing on one note. For difficulties with pitch, isolate problem notes and intervals for repetition. Encourage the singer to hear and sing individual pitches in relation to the tonic.

The singer must take care to remember the first note of each phrase. It may help to keep the pulse by tapping a foot or toe, and by humming along quietly as the piano plays. The structure of the test means that responses need to be immediate and rhythmic after each section of the tune is sounded.

Delivering the test

Use one of the tests below that suits your singer's range: you may need to play tests an octave lower for tenors and basses. If you want to use a particular test that may be beyond the range of a singer, it is acceptable to transpose it into another key.

Sound the key chord first, and then the tonic. Sound two bars of the pulse by tapping with one hand. Then play the first section of the melody twice, in strict rhythm. After this, the singer should provide the echo. Then play the second section twice, still in strict rhythm, and wait for the echo.

Assess the accuracy of the response. Listen for accurate reproduction of pitches and rhythms, and a sense of security and confidence. If you are unsure about the result, test the singer with a second passage.

Red level: aural test (a)

Red level: aural test (a) *cont.*

 Red aural test (b)

To sing, unaccompanied, a major or minor arpeggio of one octave (ascending and descending). The choir trainer will first sound the key chord and key note.

 Preparing for the test

Singers should already be familiar with the concept and sounds of triads and arpeggios through practical and theory work at Dark Blue level, and from modules A and B of the Red workbook. This test follows on from singing a scale at Light Blue level, but since there are gaps between the notes here, intonation may be a problem. Begin by singing up and down a triad, eventually extending to the top note. Singers will often find singing the minor version more challenging, so practice the minor third interval until it is secure. Take care not to push singers out of their range.

Delivering the test

Once the singer knows what is expected, simply sound the chord and the key note. The chart below indicates suitable ranges for the *starting* notes for singers at this level. To achieve this target, singers should respond with a good tone, and with sensible breathing to support the top notes.

*For newly changed voices,
begin no higher than E*

Red aural test (c)

To look at a short passage of choral music in short or open score and:

- name the key
- name the pitch of any note in the first chord
- on hearing the first chord, sing any note in it (within the singer's vocal range) as requested by the choir trainer

The test passage will:

- be in a major or minor key of up to four sharps or flats
- not necessarily begin on the tonic, and the first chord will not necessarily in be root position

Here are some sample tests. Use the criteria above to find suitable passages of your own from printed music. For the test itself, use the passages that begin overleaf. The required answers are shown by each score.

01

Key: E flat major

Soprano: B flat
Alto: D
Tenor: F
Bass: B flat

02

Key: E flat major

Soprano: B flat
Alto: G
Tenor: E flat
Bass: G

Preparing for the test

Singers who understand the theory for this level should have little difficulty with the first two parts of test (c). They may struggle to recognize minor keys, so need to understand the idea of the raised seventh degree. (It may help to revisit the material about harmonic minor scales starting on page 20 of the Dark Blue workbook.) For example if the piece has a key signature of two sharps but the music contains an A sharp, that A sharp will be the seventh note of a minor scale. If singers work out that A sharp is a semitone below B (the seventh note of a major or harmonic minor scale is always a semitone below the tonic), they will arrive at the answer – B minor.

The third part is more complex and may need careful preparation. First, play two notes and ask singers to sing the lower one. Then extend this to three-note chords, asking singers to pitch the lowest or the middle note. Then move to four-note chords. Once singers are secure with the lower notes, ask them to reproduce the higher ones.

It is also helpful to encourage singers to identify the root, third and fifth within the opening chord. Knowing which note appears in which part will help the singer to pitch the part requested by the examiner. The information about triads and arpeggios on pages 27 and 46 of the Red level workbook will help here.

The actual test allows singers to see the chord in question as well as hear it. They should work out how far up, or down the requested note is in the chord, and either work from the top or bottom note to the answer. The ability to hear the top and bottom notes is thus important to the successful outcome of the test.

Delivering the test

Choose one of the test passages below, find it in the singer's copy and give it to the singer. Allow about 15 seconds for perusal, after which the singer should name the key signature. After this, specify one of the parts and ask for the name of the first note. Finally, play the first chord in the passage. Ask the singer to sing the first note of any part – but you should only ask for notes within the range of the singer. Expect a reasonably prompt response if the test is to be passed.

In order to pass this test, singers must get all three parts correct – key identification, note-naming and pitch reproduction. You will find the answers to the first two parts to the right of each passage below.

Red level: aural test (c)

01

Key: B minor

Soprano: F sharp
Alto: B
Tenor: D
Bass: F sharp

Red level: aural test (c) *cont.*

02

Key: E major

Soprano: G sharp
Alto: E
Men: E

03

Key: E flat major

Soprano 1: B flat
Soprano 2: E flat
Alto: B flat
Tenor: G
Bass: E flat

04

Key: F major

Soprano: A
Alto: F
Tenor: C
Bass: F

05

Key: E minor

Soprano: B
Alto: G
Tenor: E
Bass: B

06

07

08

Red aural test (d)

To sing, above a given note, any major, minor or perfect interval (up to an octave).

Preparing for the test

Singers will need to be familiar with the theory of intervals and the 'feel' of them in the voice. Details are given on pages 21–23 of the Red workbook, and page 46 lists all the relevant intervals in ascending order of size, in treble and bass clefs. For reference, these are also shown here, starting on the note C.

You may have your own ideas about how to approach the teaching of intervals. Some singers learn them quickly and easily – others may need help to remember them, particularly the larger and less straightforward ones. Here are a few hints:

Some singers get confused between the minor and major sixth. For the minor sixth, singers could think of the first two notes of 'Close every door to me' from *Joseph and the Amazing Technicolor Dreamcoat*. The first two notes of 'My Bonny lies over the ocean' form a major sixth. It can be useful to practise singing these two intervals alternately to aid familiarity.

The difference between minor and major sevenths may cause problems too. The first two notes of 'There's a place for us' from *West Side Story* form a minor seventh. Examples of major sevenths are rare, but the first and third notes of 'Somewhere over the rainbow' form this interval. (And, if extra reference is necessary, the first two notes of this song form an octave.) Singers may also find it useful to think of examples of these intervals from their own repertoire or music collections.

Delivering the test

Simply play a key note, and name an interval for the singer to produce. Listen for confident, accurate pitching without too much delay. Repeat the process with two or three different intervals from a few different starting notes, to ensure that the singer's grasp of the exercise is really secure.

When choosing starting notes and intervals, make sure that the singer can comfortably reach the upper note of any interval you request. See the range guides on page 90 – the safe upper limit for each voice is an octave above the notes shown.

Red aural test (e)

To tap or clap the pulse of a passage of music and state whether it is in 2, 3 or 4 time. The passage will be played twice. On the second playing the singer should tap the pulse, stressing where the strong beat falls, then state whether the music is in 2, 3 or 4 time. The music will:

- be in 2, 3 or 4 time, simple or compound

- last long enough for the singer to identify the pulse

- be in a tempo and style where the pulse is clear and easy to identify

Preparing for the test

As at earlier levels, this test develops listening and rhythm skills. To help your singers prepare, any music with an apparent beat in simple or compound 2, 3 or 4 time is appropriate, at any tempo where the pulse remains reasonably clear.

When you play, lightly stress the first beat of each bar. Make the pulse clear but play musically without over-emphasis. At first, simply ask singers to clap along. Then encourage them to identify the stressed beats and count '1' – or clap more loudly – on each of these. They can then work out how many beats there are between each stressed beat.

This test extends what has gone before, but now includes compound time. This often causes problems, and singers need to be taught what to listen out for. Note that time signatures are not asked for – merely the number of beats in a bar. In compound times, the beat is sub-divided into threes, but the threes are usually too fast for the music to be in triple time. If the singer tries to clap each quaver of a fast passage in 6/8 time, it should be immediately obvious that the claps are too close together.

Learning to spot the two slower dotted crotchet beats is the key. If this remains difficult, check the singer has properly understood the concept of compound time signatures (see page 20 of the Red workbook). When testing passages in 6/8, play them quickly enough so that the beat is not ambiguous. Make sure that the second dotted crotchet beat is slightly lighter than the first, to show where the barline falls.

Delivering the test

Once the singer knows what is expected, simply play the music twice. (The passages for this test begin on the opposite page.) To achieve this target, singers should clap the beats clearly, emphasizing the first beat of each bar. After clapping, they should state whether there are two, three or four beats in a bar.

Red level: aural test (e)

01 — Allegro ma non troppo

02 — Allegretto

03 — Simply ($\quad$ = 80)

Red level: aural test (e) *cont.*

Introduction

There is only one sight-reading target at Red level. It assesses the ability to sing from notation. The notational elements tested will be familiar to singers who have worked on Module B of Red level.

Red sight-reading test (a)

To sing a short melody from sight, using the set words. The key chord and starting note are sounded. The singer is then given 15 seconds to look through the music. The key chord and starting note are sounded again; after this, the singer should attempt the test. Unless the first attempt is perfect, a second one will be requested. There is no piano introduction – the candidate sets the tempo and the accompanist will follow. The test will:

- be sung to a piano accompaniment (which the singer sees)

- be in simple or compound time, around eight bars long

- be in any key up to and including five sharps or flats

- cover a range of up to an octave, maybe slightly more

- not necessarily begin or end on the tonic, and may contain modulation away from the tonic chord

- contain intervals of up to a sixth

- feature semibreves, minims, crotchets and quavers (and their equivalent rests); the dotted crotchet/quaver pattern and simple syncopation may also appear

- include dynamics, phrasing and other performance directions

To get an idea of the level of complexity involved, look at the actual test passages that begin on page 111. Use the criteria above to find more test passages of your own for practice purposes. The information that begins overleaf about preparing for this test also contains some sample passages, with advice about how to use them in practice.

At this level, you must take care helping your singers to:

- feel comfortable establishing the tempo from the information in the music

- use the preparation time effectively to identify anchor points and potential pitfalls

- recognize chromatic notes and modulation points

- recognize sixths in notation, and sing them

- practise singing falling intervals

- be comfortable with compound metre

- understand dotted rhythms and simple syncopations

On the following pages you will find advice about how to integrate some of these theoretical and notational elements into sight-reading practice to enhance your singers' aural imagination.

Preparing for the test

This test is harder than its equivalent at Dark Blue level, demanding simultaneous reading of rhythm, pitch, words and performance details. Thorough knowledge of the theory in Module B of the Red workbook is essential, but this is only the start. Other vital keys to confident sight-reading are discussed here, with a few training hints.

The right attitude

Some singers (and teachers) are intimidated by sight-reading, particularly when it requires attention to a range of features and preparation time is limited. A fearful student will perform less well than a relaxed one. Your job as a teacher is to make sight-reading not only a normal activity but also a source of pleasure – a chance to encounter new music in an enquiring, open-minded, non-threatening environment.

Therefore the 15 seconds of preparation time stated in the target is definitely not to be imposed at the outset. It is a goal – a point singers need to reach before you assess them for the level. If you hurry students at first, it may instil fear. Allow them time to explore, experiment and make mistakes. After they have attempted a piece of sight-reading, encourage reflection on what was successful and what was less so, and on what they found easy and what they found harder. Only when they are confident sight-readers should you start to reduce the amount of preparation time bit by bit.

Confidence in setting the tempo

This requires recognition of tempo indicators and time signatures. Ensure that students know the meanings of the Italian tempo directions used at Dark Blue and Red levels, and that they understand the theory of time signatures.

Encourage singers to look at pieces they already know and (unaided by you) use the tempo information to count a few introductory bars of pulse and then start to sing. By removing the necessity to read unfamiliar notation, this activity focuses purely on imagining what the pulse should be and what the music should sound like.

Next, have singers look at tempo indications and time signatures in some unfamiliar music. At first ask them simply to imagine the pulse, then clap or tap it. Later you might ask them to clap the pulse and speak the text of the first few bars over the top. Once again, this can be practised independently of any pitch reading.

Security of pitch

In the Red sight-reading test, the key chord and starting note are sounded twice before the singer begins. This of course helps with pitch security but some singers fail to make best use of it when they are under pressure, forgetting the notes they have heard when they are confronted with the music itself. Avoid this by encouraging singers to scan the notation for each occurrence of the starting note. This links the heard sound to the printed music.

If the starting note is not the tonic, singers should also pay attention to the tonic when it is sounded in the key chord and hold it in the memory while looking for all instances of it in the score. (Check your singers understand the concept of the tonic.) Again, this technique is something you can practise without requesting any actual singing – it is a good aid to aural imagination. (Red level aural test (c) is also excellent preparation for note identification and pitch security.)

Rhythmic security

The ability to 'keep going' is the most important feature of successful sight-reading: it is crucial to maintain the pulse in spite of mistakes. Singers should always know where they are in the bar. You can aid this by providing plenty of clap-and-count exercises – with both familiar and unfamiliar music.

It can also help singers to read the text of the test aloud before they begin to sing. (This is in fact a feature of the Silver award sight-reading test – see page 123.) Doing this creates a rhythmic framework which can be maintained regardless of pitching errors. During training, it can also be useful to ask singers (before they attempt to sing) to speak the text in rhythm, to the established pulse. This focuses on accurate rhythm reading without worrying about pitch; and the words will often help to articulate the rhythm.

Yet you may find that, at the first sign of trouble, a student's overwhelming instinct is to stop – however encouraging you are. This is a natural reaction to a mistake (or perceived mistake), and simply exhorting a singer to 'keep going!' may not be enough. Indeed the more you do this, the more it may undermine confidence. Instead, it is important to teach strategies that give singers the security to continue. Anchor points provide this security.

Understanding anchor points

Sight-reading often takes place under pressure. When preparation time is limited, it is important that students learn to identify, before starting to sing, a few places in the notation that they can fix in the imagination and aim for as they work through the passage. A number of different elements can be anchor points:

- a pitch – especially one that is heard in the key chord that occurs at a prominent point in the music

- a group of pitches – especially repeated notes or ones that move by step (or leaps that are comfortable for the singer)

- a rhythmic pattern or feature – particularly one that repeats and is easy to reproduce

- a word or phrase in the text – particularly one that articulates the rhythm or has a particular character

- a performance direction – even a change of dynamic on a particular beat can serve as a reference point

Sometimes one anchor point is sufficient to provide shape and structure to the attempt; at others, more than one will be useful (they don't all have to be the same type). In preparatory work, you should help students to identify suitable anchors.

Playing to strengths

Some singers are stronger in certain aspects of sight-reading than others; some pitch easily but struggle with rhythm; others vice versa. Encourage students to maximize their strong points. For example, singers who pitch securely but find rhythm harder should try to get the notes right at the first attempt, then refine the rhythm at the second. Good rhythm readers may want to work the other way round, concentrating on pitch afterwards.

Red level: sight-reading test (a)

Modulation

Red level sight-reading tests may modulate away from the tonic. The accompaniment will help centre the singer in the right key, but it helps security of pitch if singers understand the difference between sharpward and flatward modulations. Here are some introductory passages to help with this. Sing them to *ah*.

Try them without accompaniment at first, but sound the tonic triad and key note. These examples are mainly stepwise or triad based, but the accidental requires careful pitching of a tone or semitone. Encourage singers to look for useful anchor points – tonic, dominant, and repeated or stepped notes.

Sharpward modulations

In the example below, the music moves into the dominant (one of the most common modulations). The clue here is the A natural, which is outside the key signature. (It will also be important to note during preparation that the A in the third bar is a flat, not a natural.)

In the example below, the music moves into the relative minor. The clue here is the D sharp in the third bar. It is important to pitch the semitone E–D sharp accurately. While in the test the accompaniment will help, the singer should be able to imagine and pitch this interval during the preparation time. This is particularly important because D natural features prominently in the accompaniment of the first two bars – the D sharp is a new pitch.

Flatward modulations

In the example below, the music moves flatwards to the subdominant. The clue here is the F natural, which is outside the key signature. Again, the singer needs to imagine the pitch of this note during preparation. It can help to be aware of the presence in the first bar of F sharp in the accompaniment. (This latter note is in conflict with the note that the singer will have to pitch in the second bar, but skilled singers may be able to use it as an anchor.) Attentive singers should also spot in advance that they have to sing F sharp too, in the third bar, and that the first chord of this bar will prepare them for this.

The example below is more complex and less obvious, moving through F minor via an imperfect cadence. The correct pitching of the D flat–C semitones is essential. Equally, singers will need to take care over the D natural leading note (back into E flat) on the last beat of the third bar. Once again, the accompaniment supports this, but it will help to have imagined the note in advance.

Here is another preparatory example. The chromatic notes are covered in the accompaniment – and are in keeping with the style of the music. The E flat in the penultimate bar is in the piano chord on the first beat. In both cases, the singer has to pitch a whole tone step. Rhythmic security is vital here too.

Here are the key training points to consider:

- The chromatic notes are supported by the accompaniment (both are a step down of a tone).

- This 'internalization' of intervals could be supported with aural work, pitching tones or semitones from a given note.

- The accompaniment helps to underpin the syncopated rhythm – including the introduction.

- The singer should count the accompanist in, or tap the beat. This needs a confident grasp of the tempo at the outset.

- The starting note (G) is sounded, but the key (C major) must be recognized quickly. The note on the word *Christmas* is the key note and should be easy to pitch. Singers should spot that the first phrase starts and finishes on the same note.

- The most likely pitfall is the unsupported perfect fifth at the beginning of the second phrase. The following fall of the fourth to the A may be more secure if the singer remembers that it is a step higher than the G the phrase started on.

- The rhythm needs to be secure at the end with the unsupported last phrase placed on the correct beats of the bar. Tapping a foot through the music will help here.

On the next few pages you will find some preparatory tests, with ideas to help successful completion. During the preparation time, singers should scan the words for potential pitfalls, such as the use of more than one note per syllable (the layout of which may confuse at first), hyphens splitting a word between notes, and so on.

- Although there is no separate rhythm test, it is still a good idea to prepare for these tests by clapping sections of the rhythm. At this level, syncopation will be encountered for the first time in the sight–reading tests and singers need to be secure.

- The key is F minor. Singers need to be familiar with keys up to five sharps or flats, and must be able to recognize the notes of the tonic triad. In minor keys, singers should expect to encounter the sharpened seventh with an accidental.

- The rhythm is quite syncopated with a repeated figure. Singers should practise this type of rhythm by clapping relevant examples. (It may help at first to clap bar 1 without the tie.)

- Bar 1 is based on the tonic; bar 2 falls to the lower dominant.

- At this level, the accompaniment is much more independent than before. Practise individual phrases without the piano to increase confidence.

- In bar 4, the accompaniment takes the music into A flat major. The singer should be confident enough to pitch the major thirds in bars 3 and 4. Looking through the music, the singer may have already pitched bar 4 from the tonic chord.

- The piano part is close to the melody in bars 4 and 5 and again in bars 7 and 8.

- Bars 5 and 6 are a falling sequence. If singers recognize where sequences occur, this makes singing more straightforward.

- Try to add the simple dynamics.

- Finally, the singer should take care with the breathing in this piece. It consists of four two-bar phrases. More than ever before, sing with a good, confident tone!

- During the preparation time, singers should try to decide where to breathe. In this piece, it is sensible to breathe in bar 5 after the word *say*, then avoid breathing again until the end of bar 7. It is also important to reserve breath for the crescendo that starts in bar 6.

- Although the beginning of the extract is *forte*, it is important not to start too loudly. The singer should keep something in reserve for the final line.

- Care should be taken with the dotted rhythms – both the articulation and the pronunciation of the words.

- It's important to read the text carefully so that there are no surprises (such as in bars 2 and 5).

- Once again, it is sensible to use the preparation time to establish good points to breathe – and to conserve breath to sustain the vocal line where necessary.

Red level: sight-reading test (a)

- Singers need to feel confident in keys like this. This can only be achieved by familiarity with key signatures and the theory, sound and feel of different scales.

- In the tests at this level, there is still plenty of reference to the tonic chord – four instances in the example above.

- The first phrase may look awkward, but is quite straightforward. Ask the singer to sing the notes on 'Past' and 'clock' – this should not be difficult. The missing note, 'three', is the tonic. Stress that it is important to look at the shape of a whole phrase, rather than reading a succession of separate intervals.

- Bars 5–6 look similarly awkward. Again, ask the singer to sing the notes on 'past' and 'clock'. As they are the tonic and dominant, this should be easy. This time, the missing notes 'three' and 'o' are one step higher than the dominant. This should help the singer sing the phrase without worrying about the major 6th.

- Add the simple dynamic contrast that starts on the last crotchet of bar 6.

Delivering the test

Select a test with a range which is suitable for the singer. Hand over the singer's copy and indicate which passage is to be attempted. Sound the key chord and tonic. Allow 15 seconds for preparation. At the end of this, sound the key chord and tonic a second time, then accompany the singer's attempt at the test. Listen out for security of rhythm and pitch, and the ability to keep going regardless of minor slips.

It is acceptable to allow the singer a second attempt. If you remain unsure as to whether the target has been achieved, test a second passage.

Red level: sight-reading test (a)

Red level: sight-reading test (a) *cont.*

02

Red level: sight-reading test (a) *cont.*

03

04

Allegretto

mp

Drip, drop, Drip, drop, lis – ten to the rain.

mp

Drip, drop, Drip, drop, lis – ten to the rain.

mp

5

mf

Pit – ter pat – ter, drip – ping drop – ping, on my win – dow pane.

mf

Pit – ter pat – ter, drip – ping drop – ping, on my win – dow pane.

05

Maestoso

mf

My soul doth mag – ni – fy the Lord,

mf

My soul doth mag – ni – fy the Lord,

Red level: sight-reading test (a) *cont.*

and my spi – rit hath re – joiced in God my sa – viour.____

and my spi – rit hath re – joiced in God my sa – viour.____

Sostenuto

mf

Ho – ly, ho – ly, ho – ly Lord, God____ of pow – er and might,

Ho – ly, ho – ly, ho – ly Lord, God____ of pow – er and might,

heav'n and earth are full of your glo – ry, ho – san – na in the high – est.

heav'n and earth are full of your glo – ry, ho – san – na in the high – est.

Red level: sight-reading test (a) *cont.*

Red level: sight-reading test (a) *cont.*

08

Cantabile

May the grace of our Lord Je - sus Christ, and the

May the grace of our Lord Je - sus Christ, and the

love of God the Fa - ther, and the fel - low - ship of the

love of God the Fa - ther, and the fel - low - ship of the

Ho - ly Spi - rit be with us for ev - er - more. A - men.

Ho - ly Spi - rit be with us for ev - er - more. A - men.

10

O be joy - ful in the Lord, all___ you lands,

O be joy - ful in the Lord, all___ you lands,

serve the Lord with_ glad - ness and come be-fore his pre-sence with a song.

serve the Lord with_ glad - ness and come be-fore his pre-sence with a song.

SILVER AWARD

The material in this section reflects the order and titles of the tests in the award exam itself. For more details see the syllabus for the RSCM singing awards, which is downloadable from **www.rscm.com** free of charge.

Singing at first and second sight: introduction

Section B1 of the Silver award exam contains just one sight-reading test. It assesses candidates' ability to sing from notation and requires the same skills as those needed for Red level, though the format is slightly different. The relevant theory and notation can be found in Module B of the Red workbook. You are advised to begin by reading the Awards syllabus, which can be downloaded from **www.rscm.com** free of charge.

How to use this section of the book

The preparatory materials for Red level sight-reading (see page 99) are also suitable for use here. There are further exercises starting on page 104 with pointers, hints and tips – these are also reproduced in the downloadable singer's copy. (You can also use the criteria below to find more practice passages of your own.) Then on page 130 you will find the script and instructions used by the examiner, together with further tests – these will enable you to conduct a mock exam with your students.

Silver award section B1, test (a)

Candidates will be asked to sing at sight, with the given English text, a short piece of two or three phrases. The examiner will play the outline accompaniment, which is seen by the candidate. The key chord and starting note will be given, but there will be no piano introduction. Candidates are expected to set their own appropriate tempo, and to pay careful attention to the printed dynamics, as well as phrasing and articulation. Two attempts will be allowed. The test:

- will be in 2/4, 3/4, 4/4, 2/2 or 6/8

- will not necessarily start on the first beat of the bar

- may include rests, ties and dotted notes

- will be in any of the following major keys: D, E flat, F, A flat, B flat; *or* any of the following minor keys: C, D, G, F, B

- will not necessarily begin or end on the tonic

- will be pitched in the range low C to upper D (candidates are offered the choice of treble or bass clef)

- may contain intervals up to and including a sixth, and additionally a perfect octave

- may contain one non-diatonic note

- will contain a range of dynamic variations between *p* and *f*, possibly containing 'hairpins'

- will have an Italian performance direction at the start, and may include indications for changes of tempo near the end

Before attempting the music, the candidate will be asked to read the text aloud (in the exam booklet, the text will be printed below the music, as shown in the following tests). If the candidate has difficulty with the words, the examiner may help with this. (For details of how the tests are conducted for candidates with dyslexia or other special educational needs, consult the syllabus.)

The examiner then names and sounds the key chord and starting note on the piano, and allows up to 15 seconds of preparation time. After this, the key chord and starting note are sounded again and the candidate sings, to the examiner's accompaniment.

Two attempts at the test will be given. (A second attempt will always be offered, unless the first is faultless in absolutely every detail.) Before the second attempt, the examiner will identify one significant point of error – such as a miscounted rhythm, mispitched interval or overlooked dynamic marking – and may go over this with the candidate once. This may include counting, playing or singing a maximum of one bar. After this, the candidate must begin the second attempt.

 What the examiner is listening for
Full marks will be given for a faultless first attempt in which the music is perfectly articulated, with a solid, confident sense of pitch and pulse; the examiner will also listen for: correct articulation and pronunciation of the words; accurate interpretation of any dynamics and tempo instructions; good breath control and appropriate shaping of phrases.

Marks will be deducted for:

- insecurity of pitch, rhythm or pulse
- irregularity of pace or rhythm
- hesitation or lack of confidence
- inconsistency of pace or tone
- failure, in the second attempt, to improve or to remedy the significant point of error identified after the first

 Preparing for the test
Preparation for this test should focus on and develop all that has been learned before. Remind your candidate that:

- in the test, the singer has to set the tempo, so must be able to understand Italian tempo markings and time signatures
- the music will be firmly rooted in a key, so it's important to look for anchors – notes and phrases based on the tonic triad
- it's important to take a snapshot of the shape, character and mood of the music during the preparation time – and reading the text at the start of the test may give useful clues about this
- the ability to read ahead is essential – and comes with practice
- it is nearly always better to keep going, in rhythm, than to stop – mistakes are rarely as bad as they feel!

Silver award: section B1, test (a)

 Here is a preparatory Silver award test. It should present few problems as long as the octaves are sung with conviction. Here are a few things for singers to bear in mind:

- The candidate sets the speed. What does *Andante* suggest?

- The singer begins and the examiner, accompanying, immediately picks up the singer's chosen pulse; so this must be confident and clear.

- In this piece there are many references to the tonic chord and, especially, the dominant note. As before, look for anchor points.

- The singer must not be put off by the accompaniment dropping out briefly just before the end!

Music divine, proceeding from above,
Whose sacred subject often-times is love.

In this preparatory test, singers should look out for the following:

- The pulse will need to be carefully set and felt throughout the passage.
- Security of pitch may be challenging against the chromatic accompaniment.
- Care will be needed with the quavers in bar 4 and the tied note over bars 6–7.
- A breath may be needed in the second line - where?
- The final note is chromatic and needs careful pitching.

The sea is his, and he made it, and his hands prepared the dry land.

Parts of the example opposite – such as the stepwise movement in the first sung bars – may seem reasonably straightforward at first, but there are some challenging elements. The singer will need to feel secure with both rhythm and pitch.

- As long as the key is recognized (G major) then the first four bars (steps and broken key chord) should be straightforward. The first note of the third phrase in bar 5 is also a key chord note. You could try asking the singer to pitch this note before attempting the exercise.

- When singing the penultimate note of the first line, some singers may be disorientated by hearing the C sharp in the accompaniment. If they can identify the note B earlier in the bar in the piano (albeit at a different octave), this should help security of pitch.

- The triplet rhythm looks daunting in the second line. The beat needs to be felt in minims to fit in the threes: this may need to be practised. In a 4/4 metre, begin clapping four crotchets per bar – then change to six crotchets in two triplets – as in this example. In both cases, the keyboard should play a minim pulse under the music – as in the example.

- An alert singer will notice that there is a quick hint of the triplets in the accompaniment just before this phrase starts. This can be used to help to construct the rhythm.

- The sixth just before the end is part of the key chord, but will rely on the E being pitched correctly on the first word *long*. Once again, take care that the keyboard part doesn't confuse! Ask for the last three notes to be pitched before attempting the exercise.

- The keyboard part is really a harmonic support here and in several places has the potential to mislead. Practise the phrases without accompaniment to encourage independence.

Tell me the tales that to me were so dear,
Long, long ago.
Sing me the songs I delighted to hear,
Long, long ago.

Though rhythmically quite straightforward, the example opposite requires the singer to be comfortable in compound metres. Pitching is more problematic in places, though this will be helped by carefully identifying anchor points and pitch preparation in the accompaniment. A good grasp of the mood and atmosphere of the music is crucial to effective delivery here.

- Before starting to sing, establish the compound metre by clapping the rhythm of the first few bars.

- The sixth in the first phrase may be helped by its proximity to the start and end notes of the phrase. Practise pitching the notes on: *kiss, eyes* (key chord); then, *kiss your eyes.*

- Similarly, the falling fourth in the second phrase may be helped by its proximity to two key-chord notes. Practise singing the notes on: *when, rise*; then, *when you rise.*

- Singers should be encouraged to spot where the accompaniment does in fact supply a melodic support – as with the next phrase. The starting note joins onto the end of the rising figure in the right hand of the keyboard, with the melody initially based on the key chord once more.

- The D flat in bar 7 is covered by the piano, but the semitone shift from the note before and to the note afterwards should be secure.

- The first note of the last phrase is covered by the keyboard and the phrase is a straightforward scale leading to a final descent of the key chord.

Golden slumbers kiss your eyes,
Smiles awake you when you rise,
Sleep pretty darlings, do not cry,
And I will sing a lullaby.

The test itself

Once your student is ready, you can perform a mock exam using the materials on the following pages (see the relevant pages of the downloadable singer's copy for this section of the book). There are four test passages, in much the same format as they appear in the exam.

It is advisable to print out only what the student needs for the practice tests at any given time. Each one is available in treble and bass clef versions. In the exam, the examiner will select a page from a leaflet to hand to the candidate, offering the choice of treble clef on one side and bass clef on the other; in the context of this book, it may be easier for you to establish which clef your candidate would prefer and print just that page. But make students aware that in the exam itself they will be offered a choice.

The entire script and instructions used by the examiner are shown below. Once again, the text spoken by the examiner is shown in *italic* type, and the instructions are shown [in square brackets].

Have a look at Test B, on this page of the leaflet. [Offer the candidate the appropriate section of the downloadable copy.] *If you'd prefer to see this test in the bass clef, please turn over the page.* [Say this to all candidates.]

First, I'd like you to read aloud the text of this piece, as printed below the music systems. [Offer help, as appropriate, with any evident difficulty or hesitation.]

I'd like you to sing me this piece, using these words, whilst I accompany, at your own chosen tempo.

Here is the key chord of E flat major: *and your first note, B flat.*

[If bass clef is chosen, play both of these an octave lower.]

Take a few moments to prepare, and you may sing out loud if you wish. [Allow a pause of 15 seconds.]

Here is the key chord again [play] *and your first note* [play, leave a short pause]. *Please begin now ...* [Accompany sensitively, allowing the candidate to set and control the tempo, but gently encouraging momentum.]

[After the first attempt:] *Thank you. Before we have a second attempt,* * *may we check again for a moment ...* [One error / slip – a miscounted rhythm, or a mispitched note/ figure, especially if either then gave rise to further insecurity; or one uncertain moment with text / underlay; or an overlooked dynamic (or performance) marking. Say precisely what it was.]

Ready now for your second attempt. Here is the key chord again [play] *and your first note* [play].

[* The second attempt must be offered with a moment's helpful advice, unless the first attempt was faultless.]

God be gracious to us and bless us, and make his face shine upon us.

Silver award: section B1, mock exam

Have a look at Test B, on this page of the leaflet. [Offer the candidate the appropriate treble or bass clef section of the downloadable copy.] *If you'd prefer to see this test in the bass clef, please turn over the page.* [Say this to all candidates.]

First, I'd like you to read aloud the text of this piece, as printed below the music systems. [Offer help, as appropriate, with any evident difficulty or hesitation.]

I'd like you to sing me this piece, using these words, whilst I accompany, at your own chosen tempo.

Here is the key chord of D major: *and your first note, D.*

[If bass clef is chosen, play both of these an octave lower.]

Take a few moments to prepare, and you may sing out loud if you wish. [Allow a pause of 15 seconds.]

Here is the key chord again [play] *and your first note* [play, leave a short pause]. *Please begin now ...* [Accompany sensitively, allowing the candidate to set and control the tempo, but gently encouraging momentum.]

[After the first attempt:] *Thank you. Before we have a second attempt,* * *may we check again for a moment ...* [One error / slip – a miscounted rhythm, or a mispitched note/ figure, especially if either then gave rise to further insecurity; or one uncertain moment with text / underlay; or an overlooked dynamic (or performance) marking. Say precisely what it was.]

Ready now for your second attempt. Here is the key chord again [play] *and your first note* [play].

[* The second attempt must be offered with a moment's helpful advice, unless the first attempt was faultless.]

Jesus Christ is holy, Jesus Christ is Lord, to the glory of God the Father.

Have a look at Test B, on this page of the leaflet. [Offer the candidate the appropriate treble or bass clef section of the downloadable copy.] *If you'd prefer to see this test in the bass clef, please turn over the page.* [Say this to all candidates.]

First, I'd like you to read aloud the text of this piece, as printed below the music systems. [Offer help, as appropriate, with any evident difficulty or hesitation.]

I'd like you to sing me this piece, using these words, whilst I accompany, at your own chosen tempo.

Here is the key chord of F major: *and your first note, F.*

[If bass clef is chosen, play both of these an octave lower.]

Take a few moments to prepare, and you may sing out loud if you wish. [Allow a pause of 15 seconds.]

Here is the key chord again [play] *and your first note* [play, leave a short pause]. *Please begin now ...* [Accompany sensitively, allowing the candidate to set and control the tempo, but gently encouraging momentum.]

[After the first attempt:] *Thank you. Before we have a second attempt,* may we check again for a moment ...* [One error / slip – a miscounted rhythm, or a mispitched note/ figure, especially if either then gave rise to further insecurity; or one uncertain moment with text / underlay; or an overlooked dynamic (or performance) marking. Say precisely what it was.]

Ready now for your second attempt. Here is the key chord again [play] *and your first note* [play].

[* The second attempt must be offered with a moment's helpful advice, unless the first attempt was faultless.]

O be joyful in God, all ye lands!
Serve the Lord with gladness,
Come before his face with songs of joy!

Have a look at Test B, on this page of the leaflet. [Offer the candidate the appropriate treble or bass clef section of the downloadable copy.] *If you'd prefer to see this test in the bass clef, please turn over the page.* [Say this to all candidates.]

First, I'd like you to read aloud the text of this piece, as printed below the music systems. [Offer help, as appropriate, with any evident difficulty or hesitation.]

I'd like you to sing me this piece, using these words, whilst I accompany, at your own chosen tempo.

Here is the key chord of D minor: *and your first note, D.*

[If bass clef is chosen, play both of these an octave lower.]

Take a few moments to prepare, and you may sing out loud if you wish. [Allow a pause of 15 seconds.]

Here is the key chord again [play] *and your first note* [play, leave a short pause]. *Please begin now ...* [Accompany sensitively, allowing the candidate to set and control the tempo, but gently encouraging momentum.]

[After the first attempt:] *Thank you. Before we have a second attempt,* * *may we check again for a moment ...* [One error / slip – a miscounted rhythm, or a mispitched note/ figure, especially if either then gave rise to further insecurity; or one uncertain moment with text / underlay; or an overlooked dynamic (or performance) marking. Say precisely what it was.]

Ready now for your second attempt. Here is the key chord again [play] *and your first note* [play].

[* The second attempt must be offered with a moment's helpful advice, unless the first attempt was faultless.]

You are my hiding place and my shield;
My hope is in your word.

Introduction
The four aural tests for the Silver award assess similar skills to those needed at Red level, but examine them slightly differently. Singers are required to: clap the pulse of a melody played by the examiner and state whether it is in 2, 3 or 4 time; sing as echoes two melodic phrases played by the examiner; listen to a triad, sing back the middle or lowest note and identify it as major or minor; and sing intervals above a given key note.

 The 'Tone and range' exercises in Module A of the Red workbook (pages 11–14) will prepare singers technically for these tests. The theory activities in Module B (pages 17–29) supply the vocabulary and concepts singers need to understand what is being asked. All necessary keys and key signatures are covered there too.

 Silver award section B2, test (a): clap the pulse and identify the beat
Candidates are required to clap or tap the pulse of a melody (played by the examiner) in simple or compound time. The phrase will be played twice; the candidate should listen during the first playing and clap along with the second. After this, the candidate must state whether the melody was in 2, 3 or 4 time. The melody will:

- be in 2/4, 3/4, 4/4 or 6/8, around eight bars long

- not necessarily begin on the first beat of the bar – up-beats are possible

- contain a variety of note and rest values which may include minims, crotchets, quavers and semiquavers; dotted notes may be used, including dotted quaver/semiquaver patterns

- be in a major or minor key

- begin or end on the tonic but not necessarily both

 Preparing for the test
Singers who have successfully completed Red level aural test (e) (see page 96) should have little difficulty with this. For practice purposes, you can play to your students any music with the time signatures listed above – use around eight bars of any example you choose. Encourage singers to feel the pulse from the outset, perhaps by tapping a foot or finger. It is also useful if singers learn to do this – almost as a reflex action – with any music they hear.

 The test itself
On the opposite page, the text spoken by the examiner is shown in *italic* type, and the instructions to the examiner [in square brackets]. This will enable you to conduct a mock test with your singer before the exam, using any of the six test passages.

Clap or tap the pulse, when I play this melody for the second time. Listen now to the first playing. [Begin immediately, with no further introduction or elaboration.]

Please join in this time, indicating the pulse. [Repeat.] *Was the melody in 2 time, 3 time or 4 time?*

Use the examples below in a similar way.

Silver award section B2, test (b): echo test (singing)
Candidates are required to sing (as an echo and in strict time) two two-bar melodic phrases; each phrase is heard twice. The key chord and starting note will be sounded, and the pulse indicated, before the passage begins. The melody will:

- be in a major or minor key

- not necessarily begin or end on the tonic

- be in 3/4, 4/4 or 6/8

- contain stepwise movement, and also leaps of up to a sixth, and additionally a perfect octave

- contain a variety of note and rests which may include minims crotchets, quavers and semiquavers; dotted notes may be used

The sample test below shows you the 'mechanics' of the test – what the examiner plays and when the candidate is expected to sing. On the opposite page, you will find more examples which follow the same format. If you feel it necessary, you can transpose any of these into a key more suitable for your singers. You can also use the criteria above to create more of your own for practice purposes.

Preparing for the test
Singers who have passed aural test (a) at Red level will have little difficulty with this. The preparatory materials that begin on page 88 are also suitable for use here. As before, you should encourage singers to:

- identify the tonic and dominant notes and use them as anchors

- keep a steady pulse (tapping a foot or finger, for example)

- listen for repeating rhythmic, melodic or intervallic patterns

The test itself
On the opposite page, the text spoken by the examiner is shown in *italic* type, and the instructions to the examiner [in square brackets]. This will enable you to conduct a mock test with your singer before the exam, using any of the six test passages.

Silver award: section B2, test (b)

ⓘ **The test itself**
Below, the text spoken by the examiner is shown in *italic* type, and the instructions to the examiner [in square brackets]. This will enable you to conduct a mock test with your singer before the exam, using any of the six test passages.

Next, I'd like you to sing, as echoes, these two phrases, after you have heard each of them for the second *time. The repeat of each phrase will be played without a break, then* you *must echo it by singing it once. Sing your echo immediately and in strict time.*

Here is the key chord ... this is your first note ... and I will count aloud two bars of the pulse.

[Choose a tempo helpful to the candidate, and indicate it precisely by your counting aloud, as introduction. Play the whole example an octave lower, or another transposition, if necessary to suit the candidate's range.]

Silver award section B2, test (c): triads

Candidates are required to sing (as requested by the examiner) the middle or lowest note of a triad which will be played twice, and to identify the triad as major or minor. The key note will be played, then the triad in close position in any inversion. At least two chords will be tested in the exam. Here are examples of the triads candidates will encounter. They are given here in C major and C minor: you will need to vary the keys as you help your students to prepare.

Preparing for the test

This test draws on concepts and skills encountered at earlier stages of *Voice for Life*. For instance, Dark Blue aural test (c) requires the identification of major or minor triads (see page 39); and singers who have completed Module B of Red level will have the necessary skills for this. You may wish to check that they are familiar with the idea of major and minor tonalities (see page 26 of the Dark Blue workbook).

To prepare singers for the pitching part of the test, ask them first to sing *all* the pitches in triads you play – perhaps as an arpeggio, ascending and descending. Play major and minor triads in various inversions. Once singers can comfortably sing the arpeggio, it should be easy for them to sing individual notes that you nominate.

Identifying modality can be more tricky. As the triads may occur in inversion, candidates cannot rely on 'measuring' the lower interval (this only works with root-position triads). However by this stage most singers will be able to discern major and minor triads from their sounds, regardless of inversion. To check that your singers can do this, play a number of differently inverted triads. (Bear in mind that the test does not require candidates to identify inversions, or even to know about them.)

Candidates may be confused by hearing a minor third at the bottom of a major triad in first inversion, or the major third at the bottom of a minor triad in first inversion. If this is the case, suggest they first try to identify whether the triad sounds 'bright' (major) or 'dark' (minor). This is not infallible but can be a good first step.

It is also important for candidates to hang on to the tonic note which the examiner sounds before the chord; this will help with the major/minor question. Having identified the tonic, 'measuring' the size of the interval from it to the third above it, and calculating it as major or minor, will then aid identification.

Bear in mind that when you use the sustain pedal on a piano, it allows the strings to resonate. Singers with good hearing may detect the upper partials, which can be confusing. So when you play the chord for this test, avoid the sustain pedal; it is better to play and hold the chord via the keyboard.

The test itself

Below, the text spoken by the examiner is shown in *italic* type, and the instructions to the examiner [in square brackets]. This will enable you to conduct a mock test with your singer before the exam.

Now, I should like you to listen to a triad, and I will ask you questions after you have heard it twice.

Here is the key note ... and listen now to its tonic triad for the first time ... [Play the notes simultaneously, not arpeggiated; sustain them for a thoughtful length of time.]

I will play it again, and then please sing me the middle (or *lowest*) *note.* [Wait for the sung response, and maybe a second try.] *Was that triad major or minor?*

Here is a second one. This is the key note [play a different note] *and here is the triad* [not necessarily a different modality] *for the first time ...*

I will play it again, and then please sing me the lowest (or, *middle*) *note.* [Wait for the sung response, and maybe a second try.] *Was that triad major or minor?*

[A third one, using the same script, should only be requested if one of the two modality answers is incorrect.]

Here are some examples of the types of triads you might use. Play them an octave lower, or another transposition or inversion, if necessary to suit the candidate's range.

Silver award section B2, test (d): intervals
Candidates are required to sing a variety of intervals. A key note will be given in the lower range of the singer's voice, and the examiner will name the interval the candidate should sing above it. Two or three examples will be given, based on different key notes. (The required intervals are shown here, starting on the note C.)

Preparing for the test
This test is similar to Red level aural test (d), and singers who have achieved that target should have little difficulty with this. Several intervals in succession are tested, from different starting notes, so it may be useful to practise this in advance.

A possible complication is that singers will find it hard to 'clear' the tonic of the first instance of the test when the second tonic is sounded, so there may be some 'interference' from one to the other. Plenty of practice should help with this. A useful preparatory routine is to ask the singer to add the major third or the fifth above a series of tonics you play, gradually increasing the pace until the singer can swiftly react to each new starting note. Once this is secure, proceed to the other intervals.

The test itself
Below, the text spoken by the examiner is shown in *italic* type, and the instructions to the examiner [in square brackets]. This will enable you to conduct a mock test with your singer before the exam.

The final aural exercise is for you to sing me some intervals. You might be asked for a major second, a major or minor third or sixth, or a perfect fourth or fifth.

Please sing me this key note ... [in the lower part of the candidate's range] *and, above it, please sing ...* [The first one requested should not be a sixth. Be ready to repeat the key note, or the request, if asked.]

Now, a second one: [and maybe a third; use the same script but different key notes and requested intervals. A third example is not necessary if the first two responses were faultless.]

Section B3: technical questions

In section B3, the examiner refers the candidate to the piece he or she sang in section A3 or A4 of the exam (at the examiner's choice) and uses the music as the basis for questions about aspects of notation and theory, such as:

- note names in the treble or bass clef (including leger lines) – in the candidate's chosen part and in other parts too

- note values (including dotted or tied notes and syncopations), and places in which rhythmic patterns identified are repeated elsewhere in the score

- time signatures (simple or compound, crotchet or minim pulse)

- key signatures up to five sharps or flats (or, in renaissance music, the piece's tonal centres); related keys (such as relative minor, tonic, or dominant); accidentals and their significance

- dynamic markings and performance instructions

Preparing for the test

Candidates who have successfully completed modules B and C of Red level will have sufficient technical knowledge to answer these questions. The performance instructions on page 28 of the workbook and the reference section on pages 44–46 are important reading in this context. The questions about performance instructions, for example, are drawn from those in the Red workbook and all earlier levels.

It is not possible here to provide sample questions about all the pieces on the syllabus list. Make sure your candidate is prepared for the sort of questions that might be asked about the chosen songs or anthems. All the pieces in section A3 are available in the *RSCM Silver Collection*, books 1 and 2; and each has training notes that you should consult by way of preparation. You should also ensure (by testing) that your candidate knows the following details of the piece:

- the names of all the pitches in all the clefs (including sharp or flat names as dictated by key signature or accidentals)

- the time signature and what it means (the number and type of beats in a bar); and also the meaning of other time signatures

- the names of all the note values (British or American terms) and their durations (including tied and dotted notes and patterns)

- the key signature and tonality of the piece (major or minor), and related key signatures of up to five sharps or three flats)

- the meaning of all performance directions in the piece, including tempo markings (and tempo changes); dynamics (and dynamic changes); repeat marks; and marks of articulation

- the meaning and use of the words and abbreviations on pages 28–29 of the Red workbook

Test candidates' knowledge of the chosen piece by frequent and regular questions about these different elements of the music; and test wider knowledge by asking similar questions about other music too.

YELLOW LEVEL

Introduction

The five aural tests at Yellow level assess singers' ability to: identify notes, chords and inversions (from printed notation and heard music); sing any interval up to an octave from a given note; sing a melodic or harmonic minor scale (at the singer's choice), ascending and descending, after hearing the key chord and key note; identify different types of cadences; state the number of beats in a bar after hearing a passage of music (complex time signatures may be involved).

The 'Tone and range' exercises in Module A of the Yellow workbook (pages 9–12) will prepare singers technically for these tests. The theory in Module B (pages 19–35) will supply the vocabulary and concepts singers need to understand what is being asked of them. All the necessary intervals, keys, key signatures and time signatures are covered there too, and in the reference section which begins on page 51.

Yellow aural test (a)

To look at a short passage of music and:

- name the key signature

- name the pitch of any note in the first chord

- name the first chord and its inversion

- name the relation of the chord to the key (by means of Roman numerals or the degree of the scale – dominant, tonic etc.)

- sing any note of the first chord (within the singer's range) after hearing it played

The passage will:

- be in any major or minor key

- be in open or closed score, up to four parts

- start on a chord based on any degree of the scale, in any inversion

Here are some sample tests and answers. Use the criteria above to create more of your own for practice purposes. For the test itself, use the passages that begin on page 151.

Key signature: Note names:
B flat major Soprano: F Alto: F Tenor: C Bass: A

First chord: F major in first inversion

Relation of chord to key: Dominant (or chord V)

Sen - su - um de -fec - tu - i.

Key signature: Note names:
B flat major   Soprano: B flat   Alto: E flat   Tenor: G   Bass: E flat

First chord: E flat major in root position

Relation of chord to key: Subdominant (or chord IV)

Preparing for the test
Test (a) builds on work done at earlier levels and in order to succeed, singers will
need to have understood all the theory material in Module B of the Yellow workbook.
Perhaps the most challenging aspect is the third part of the test – naming the first
chord and its inversion. Here are some hints on how to help with this. Begin by
looking at the passage below:

it be - gan _ to   sail

For the first part of the question, the singer must establish the key signature. Two
flats is either B flat major or G minor – the F sharp in bar 1 signals G minor (and
this is confirmed by the first chord in bar 2). For the second part of the question, if
the singer observes the clefs and key signature carefully, it should not be difficult to
name the pitches in the first chord. (Reading up from the bottom, these notes are E
flat, G and C.)

To identify this chord for the third part of the test, the singer must now think of these
notes as a root position triad in closed position. This means imagining them as two
intervals of a third, one on top of the other. The only possible solution to this is, from
the bottom upwards, C, E flat and G. The lower interval indicates whether the triad
is minor or major. In this instance, because C to E flat is a minor third, we know the
triad is minor. Because the lowest note is C, we know it is C minor.

Now singers must identify the inversion of the first chord in the passage. The middle
note of the triad is at the bottom of the chord, so it is in first inversion. So the answer
to the third part of the question is: C minor, first inversion.

| Root | First | Second |
| position | inversion | inversion |

The fourth part of the question requires an explanation of how the first chord in the passage relates to the tonic. The theory on pages 27, 28 and 52 of the Yellow workbook will help with this. For the passage above, the singer should be able to work out that C is the fourth note of the G minor scale, and that the fourth note of the scale is the subdominant.

 Confusion could occur if the singer fails to realize that the chord takes its name from the root of the chord, regardless of the inversion in which it appears in the music. You may need to reinforce this idea when preparing for the test.

 If the chord consists of four different notes, in the context of this test it will be a seventh chord (see page 30 of the Yellow workbook). Seventh chords can appear in root position or in any one of three inversions:

For the singing element of this test, singers should not find any problem pitching notes of the first chord if they have already accurately imagined them. But do not forget to practise this part of the test as well as the earlier parts of it.

 Delivering the test
Choose one of the tests that begin on the opposite page, find it in the singer's copy and give it to the singer. Allow about 15 seconds of preparation time. After this, the singer should name the key signature. Next, specify one of the parts and ask for the name of the first note. Then ask the singer to give you the name and inversion of the first chord, and to describe it in relation to the key. Finally, play the first chord in the passage. Ask the singer to sing the first note of any part – but you should only ask for notes within the range of the singer.

In order to pass this test, singers must get all five parts correct – key identification; note-naming; the name of the first chord and its inversion; the description of its relation to the key; and pitch reproduction. Beneath each of the passages, you will find the answers to the first four parts of the question.

01

Key signature: *Note names:*
C major   *Soprano: E   Alto: C   Tenor: G   Bass: B flat*

First chord: C major 7th in third inversion

Relation of chord to key: Tonic (or chord I) with an added 7th

02

Key signature: *Note names:*
C minor   *Soprano: G   Alto: B natural   Tenor: F   Bass: D*

First chord: G major 7th in second inversion

Relation of chord to key: Dominant 7th (or chord V7)

03

Key signature: *Note names:*
C major   *Soprano: A   Alto: F   Tenor: C   Bass: C*

First chord: F major in second inversion

Relation of chord to key: Subdominant (or chord IV)

Yellow level: aural test (a) *cont.*

04

cre - do, cre - do, cre - do

Key signature: *Note names:*
C major   *Soprano: G   Alto: E   Tenor: C   Bass: B flat*

First chord: C major 7th in third inversion

Relation of chord to key: Tonic (or chord I) with an added 7th

05

mi - se - re - re,

Key signature: *Note names:*
F minor   *Soprano: F   Alto: F   Tenor: C   Bass: A flat*

First chord: F minor in first inversion

Relation of chord to key: Tonic (or chord I)

06

Soprano — Hide not thou thy face from us
Alto — Hide not thou thy face from us
Tenor — Hide not thou thy face from us
Bass — Hide not thou thy face from us

Key signature: *Note names:*
E minor   *Soprano: B   Alto: D sharp   Tenor: F sharp   Bass: B*

First chord: B major in root position

Relation of chord to key: Dominant (or chord V)

Yellow level: aural test (a) *cont.*

07

Key signature: Note names:

A flat major   Soprano: A flat   Alto: F   Tenor: A flat   Bass: D flat

First chord: D flat major in root position

Relation of chord to key: Subdominant (chord IV)

08

Key signature: Note names:

E major   Soprano: C sharp   Alto: E   Tenor: C sharp   Bass: G sharp

First chord: C sharp minor in second inversion

Relation of chord to key: Submediant (chord VI); or relative minor

Yellow aural test (b)

To sing any interval (up to an octave) above a given starting note.

Preparing for the test

The intervals in question are given on page 54 of the Yellow workbook.

Some singers learn intervals quite easily: others may need help to remember them, particularly the less straightforward ones. The important addition at Yellow level is the augmented fourth or diminished fifth, two intervals which sound the same. A well-known example is found in the first two notes of 'Maria' from *West Side Story*. To explain the interval technically, play it as a fourth plus a semitone, or a fifth minus a semitone. It may help singers to think of examples of these intervals from their own repertoire or music collections. And you may have ideas of your own, too.

Delivering the test

It is important that the upper note of the interval you request is easily within the singer's range. Decide which interval you want to test before you sound the lower note.

Yellow aural test (c)

To sing, unaccompanied, a minor scale (harmonic or melodic at the singer's choice) of one octave (ascending and descending). The choir trainer will first play the key chord and key note.

Preparing for the test

Singers should already be familiar with the concept and sounds of minor scales, and the theory for these is covered in the Red and Yellow workbooks. Even so the test is harder than it may seem, because of the intonation problems many singers encounter at the top end of both versions of the minor scale.

The harmonic version features the awkward augmented second at the top; and the melodic version is different at the top end depending on whether it is ascending or descending. Whichever version singers choose to sing for the target, they must demonstrate accurate intonation to pass the test.

The following exercise is useful for practising the top end of the harmonic minor scale. Ask singers to sing it to *ah*, paying particular attention to the augmented second. Point this interval out as the scale ascends and descends.

For the top end of the melodic minor scale, try the following (to *ah*). In this case, point out the differences between the ascending intervals and the descending ones.

Delivering the test

Once the singer knows what is expected, simply sound the chord and the key note. Below are suitable ranges for the starting notes for singers at this level. To achieve this target, singers should respond with a good tone, and with sensible breathing to support the top notes.

For newly changed voices,
begin no higher than E

Yellow aural test (d)
To identify the cadence at the end of an extract of music. The cadence will be perfect, imperfect, plagal or interrupted. The extract will:

- be up to eight bars long, in simple or compound time

- begin on the tonic (which is sounded before the test is played)

- be played twice

- be reasonably straightforward harmonically, in a classical style, with few chordal 'distractions'

Preparing for the test
The cadences in this test are given on page 31 of the Yellow workbook. The examples there contain only major chords in root position, as this is the simplest way to explain the concept. Help singers to identify them by playing these examples, and also by playing other extracts – hymns are particularly useful here.

It can help to describe the sound of each cadence to your singers. For example, in a **perfect cadence** the progression dominant–tonic makes the ending sound quite final, as if the music has reached a conclusion.

An **imperfect cadence** sounds unfinished, as if the music wants to keep going.

A **plagal cadence** ends on the tonic, but sounds less emphatically final because it is approached from the subdominant rather than the dominant.

In major keys, an **interrupted cadence** finishes on a minor chord. This 'reversal of polarity' is a useful means of identification.

(Note that in minor keys, an interrupted cadence will often be two major chords: sharpened dominant followed by major submediant).

Bear in mind that 'real' music is often more complex than the model cadences in the workbook, and this may be reflected in the test. Various things may distract singers. For example cadences occur in both major and minor keys; they may contain inversions, passing notes or seventh chords; a minor cadence may end on a major tonic ('tierce de Picardie').

 Play plenty of examples to your singers in the context of longer passages, and point out cadences in the music they sing. Ask them to identify cadential points (the two chords approaching a pause in the music, often called the 'preparation chord' and the 'resolution chord'). Help them to recognize the chords in each one, and hence to name the cadence.

In the context of this test, in which the passage begins on the tonic, it is important that singers keep the tonic chord in mind and identify the last chord in relation to it. It can also help to ask singers to indentify cadential chords by their names or degree numbers. This links to other aural tests at this level and enhances the connection between theoretical understanding and aural perception.

 The passages that follow contain the four cadences in the test, first in a major key (on this page) and then in a minor (opposite). Play the complete passages so that your singers can hear the difference in character between each cadence; then select individual two–bar sections and encourage your singers to name the cadence. Some of the examples contain special features which are shaded in the music and explained in the labels on the right. Your singers may be able to identify these – if not, try pointing them out within the context of the cadence.

The preparation chord is in first inversion (IIb)

The preparation chord contains a passing note of a falling 7th

PLAGAL

IMPERFECT

The preparation chord is in second inversion (Ic V)

INTERRUPTED

Passing notes in the tenor – one forms V7 in the preparation chord

PERFECT

Minor example ends on the major tonic ('tierce de Picardie')

Delivering the test
Select one of the test passages below. Tell the singer you will sound the tonic chord, then play the passage twice. When you have finished playing, expect the answer promptly. (The correct answer is given below each test.) If you are unsure of the validity of the outcome, it is acceptable to repeat the test using a second passage.

Yellow level: aural test (d)

01

Perfect

02

Perfect

Yellow level: aural test (d) *cont.*

Perfect

Imperfect

Imperfect

Imperfect

Plagal

Plagal

09 **Andante**

Plagal

10 **Andante**

Interrupted

11

Interrupted

12

Interrupted

Yellow aural test (e)
To identify the time signature of a passage of music, which will be played twice. After the second playing the singer should state the number of beats in each bar. The music will:

- be in 5/4, 5/8, 7/4 or 7/8

- be in a tempo and style where the pulse is clear and easy to identify

Preparing for the test
As at earlier levels, this test develops listening and rhythm skills – but this time it concentrates on the 'odd-number' time signatures that are introduced on page 32 of the Yellow workbook. Listening to, or singing, any music with an easily-heard beat in the time signatures listed above will be good preparation for the test.

In metres such as 5/8 and 7/8, the beats will (for the purposes of the test at least) always be grouped into smaller units within the bar. In the example below, the beat is counted as 1-2-3, 1-2 ¦ 1-2-3, 1-2 and so on.

Likewise, in the example below, the beat is heard as 1-2, 1-2, 1-2-3 ¦ 1-2, 1-2, 1-2-3 and so on (or possibly 1-2-3-4, 1-2-3). By adding these groupings together, singers will arrive at the answer: seven beats in a bar.

As you play preparatory examples, lightly stress the first beat of each bar. Emphasize slightly the first beat of each subdivision. At first it may help to ask singers to clap along and count the claps.

Singers may find it difficult to differentiate at first between the crotchet time signatures (5/4 and 7/4) and the quaver ones (5/8 and 7/8). This is partly a matter of tempo – the faster the pulse, the more likely the beats are to be quavers. But 5/8 and 7/8 tend to share a quality with the compound time signatures learned at earlier levels in that an underlying slower pulse (albeit an uneven one) can usually be heard in the note groupings.

So in the first example above, the slower pulse is dotted crotchet / crotchet. In the second example, it is crotchet / crotchet / dotted crotchet. It can help to ask singers to clap these underlying slower pulses and to notice that, in 5/4 and 7/4, this is much harder (if not impossible) to do.

ℹ️ **Delivering the test**
Once the singer knows what is expected, simply play the music twice. The test passages begin below. The singer should then state the time signature.

Yellow level: aural test (e)

04   **Happily** ♩ = 150

05   **Lively and fast**

06   **Andante**

Introduction

There is only one sight-reading test at Yellow level. It assesses singers' ability to reproduce melodies from notation. The notational and theoretical elements tested will be familiar to singers who have worked on Module B of Yellow level.

Yellow sight-reading test (a)

To sing a piece of music of moderate difficulty, using the set words. The key chord and tonic are sounded. The singer is then given 30 seconds to look through the music. The key chord and tonic are sounded again before the test is attempted. The test will:

- be sung to a piano accompaniment which will have a high degree of independence from the vocal line and may modulate

- be in any time signature and any key

- be around 12 bars in length (not including the piano introduction)

- cover a range that is likely to exceed an octave

- not necessarily begin or end on the tonic

- contain a variety of intervals, possibly including sevenths and augmented fourths or diminished fifths

- feature a variety of rhythms including triplets, duplets, dotted notes, syncopations and changing time signatures

- include dynamics, phrasing, expression and breath marks which the singer should reproduce when singing

To get an idea of the level of complexity required, look at the actual test passages that begin on page 168. Use the criteria above to find more test passages of your own for practice purposes. The information below about preparing for this test also contains suitable sample passages, together with advice about how to use them in practice.

Preparing for the test

At Yellow level, singers should be encouraged to sight-read almost any music. When preparing singers for this test, choose music that is consistent with the level of music theory introduced in the Yellow workbook. This, and the aural tests for this level, will prepare singers for such notational challenges as complex intervals, unusual time signatures and so on. In particular, you should encourage singers to:

- practise singing a range of intervals, up and down, from notation

- be comfortable with more complex time signatures

- read ahead to spot anchor points and potential pitfalls

- read and sing dynamics, phrasing, expression and breath marks

The preparatory exercises that follow contain advice about integrating elements of theory and notation into sight-reading to improve singers' confidence and aural imagination. As ever, careful preparation is the key. There is no such thing as 'too much' sight-reading practice. The advice on pages 100–101 is also relevant here.

Though quite straightforward, this preparatory example contains challenging details.

- In bars 5, 10 and 16 the left hand of the piano will help to delineate the rhythm in the vocal part, so use that as an anchor.

- It may feel odd to sing the G sharp in bar 8, as it follows a G natural in the piano in bar 7. Encourage singers to have the courage of their convictions.

- Singers should spot the climactic point in bar 15 and reserve enough breath (and volume) to carry it off.

The example overleaf, *Full Fathom Five*, is quite challenging – at the top end of tests at this level. However, among the key and time signature changes, much of the music should be approachable if the sight-reading techniques learned at previous levels are borne in mind – and if the singer is able to read ahead to spot any potential pitfalls. Certain elements in the piece are discussed below, followed by related general advice in *italic type* which is applicable to all sight-reading. Encourage singers to think about the specific points and their general application.

- The first eight bars consist of intervals firmly in the key of F minor (with a key change in bar 8). Pitching these should be straightforward for singers at this level. However the vocal line clashes with the keyboard ostinato, and this may prove to be a distraction. At Yellow level, it is reasonable to expect singers to be able to sing these bars unaccompanied as part of their preparation. *Independence from the accompaniment is absolutely essential in these tests.*

- The first awkward moment is the descending major seventh in bar 9, followed by the rising scale of whole tone steps. It is a good idea to practise short chromatic passages similar to this independently of the tests. *In the test itself, during the preparation period, singers should identify intervals that may be difficult to pitch and try them out quietly.*

- In bars 12–15, some of the difficult notes to pitch are doubled by the keyboard part. *It is always useful to identify places where the accompaniment 'tracks' the melody line as this provides useful anchor points.*

- Despite the time signature changes, the minim pulse is constant. *It is important to identify which rhythmic unit is constant and use it to keep the pulse in mind at all times – tap a foot gently if necessary.*

- In bar 17, the music returns to the tonic major. After this the pitching is reasonably easy, but there is a cross-rhythm in the left hand of the keyboard part. During preparation, it is important to identify where the pulse is regular (in this case, in the right hand) and use that as an anchor. *Identify rhythmic anomalies and work out which part of the accompaniment to follow.*

- Singers should sing with a good tone, and sensible breathing. A good degree of fluency is expected, so encourage them to keep going at all costs!

Delivering the test
Select a test in a range which is suitable for the singer, find it in the downloadable singer's copy and hand it to the singer. (Some passages may be more than one page long; make sure you print the complete test.)

Sound the key chord and tonic. Allow 30 seconds for preparation. At the end of this, sound the key chord and tonic a second time, then accompany the singer's attempt at the test. Listen out for security of rhythm and pitch, and the ability to keep going regardless of minor slips.

Yellow level: sight-reading test (a)

Yellow level: sight-reading test (a) *cont.*

Yellow level: sight-reading test (a) *cont.*

Yellow level: sight-reading test (a) *cont.*

06

Yellow level: sight-reading test (a) *cont.*

Yellow level: sight-reading test (a) *cont.*

dwel- ling: Sing to him! Je - sus Christ has_

dwel- ling: Sing to him! Je - sus Christ has_

ri - sen: Lord of all the Earth.

ri - sen: Lord of all the Earth.

10

GOLD AWARD

The material in this section reflects the structure of the award exam itself. For more details see the syllabus for the RSCM Gold Award, which is downloadable from **www.rscm.com** free of charge.

Introduction

In the exam for the RSCM Gold Award, singers are expected to demonstrate their skill and musicality in solo singing, as well as effective leadership and stylistic awareness as choristers in their RSCM–affiliated church or school. The examiners expect that candidates will already have achieved considerable success at earlier stages of the *Voice for Life* scheme, normally by completion of the workbooks to Yellow level and by passing the Bronze and Silver awards.

Because a very high level of musical skill is assumed for Gold award candidates, the exam has a different structure. For example there are no separate formal aural tests, as the examiners assume that aural awareness will be highly developed by this stage. Aural skills are examined indirectly in other parts of the syllabus. A candidate who has successfully completed the aural tests at Yellow level will be adequately prepared in this respect for the Gold award.

Gold sight-reading test (a)

Below is an extract from the Gold award exam syllabus for this test, followed by some notes of explanation to help you prepare singers for it.

'Candidates will be expected to sing at sight any appropriate voice part, in treble or bass clef, in a section of an unprepared anthem, in 16th/17th century or 20th/21st century tonal style, given to them by the examiner. The standard of difficulty will be comparable with Philips: *Ascendit Deus* or Joubert: *O Lorde the maker of al thing*. The duration of the section to be attempted will be at least one minute. The successful production of the words, which will be in either English or Latin, is an integral element of this assessment.

The examiner will first offer the candidate a short period of guided preparation of part of the test, the key chord, starting note and an indication of tempo having been given. (A candidate who, at the time of entry, submits supporting evidence of dyslexia, will be given an initial period of up to one minute to read aloud and practise the words of the section of the anthem to be attempted.) Then, after a pause of 30 seconds for private study, the key chord, starting note and tempo indication will be repeated before the candidate begins the assessed attempt; the examiner will play the accompaniment (or, where unaccompanied, a sketch of the other voice parts) on the piano. One assessed attempt only is allowed.'

Preparing for the test

Gold award candidates are likely to be proficient sight-readers who already tackle a range of music during their regular choral activities. When preparing singers for the exam you need to make sure that they:

- encounter music in as wide a variety of styles as possible

- have the necessary theoretical and technical capabilities to read and reproduce music at this level of difficulty

- can approach the task calmly and in a focused way, making maximum use of the guided and unguided preparation time

The best preparation for this is regular practice! Make sure your candidates sing at sight regularly so that it becomes a matter of habit, not a cause of anxiety.

About guided preparation

At the start of the test, the examiner will point out to the candidate certain aspects of the passage in question – tempo, mood and any important technical or interpretative details. (As a choir trainer, you will probably do this naturally when working with singers.) This guidance period should not last more than two minutes and not be exhaustive, but it should help to prepare the candidate to give a convincing performance at sight.

In the sample tests that follow, the music is labelled with some suggestions of things that can usefully be addressed during guided preparation. However these are not exhaustive: you may have other ideas of your own.

The test itself

The procedure for the test is shown below. The text spoken by the examiner is shown in *italic* type, and the instructions to the examiner [in square brackets]. This will enable you to conduct mock tests with your singers before the exam. Use the tests that start on the next page. You will find these in the singer's copy too.

Now it's time for your sight reading, after guided preparation.

Have a look at this piece. I am going to ask you to sing the ... line [name the part], *beginning at... and finishing at...* [give the bar numbers or the relevant words or performance marks].*

Here is the key chord, and your starting note. [Play these. Always give both first, before starting any other helpful explanation of the music.]

I suggest that we try over the opening bars / the passage beginning ... / to get the feel of the music. I can help you with any tricky moments. [Here, begin the guided preparation. Never play the whole piece. Only use the full two minutes guided preparation time if it is really needed.]

*Now you can have half a minute * for private study. You can sing out loud if you like! Let me just remind you of the chord, and your starting note, again.*

After a timed pause:

Now for the assessment. I will play a sketch of the accompaniment with you, but not including your voice part if I can help it. Try to keep going firmly all the way: I'll rescue you if really needed! Are you ready? ... Here is the chord... your starting note... and I'm counting you in...

[Only stop the assessment mid-way in dire emergency: considerable marks are lost by not keeping going. At the end, ask for the copy back from the candidate immediately.]

* Different procedures, where dyslexia is declared on the entry form:

1) Go over the words thoroughly together at the start, before giving the starting chord

2) half a minute, or longer if you wish ... Are you ready?

Gold award: section B, test 1

Make sure the dynamics are well articulated here

Shape these longer phrases carefully

Pay attention to pitching here

*Achieve a good contrast
here with the previous bars*

*This music is quite chromatic, so be careful to sing
what you see, not what you have heard*

Make dotted quavers crisp here

Pitch the accidentals carefully here

And with thy Saints _____ a - dore. _____

Section B, test 2: Rehearsal and interpretation
In section B2 of the Gold award exam, candidates must prepare their chosen voice part in five different pieces (see the syllabus for the full list). The examiner will choose three of the five pieces to rehearse, and will ask the candidate to:

- sing short excerpts, some unaccompanied, others with minimal accompaniment provided by the examiner; the examiner may also ask the candidate to respond to varied stylistic requests

- answer a variety of straightforward technical, interpretative and stylistic questions on each tested piece

- sing, with accompaniment, an alternative voice part (which may be in a different clef) for a few bars in one of the tested pieces

Candidates may expect technical questions to include: tonality (including key signatures and modulation), rhythmic features, imitative entries, common Italian terms, and basic harmonic understanding (such as cadences, sequences and suspensions).

Preparing for the test
The 'rehearsal' of each piece will begin with the singing of a section of the music, not necessarily starting at the beginning, and maybe with just a given note, and little or no accompaniment support for a while. Examiners want to know how alertly candidates can perform in this situation, helping to sustain their own line in the choir, and then sensitively react to some specific choral directions, maybe about phrasing, diction, dynamics or style.

This means that candidates who are already note-perfect have a distinct advantage: those who need help to sing the right notes in these pieces will fail to respond quickly enough. All relevant parts in a piece should be prepared. If the candidate's voice part has more than one line to sing in the score, the examiner may ask, for example: 'Would you prefer to start singing soprano 1 or soprano 2?' But after a short time the candidate will be asked to sing some phrases from the other line too. A significant proportion of the marks awarded relate to the response to this test.

When the examiner feels that section (a) has been adequately examined, the technical questions in section (b) will follow. Candidates who have successfully completed modules B and C of Yellow level will have sufficient technical knowledge to answer these. The performance instructions on page 18 of the workbook and the reference section on pages 51–54 are important reading in this context.

It is not possible here to provide sample questions about all the pieces on the syllabus list. Make sure your candidate is prepared for the sort of questions that might be asked about the chosen songs or anthems. You should also ensure (by testing) that your candidate knows the following details of the piece:

- the names of all the pitches in all the clefs (including sharp or flat names as dictated by key signature or accidentals)

- the time signature and what it means (the number and type of beats in a bar); and also the meaning of other time signatures

- the names of all the note values (British or American terms) and their durations (including tied and dotted notes); syncopations and alterations to time signatures

- the key signature and tonality of the piece (major or minor), and related key signatures of up to five sharps or three flats); modulations and cadences as well as other melodic and harmonic features

- the meaning of all performance directions in the piece, including tempo markings (and tempo changes); dynamics (and dynamic changes); repeat marks; and marks of articulation

Test candidates' knowledge of the music for the chosen pieces using frequent and regular questions about these different elements of the music; and you should try to test wider knowledge by asking similar questions about other music too. At this level singers should be perfectly confident to discuss a range of technical and interpretative topics related to any music in their repertoire.

Using the downloadable singer's copies

The downloadable singer's copies for *Musicianship* are available from the RSCM's website at **www.rscm.com** free of charge: follow links to Voice for Life\Musicianship. There you will find files for each section of this book ('colour' levels and awards), in treble and bass clef versions. Here is some help with navigation, taking page 23 of this book as an example.

You are in the Light Blue section of the book, so you need the Light Blue singer's copy (treble or bass clef version depending on singer)

This icon means the singer needs to see a printed copy

Tests within a section are numbered for ease of reference

Materials appear in the downloadable copies in exactly the same order as they do in this book.

Each individual group of tests is identified by the page heading.

Material in the copy is identified by its page number in this book.

You are on page 23 of this book, so you need to find that material in the copy.

The foot of the page shows which version you are using (treble or bass clef)

Kaplan Publishing are constantly finding new ways to s̶u̶̶ ̶̶ ̶̶ ̶̶ents looking for exam success and our online resou̶̶ ̶̶ extra dimension to your studies.

This book comes with free MyKaplan on̶̶ study anytime, anywhere. **This free onli̶̶ separately and is included in the price**

Having purchased this book, you have access to the following online study materials:

CONTENT	AAT	
	Text	Kit
Electronic version of the book	✓	✓
Knowledge Check tests with instant answers	✓	
Mock assessments online	✓	✓
Material updates	✓	✓

How to access your online resources

Received this book as part of your Kaplan course?
If you have a MyKaplan account, your full online resources will be added automatically, in line with the information in your course confirmation email. If you've not used MyKaplan before, you'll be sent an activation email once your resources are ready.

Bought your book from Kaplan?
We'll automatically add your online resources to your MyKaplan account. If you've not used MyKaplan before, you'll be sent an activation email.

Bought your book from elsewhere?
Go to **www.mykaplan.co.uk/add-online-resources**
Enter the ISBN number found on the title page and back cover of this book.
Add the unique pass key number contained in the scratch panel below.
You may be required to enter additional information during this process to set up or confirm your account details.

This code can only be used once for the registration of this book online. This registration and your online content will expire when the examinations covered by this book have taken place. Please allow one hour from the time you submit your book details for us to process your request.

Please scratch the film to access your unique code.

Please be aware that this code is case-sensitive and you will need to include the dashes within the passcode, but not when entering the ISBN.

INTERNAL ACCOUNTING SYSTEMS AND CONTROLS

STUDY TEXT

Qualifications and Credit Framework

Q2022

The Study Text supports study for the following AAT qualifications:

AAT Level 4 Diploma in Professional Accounting

AAT Diploma in Professional Accounting at SCQF Level 8

KAPLAN PUBLISHING'S STATEMENT OF PRINCIPLES

LINGUISTIC DIVERSITY, EQUALITY AND INCLUSION

We are committed to diversity, equality and inclusion and strive to deliver content that all users can relate to.

We are here to make a difference to the success of every learner.

Clarity, accessibility and ease of use for our learners are key to our approach.

We will use contemporary examples that are rich, engaging and representative of a diverse workplace.

We will include a representative mix of race and gender at the various levels of seniority within the businesses in our examples to support all our learners in aspiring to achieve their potential within their chosen careers.

Roles played by characters in our examples will demonstrate richness and diversity by the use of different names, backgrounds, ethnicity and gender, with a mix of sexuality, relationships and beliefs where these are relevant to the syllabus.

It must always be obvious who is being referred to in each stage of any example so that we do not detract from clarity and ease of use for each of our learners.

We will actively seek feedback from our learners on our approach and keep our policy under continuous review. If you would like to provide any feedback on our linguistic approach, please use this form (you will need to enter the link below into your browser).

https://forms.gle/U8oR3abiPpGRDY158

We will seek to devise simple measures that can be used by independent assessors to randomly check our success in the implementation of our Linguistic Equality, Diversity and Inclusion Policy.

British Library Cataloguing–in–Publication Data

A catalogue record for this book is available from the British Library.

Published by
Kaplan Publishing UK
Unit 2, The Business Centre
Molly Millars Lane
Wokingham
Berkshire
RG41 2QZ

ISBN: 978-1-83996-573-9

We are grateful to the Association of Accounting Technicians for permission to reproduce past assessment materials and example tasks based on the new syllabus. The solutions to past answers and similar activities in the style of the new syllabus have been prepared by Kaplan Publishing.

This Product includes content from the International Ethics Standards Board for Accountants (IESBA), published by the International Federation of Accountants (IFAC) in 2022 and is used with permission of IFAC.

CONTENTS

STUDY TEXT

PART A – ACCOUNTING SYSTEMS AND CONTROL

Chapter

PART B – ASSESSMENTS

KAPLAN PUBLISHING

INTRODUCTION

HOW TO USE THESE MATERIALS

These Kaplan Publishing learning materials have been carefully designed to make your learning experience as easy as possible and to give you the best chance of success in your AAT assessments.

They contain a number of features to help you in the study process.

The sections on the Unit Guide, the Assessment and Study Skills should be read before you commence your studies.

They are designed to familiarise you with the nature and content of the assessment and to give you tips on how best to approach your studies.

STUDY TEXT

This study text has been specially prepared for the revised AAT qualification introduced in 2022.

It is written in a practical and interactive style:

- key terms and concepts are clearly defined

- all topics are illustrated with practical examples with clearly worked solutions based on sample tasks provided by the AAT in the new examining style

- frequent activities throughout the chapters ensure that what you have learnt is regularly reinforced

- 'examination tips' help you avoid commonly made mistakes and help you focus on what is required to perform well in your examination

- 'Test your understanding' activities are included within each chapter to apply your learning and develop your understanding.

ICONS

The chapters include the following icons throughout.

They are designed to assist you in your studies by identifying key definitions and the points at which you can test yourself on the knowledge gained.

 Definition

These sections explain important areas of Knowledge which must be understood and reproduced in an assessment.

 Example

The illustrative examples can be used to help develop an understanding of topics before attempting the activity exercises.

 Test your understanding

These are exercises which give the opportunity to assess your understanding of all the assessment areas.

 Foundation activities

These are questions to help ground your knowledge and consolidate your understanding on areas you're finding tricky.

 Extension activities

These questions are for if you're feeling confident or wish to develop your higher level skills.

Quality and accuracy are of the utmost importance to us so if you spot an error in any of our products, please send an email to mykaplanreporting@kaplan.com with full details, or follow the link to the feedback form in MyKaplan.

Our Quality Co–ordinator will work with our technical team to verify the error and take action to ensure it is corrected in future editions.

KAPLAN PUBLISHING

Progression

There are two elements of progression that we can measure: first how quickly students move through individual topics within a subject; and second how quickly they move from one course to the next. We know that there is an optimum for both, but it can vary from subject to subject and from student to student. However, using data and our experience of student performance over many years, we can make some generalisations.

A fixed period of study set out at the start of a course with key milestones is important. This can be within a subject, for example 'I will finish this topic by 30 June', or for overall achievement, such as 'I want to be qualified by the end of next year'.

Your qualification is cumulative, as earlier papers provide a foundation for your subsequent studies, so do not allow there to be too big a gap between one subject and another.

We know that exams encourage techniques that lead to some degree of short term retention, the result being that you will simply forget much of what you have already learned unless it is refreshed (look up Ebbinghaus Forgetting Curve for more details on this). This makes it more difficult as you move from one subject to another: not only will you have to learn the new subject, you will also have to relearn all the underpinning knowledge as well. This is very inefficient and slows down your overall progression which makes it more likely you may not succeed at all.

In addition, delaying your studies slows your path to qualification which can have negative impacts on your career, postponing the opportunity to apply for higher level positions and therefore higher pay.

You can use the following diagram showing the whole structure of your qualification to help you keep track of your progress.

UNIT GUIDE

Introduction

All organisations must guard against fraud through good control systems. However, many businesses underestimate both the probability and impact of employee fraud. Those working within the accounts department play a pivotal role in guarding against misuse of resources, and the key aim of this unit is to provide students with the tools to evaluate internal controls and to recommend improvements.

The unit teaches students to consider the role and responsibilities of the accounting function, including the needs of key stakeholders who use financial reports to make decisions. Students will review accounting systems to identify weaknesses and will make recommendations to mitigate identified weaknesses in future operations.

Students will apply several analytical methods to evaluate the implications of any changes to operating procedures.

The structure of the accounting function, which varies depending on the size of the organisation, must comply with statutory requirements. Students will learn to identify appropriate controls, assess their impact in terms of cost-effectiveness, reliability and timeliness, and ensure that all functions adapt their working practices to meet new requirements in an ethical and sustainable way.

Technology is changing the way that accountancy information is processed, and this unit requires knowledge of the fundamental principles of data analytics and artificial intelligence (AI), which may be used as an alternative way to gather and analyse information. Cloud accounting is changing the way accountants work and visualisation, including dashboards, is increasingly used to present information in a way that is easier for stakeholders to understand. Data security and breaches are regularly reported in the press, and therefore it is imperative that students are aware of the importance of keeping all data secure and consider the confidential nature of the data that they will be processing as part of their everyday role.

Finally, students will evaluate the impact of changes on the system and its users, identifying different methods of support that can be given to users of the accounting system to assist them in adapting to the recommended improvements.

This unit is **mandatory** in the Level 4 Diploma in Professional Accounting.

Learning outcomes

- Understand the role and responsibilities of the accounting function within an organisation

- Evaluate internal control systems

- Evaluate an organisation's accounting system and underpinning procedures

- Understand the impact of technology on accounting systems

- Recommend improvements to an organisation's accounting system

Scope of content

To perform this unit effectively you will need to know and understand the following:

Chapter

1 Understand the role and responsibilities of the accounting function within an organisation

1.1 The accounting function

Learners need to understand:

1, 9

- the importance of ethics and sustainability within the accounting function

- the importance of accuracy and cost-effectiveness within the accounting system

- why different types and sizes of organisation or departments within an organisation will require different accounting information and systems

- the different accounting team staffing structures (centralised and decentralised) that will be required by different types or sizes of organisation:

  - length of scalar chain

  - levels of management

  - span of control.

1.2 Financial information used by stakeholders

Learners need to understand:

2

- different stakeholders of an organisation:

  - internal

  - external

- the purpose of financial information produced for:

  - internal use

  - external use

- how financial information is used by stakeholders

- that financial information must comply with legislation and regulation

- the importance of ethical information and sustainability practices to stakeholders

- that stakeholders use the following types of financial reports:

  - statement of profit or loss

  - statement of changes in equity

  - statement of financial position

  - statement of cash flow

  - budgetary control reports.

1.3 Changes to management information

Learners need to understand: 3, 5, 7

- how organisational requirements will inform the management information system:

  - size of organisation

  - strategic goals

  - legislation and regulation

- how management information systems should enable the calculation of performance indicators:

  - gross profit margin

  - operating profit margin

  - current ratio

  - quick (acid test) ratio

  - inventory turnover

  - inventory holding period (days)

  - trade receivables collection period

  - trade payables collection period

  - gearing

  - return on capital employed (ROCE)

- why changes may be required to existing systems to meet:

  - revised organisation requirements.

Chapter

2 Evaluate internal control systems

2.1 Internal controls

Learners need to understand:

3, 4

- the purpose of internal controls:
    - facilitate operations
    - safeguard assets
    - prevent and detect fraud
    - ensure quality of internal and external reporting
    - compliance

- the types of internal controls used in different parts of the accounting function:
    - segregation of duties
    - organisational controls
    - authorisation and approval
    - physical controls
    - supervision
    - personnel
    - arithmetical and accounting
    - management

- how different types of internal controls suit different types of organisations:
    - size (small, medium, large)
    - nature (cash-based, credit-based, online).

Learners need to be able to:

- assess how a strong system of internal controls can minimise the risk of loss to an organisation

- assess how a strong system of internal controls can ensure ethical standards in an organisation.

2.2 Prevent and detect fraud and systemic weaknesses

Learners need to understand:

6

- the common types of fraud within a business:

    - misappropriation of funds (monetary, inventory)

    - misstatement of financial statements (singularity, over time)

- systemic weaknesses and their causes:

    - lack of controls

    - poor implementation of controls

    - lack of monitoring

    - lack of leadership

- implications for an organisation if fraud occurs:

    - financial

    - non-financial

- the role of internal controls in:

    - preventing fraud and errors

    - detecting fraud and errors

Learners need to be able to:

- identify the circumstances when fraud may occur

- evaluate the impact of fraud on an organisation:

    - financial

    - non-financial

- assess how internal controls can be used in preventing and detecting fraud

- make suggestions for internal controls to detect and prevent fraud

- assess the cause of systemic weaknesses in internal control systems

KAPLAN PUBLISHING

3 Evaluate an organisation's accounting system and underpinning procedures

3.1 An organisation's accounting system and its effectiveness

Learners need to understand:

3, 9

- control objectives, risks and control procedures for accounting systems:
  - purchasing
  - sales
  - expenses
  - payroll
  - inventory
  - non-current assets
  - bank and cash
- how an organisation's accounting system can support ethical standards and sustainable practice.

Learners need to be able to:

- identify deficiencies in accounting systems that have an impact on:
  - cost-effectiveness
  - reliability
  - timeliness
- analyse the cause of deficiencies in accounting systems
- evaluate impact of deficiencies in an accounting system including:
  - time
  - money
  - reputation.

3.2 Risk of fraud

Learners need to understand:

6

- the risk assessment process:
  - identify the risk
  - evaluate the risk
  - respond to the risk (manage/mitigate risk by taking appropriate action)
  - ensure compliance (legal and regulatory)
  - monitor, review and report.

Learners need to be able to:

- assess the impact of poor internal controls on an organisation's exposure to risk
- assess risk using the following measures:
  - risk matrix
  - low, medium, high
  - numerical grade (where the number increases as the risk becomes more serious).
- recommend a response to risk, ensuring compliance with regulatory and legal requirements
- propose monitoring review and report actions in response to an identified risk.

3.3 Operating practice

Learners need to understand:

8

- why accounting systems should be reviewed regularly to ensure that they are fit for purpose
- that the accounting systems used by an organisation should:
  - be cost-effective
  - encourage ethical principles and practice
  - support sustainability principles and practice
  - meet the specific information needs of the organisation.

4   Understand the impact of technology on accounting systems

4.1 Reporting information using technology

Learners need to understand:

5

- how accounting software presents data to non-financial managers

- how visualisation improves financial understanding of managers and clients.

4.2 Using technology within the accounting system

Learners need to understand:

5

- how technological changes may affect the accounting system:

  - cloud accounting:

    - remote access

    - shared access

    - improved sustainability

    - control of data

    - reliance on access to technology

  - artificial intelligence (AI) and machine learning:

    - change in staffing levels

    - change in error rates

    - implementation and running costs

  - data analytics:

    - speeds up processes and decision making

    - may reduce risk of fraud

    - identifying opportunities in a business to work smarter, focus and prioritise

- that there are different types of data analytics:
  - descriptive
  - diagnostic
  - predictive
  - prescriptive
- the requirement for data security
- the risks to data and operation caused by:
  - cyberattacks (phishing, malware, denial of service)
  - unauthorised access (remote or physical)
  - physical loss of equipment
  - data issued in error.

5 Recommend improvements to an organisation's accounting system

5.1 Changes to the accounting system

Learners need to understand:

8

- the principles of a SWOT (Strengths, Weaknesses, Opportunities, Threats) analysis
- how to apply a SWOT analysis to an accounting system
- the principles of a PESTLE (Political, Economic, Social, Technological, Legal and Environmental) analysis
- how to apply a PESTLE analysis to an accounting system.

Learners need to be able to:

- undertake a SWOT analysis
- undertake a PESTLE analysis
- recommend changes to the accounting system
- provide a clear rationale to support recommendations.

KAPLAN PUBLISHING

5.2 Cost and benefit of changes to the accounting system

8

Learners need to understand:

- cost-benefit analysis.

Learners need to be able to:

- quantify the cost of recommendations, stating assumptions made

- review recommendations against

- ethical and sustainability principles:

    - social issues

    - corporate issues

    - environmental issues

- undertake a cost-benefit analysis

- recommend changes to the accounting system

- provide a clear rationale to support recommendations.

5.3 The effects of changes on users of the system

Learners need to understand:

8

- the changes that users may be required to make to working practices to comply with changes to statutory and organisational requirements

- that appropriate controls need to be in place during the transition from one system to another

- that problems might occur during transition

- different methods of support that can be given to users of the accounting system to assist them in adapting to the recommended changes:

    - testing

    - piloting

    - direct changeover

    - dual/parallel running

    - phased implementation

Learners need to be able to:

- evaluate the implications of the changes to operating procedures and time spent.

Delivering this unit

This unit has close links with:

- Level 3 Business Awareness
- Level 4 Applied Management Accounting
- Level 4 Audit and Assurance.

THE ASSESSMENT

Test specification for this synoptic assessment

Assessment type
Computer based
assessment

Marking type
Partially computer/
partially human marked

Duration of exam
2 hours 30 minutes

	Learning outcomes	Weighting
1	Understand the role and responsibilities of the accounting function within an organisation	10%
2	Evaluate internal control systems	25%
3	Evaluate an organisation's accounting system and underpinning procedures	25%
4	Understand the impact of technology on accounting systems	15%
5	Recommend improvements to an organisation's accounting system	25%
	Total	100%

Pre-release scenario and reference material is made available on the AAT website before the assessment.

The assessment tasks will be based on the business included within the pre-release material. You should familiarise yourself with the business and how it operates before the assessment. Key areas to focus on include:

- company background/history
- recent developments
- staff who are employed by the business.

Reviewing the pre-release material in advance of the assessment will help you think of which areas may be tested on the real exam day.

STUDY SKILLS

Preparing to study

Devise a study plan

Determine which times of the week you will study.

Split these times into sessions of at least one hour for study of new material. Any shorter periods could be used for revision or practice.

Put the times you plan to study onto a study plan for the weeks from now until the assessment and set yourself targets for each period of study – in your sessions make sure you cover the whole course, activities and the associated questions in the workbook at the back of the manual.

If you are studying more than one unit at a time, try to vary your subjects as this can help to keep you interested and see subjects as part of wider knowledge.

When working through your course, compare your progress with your plan and, if necessary, re-plan your work (perhaps including extra sessions) or, if you are ahead, do some extra revision/practice questions.

Effective studying

Active reading

You are not expected to learn the text by rote, rather, you must understand what you are reading and be able to use it to pass the assessment and develop good practice.

A good technique is to use SQ3Rs – Survey, Question, Read, Recall, Review:

1   **Survey the chapter**

    Look at the headings and read the introduction, knowledge, skills and content, so as to get an overview of what the chapter deals with.

2   **Question**

    Whilst undertaking the survey ask yourself the questions you hope the chapter will answer for you.

KAPLAN PUBLISHING

3   Read

Read through the chapter thoroughly working through the activities and, at the end, making sure that you can meet the learning objectives highlighted on the first page.

4   Recall

At the end of each section and at the end of the chapter, try to recall the main ideas of the section/chapter without referring to the text. This is best done after a short break of a couple of minutes after the reading stage.

5   Review

Check that your recall notes are correct.

You may also find it helpful to re-read the chapter to try and see the topic(s) it deals with as a whole.

Note taking

Taking notes is a useful way of learning, but do not simply copy out the text.

The notes must:

- be in your own words
- be concise
- cover the key points
- be well organised
- be modified as you study further chapters in this text or in related ones.

Trying to summarise a chapter without referring to the text can be a useful way of determining which areas you know and which you don't.

Three ways of taking notes

1   Summarise the key points of a chapter

2   Make linear notes

A list of headings, subdivided with sub-headings listing the key points.

If you use linear notes, you can use different colours to highlight key points and keep topic areas together.

Use plenty of space to make your notes easy to use.

3 Try a diagrammatic form

The most common of which is a mind map.

To make a mind map, put the main heading in the centre of the paper and put a circle around it.

Draw lines radiating from this to the main sub-headings which again have circles around them.

Continue the process from the sub-headings to sub-sub-headings.

Highlighting and underlining

You may find it useful to underline or highlight key points in your study text – but do be selective.

You may also wish to make notes in the margins.

Revision phase

Kaplan has produced material specifically designed for your final examination preparation for this unit.

These include pocket revision notes and a bank of revision questions specifically in the style of the current syllabus.

Further guidance on how to approach the final stage of your studies is given in these materials.

Further reading

In addition to this text, you should also read the 'Accounting Technician' magazine every month to keep abreast of any guidance from the examiners.

The accounting function

Introduction

The accounting function is an important part of any organisation. It needs to reflect the organisation's needs at all times.

PERFORMANCE CRITERIA
1.1   The accounting function

CONTENTS

1   Introduction

2   The accounting/finance function

3   Understanding systems

1 Introduction

1.1 Organisations and the need for control

There are many different types of organisations but they all share the following key characteristics:

 Definition

'Organisations are social arrangements for the controlled performance of collective goals'.

The key aspects of this definition are:

- **Collective goals** – organisations are defined primarily by their goals. A school has the main goal of educating pupils and will be organised differently from a company where the main objectives are to make profits and pay dividends to shareholders.

- **Social arrangements** – someone working on their own does not constitute an organisation. Organisations have structure to enable people to work together towards common goals.

- **Controlled performance** – organisations have systems or procedures to ensure goals are achieved.

In this unit we will focus on the third of these:

- How do organisations ensure that they achieve their objectives?

- What control mechanisms can they introduce to help managers and other employees work in such a way that the organisation is successful?

1.2 Control mechanisms

There are a number of types of control which can be used within an organisation, including the following:

- Organisational **structure** – breaking the organisation down into smaller units, such as a dedicated accounts department, with clearly defined roles, responsibilities and authority. This can be reflected in many ways, for example, insisting that all capital expenditure over £1,000 must be authorised by the Finance Director.

- **Target** setting and **budgeting** – so that employees are aware of what is expected of them.

- Direct **supervision** of employees by managers.

- The **culture** of the organisation – for example, where mistakes are not tolerated.

- **Self-control** where employees are encouraged to work independently and take responsibility for their own results.

- Control **systems** – for example where actual results are compared to the budget each month and variances calculated. These allow managers to identify, and focus on, areas where performance is not as expected and take corrective action.

- Specific control **processes** – for example, purchase ledger control account reconciliations may identify errors in processing purchase invoices. Note: the purchase ledger control account can also be known as the payables ledger control account.

In this chapter, and the Chapters that follow, we shall look in particular at how some of these impact the running of the accounting function and the role of internal controls within an accounting system.

 Test your understanding 1

Jersey Ltd is a small business that manufactures high quality portable loudspeakers. The business is small and has only twenty members of staff, with one supervisor. The work is highly skilled and complex, with staff divided into four teams – each with very different sets of required skills.

Currently there are no control procedures or any work guidance for employees, meaning that each member of staff often works in the way they individually feel is best. The twenty employees are moderately well paid, though there are few, if any, real promotion prospects and several employees have expressed their dissatisfaction with the working conditions within Jersey.

Jersey is owned and run by one person, H. H is concerned that the quality of production has fallen in recent months, as evidenced by an increase in wastage and a decrease in output. H is concerned about the effect this is having on the profitability of the company. As such, H is examining the possibility of introducing control processes to ensure that all units produced are of adequate quality.

Task

Discuss the appropriateness of each of the following possible controls for Jersey:

(a) Direct supervision of manufacturing staff

(b) Setting performance targets for employees based on quality of output

(c) Relying on individual employees to control their own work.

1.3   Organisational structure

Organisational structure is concerned with the way in which work is divided up and allocated and can involve considering the following:

- **The division of responsibility:** some organisations may be split on divisional lines based on geography, e.g. having a UK division. Others will be on divisional lines based on products, e.g. having a motorbikes division, some on functional lines, e.g. having a marketing department, and others a mixture of these elements.

- **The degree of decentralisation:** This refers to the level at which decisions are made.

    In a centralised structure, the upper levels of an organisation's hierarchy retain the authority to make decisions. In a decentralised structure the authority to take decisions is passed down to units and people at lower levels.

    For example, a company may have a division responsible for developing a new mobile phone but the manager concerned may find that all key decisions are made by the main Board of Directors, rather than by themselves.

    Decentralisation can also refer to where certain functions operate. For example, within a divisional company each division could have its own decentralised accounts department, or there could be just one centralised head office.

- **The length of the scalar chain:** This is the line of authority which can be traced up or down the chain of command, from the most senior member of staff to the most junior.

    It therefore relates to the number of levels of management within an organisation.

- **The size of the span of control:** A manager's span of control is the number of people for whom he/she/they are directly responsible.

- **Whether organisations are 'tall' or 'flat':** A 'tall' organisation has many levels of management (a long scalar chain) and a narrow span of control. A 'flat' organisation has few levels of management (a short scalar chain) and a wide span of control.

Tall and flat organisations

Tall organisations have many 'layers' of management, who oversee relatively few subordinates.

'Tall' organisation with 'narrow' spans of control

Flat organisations have few layers of management, who oversee a larger number of subordinates.

'Flat' organisation with 'wide' spans of control

In order to discuss these issues, it is important to distinguish between authority, responsibility and accountability:

- **Authority:** if an organisation is to function as a co-operative system of individuals, some people must have authority or power over others. Authority and power flow downwards through the formal organisation.

- **Responsibility:** tasks may be allocated to individuals and groups within the organisation, and those individuals or groups are responsible completing those tasks. It means that the individuals or groups are held accountable for personal performance and achievement of targets specified by the organisation's plans.

- **Accountability:** individuals need to explain and justify any failure to fulfil their responsibilities to their superiors in the hierarchy. It is the extent to which persons are answerable for their actions, the consequences of those actions and the measured effect on results.

2 The accounting/finance function

2.1 The role of the accounting function

Accounting is the systematic recording, reporting and analysis of financial transactions within a business. Within this, accuracy and cost-effectiveness are critical.

The accounting function affects all areas of an organisation and should be capable of producing information to assist management with decision-making, monitoring and control, as well as producing financial information to meet statutory obligations.

Accountants thus have to provide information to very diverse stakeholder groups, both internally and externally. The specific needs of each group determine whether these can best be served by the financial accounting or the management accounting function of the business organisation.

- **Financial accounting** is concerned with the recording and processing of transactions as they occur. Accounts are kept of all sales and purchases transactions and of all monies paid to and by the business.

  Coupled with this will be the preparation of the annual accounts in the form required by the accounting standards for use by both shareholders and HMRC, and also periodic financial statements (e.g. cash flow statements, receivable and payable balances, draft monthly statements of profit or loss and statements of financial position). For these there will be the need to incorporate adjustments for items such as depreciation, asset valuation, accruals and provisions.

- **Management accounting** involves the preparation and presentation of internal accounting information in such a way as to assist management in formulating policies, planning and controlling activities.

  Based mainly on the information provided by the cost accounts, data is analysed and information is presented to management to provide a basis for decision-making.

  Associated with this will be the operation of systems of budgeting control and standard costing.

  Information requirements could thus involve anything from monitoring inventory levels to monthly variance analysis to setting and monitoring key performance indicators (KPIs).

As you will know, the preparation of cost accounts involves a separate approach from financial accounting and will therefore have a separate role within the accounting function.

An **integrated** accounting system combines the needs of external and internal users of the accounts.

This type of system is increasingly common and can:

- be cheaper to operate than two or more separate systems

- provide greater consistency of data

- increase the confidence in the data.

Normally other subdivisions of the accounting function include the cashiers' department and the wages department. The cashiers are responsible for all the transactions involving cash, such as receipts from customers, payments to suppliers and payments of wages. The wages department, in addition to the calculation of remuneration due to employees, will also provide basic data for both the financial and costing systems.

The role of internal auditor is very often part of the accounting function, but ideally should be a separate function.

Note: Larger organisations may also have a separate **treasury** function. Treasury management is the corporate handling of all financial matters, the generation of external and internal funds for business, the management of currencies and cash flows, and the complex strategies, policies and procedures of corporate finance. These activities are beyond the scope of this module.

2.2 Sections in the accounts department

The financial accounts department may be further divided with a supervisor or manager responsible for each section e.g. sales ledger (can also be known as the receivables ledger), purchase ledger (can also be known as the payables ledger), credit control and payroll.

Management accounting work may also be divided up with accountants as supervisors of sections responsible for keeping different cost records e.g. materials, production and marketing.

Taking a section of the cost accounts department, we can outline a possible structure:

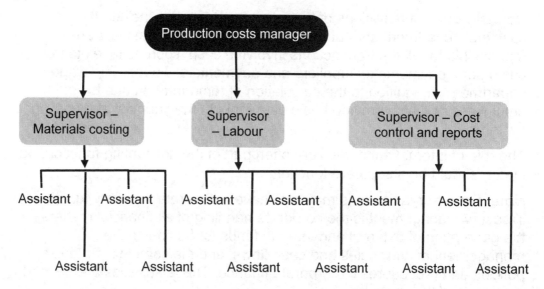

2.3 Location of the accounts department(s)

For organisations with different sites, the overall policy on centralisation versus decentralisation and organisational structure will have important effects on the location of the accounts departments.

In some cases the accounting function may be carried out entirely at the head office. In others each location could be responsible for all its own accounting procedures, with only interim and final financial statements being forwarded to head office.

With centralisation there is the opportunity to employ specialist accounting staff and advanced management information systems more effectively and economically.

When staff are in one central office, supervision may be improved and there is greater flexibility of staff and easier handling of peak loads. However day-to-day control over financial control systems may be lost and there may be delays in the flow of information and documents. In addition, head office staff are quite often regarded with suspicion and resentment and there may be the danger of head office becoming out of touch with the methods of working at each location.

KAPLAN PUBLISHING

Organisational structure may influence the location of departments. A divisional structure with different activities within each division may lend itself to separate accounts departments for each division. On the other hand a major chain of retail stores may install strong control systems at each outlet, with basic data being transmitted daily for processing and reporting by a centrally located accounts department.

2.4 Relationships between the accounting function and other departments/functions within the organisation

Within any organisation, departments, sections and individuals must all be organised to ensure that:

- the overall objectives of the organisation are achieved

- each department, section and individual makes a valid contribution.

It is therefore essential that the efforts of each contributor are co-ordinated to ensure that objectives are met.

In addition to the initial communication of expected objectives to contributors, it is essential that the organisational structure permits the flow of required information in all directions so that the attainment and achievement may be measured or forecast at any one moment. Reporting procedures should ensure that progress is constantly monitored and that the work plan is kept on schedule.

If we briefly consider the role of the accounting/finance function, then we can see that it has an important relationship with other major areas.

The main roles of finance include:

(i)   It is a resource that can be deployed so that objectives are met.

(ii)   Financial controls are often used to plan and control the implementation of strategies and financial indicators are often used to assess detailed performance.

The accounting department can be viewed as having responsibility for handling and processing information within the organisation. This information and any control procedures are provided as a service to the other departments.

Other relationships involving the accounting function include the following:

(a)   The marketing department will rely on an analysis of sales by region, sales person, customer or town in order to formulate an advertising strategy or sales promotion effort.

(b) There is a relationship between the personnel department and the wages department, because employee details must be updated for any changes. This relationship could be extended to include the industrial relations officer, who may be employed by the production department and be responsible for initiating these changes.

(c) The IT department, whether considered part of the accounting function or not, has a very wide span of responsibility in any organisation.

Most of the department managers will expect regular reports from this department and must therefore be in constant liaison with the IT staff to make sure the information is relevant to their current needs. Any suggestions for changes to the system would be negotiated here.

(d) The statistician will have responsibilities for providing information on such things as production output, variations from quality standards, comparisons of efficiency in the sales department, analysis of questionnaires for the market research staff and comparative information on wastage of materials from different suppliers.

Test your understanding 2

BBO Ltd makes luxury cakes and desserts. Most of the cakes manufactured are for large food retailers who sell the cakes as their own brand. BBO packages the cakes using the brand required by each retailer. Some cakes and desserts are sold to small independent food retailers, such as hotels and coffee shops, under BBO's own brand. The smaller retailers typically take longer to pay invoices than larger retailers. Currently the Junior Accountants cover the role of credit control between them.

The board of BBO are keen to expand sales to smaller retailers under the BBO brand as margins are higher and they feel that it is important to strengthen BBO brand awareness to help in negotiations with larger retailers.

Task

Assess the impact of the proposed expansion on the finance function, highlighting key risks and outlining two ways risk can be mitigated.

3 Understanding systems

3.1 Systems

Before looking in detail at accounting control systems, it is worth considering the wider topic of what is meant by a 'system' and what are typical features of such 'systems'.

The term 'system' can be defined as a set of interacting elements responding to inputs to produce outputs.

Every system, whatever its nature and purpose (e.g. central heating system, banking system, payments system) is a way of viewing a group of components or elements and the way in which they interact.

The elements of a system are outlined in the diagram below.

Every system exists within an environment. This is the set of elements that affect the system, but are not controlled by it. The system boundary is the limit of the system. Within it is the system and outside it is the environment.

A boundary is often a matter of definition. For example, if the system under examination is 'the whole company' then within the boundary will be found the subsystems of the system, for instance, the employees and procedures contained within departments such as production, purchasing, sales and finance. The sub-systems communicate by passing messages between themselves.

Outside the boundary is the environment, which includes customers, suppliers, the labour market, shareholders, lenders, competitors and the local community as well as more abstract and indirect influences such as the law and the economy.

If we are concentrating on the finance system, then sales, production and purchasing become part of the environment, and within the system boundary will be found smaller subsystems such as product costing, financial accounting and treasury.

Financial accounting staff responsible for the preparation of the annual accounts might rely on the management accounting staff for data about inventory records, so as to place a value on closing inventory in the accounts.

The receivables section relies on sales staff to send copies of sales orders or confirmation of goods delivered to customers and on the cashier to pass on information about payments received. It must also co-operate with debt collection staff by helping to prepare monthly statements and lists of aged debtors.

The payables section relies on the purchasing department to send copies of purchase orders and confirm the validity of invoices received from suppliers and also inform the purchase ledger staff about any despatches concerning goods received or purchases returned. The section also relies on the cashier to inform it of all payments of invoices.

3.2　The systems approach

The systems that operate within organisations can be viewed in many ways, for example:

- Social systems – composed of people and their relationships
- Information systems – relying on information to support decisions
- Accounting systems – emphasising the organisation's cash flows
- Economic systems – utilising resources to produce economic welfare.

Our focus is solely on the accounting system.

The accounting system receives inputs from other systems (e.g. production), it converts that data in to meaningful financial information (its output). Clearly anything outside the accounting system is its environment (the wider organisation for example).

3.3　Control systems

Organisations have many control systems such as quality control/management, stock control and budgetary control. Control is the activity that monitors changes or deviations from those originally planned. The control of an organisation is exercised by managers obtaining and using information.

To get a better understanding of control systems, it is useful to start with an example that is in everyday use – a thermostat. All central heating systems contain thermostats to regulate the temperature of the rooms they are heating. The user sets the thermostat to the required temperature on the dial. There is a thermometer in the system, which measures the temperature of the rooms. The room temperature is continually compared with the pre-set temperature on the thermostat dial. If the room temperature is above the dial temperature, the power (e.g. gas) is switched off. When room temperature falls below the dial temperature, the power is switched on.

KAPLAN PUBLISHING

The elements of a control system are:

- **Standard** – is what the system is aiming for. In the thermostat system it is the pre-set temperature.

- **Sensor** (or detector) – measures the output of the system. In the thermostat system it is the thermometer.

- **Comparator** – compares the information from the standard and the sensor.

- **Effector** (or activator) – initiates the control action. In the thermostat system it is the switch.

- **Feedback** – is the information that is taken from the system output and used to adjust the system. In the thermostat example the feedback is the actual room temperature.

In an organisational system, information about how the system actually performs is recorded and this information is available to the managers responsible for their achievement of the target performance. For effective and accurate control it is essential that timely and efficiently detailed feedback is provided so that corrective action can be taken. This may be a minor operating adjustment or it may involve a complete redesign of the system.

A good example of such a system is variance analysis:

1   Standard costs are developed and a budget produced detailing what should happen – this is the 'standard'.

2   Actual results are measured – this is the 'sensor'.

3   Actual results are compared against budget in the form of variance analysis – this is the 'comparator'.

4   Managers then decide which variances are significant and worth further investigation – this is the 'activator'.

5   Managers can then take appropriate action, whether this is changing the budget or addressing operational issues – this is 'feedback'.

Controls within an accounting function are covered in more detail in Chapter 3.

3.4 Systems and procedures best practice

As with most aspects of business administration, there are certain best-practice principles, including the following:

- There should be a smooth flow of work with no bottlenecks.
- Movement of staff should be kept to a minimum.
- Duplication of work should be avoided.
- The best and most effective use of existing specialist attributes should be made.
- Simplicity within systems should be sought. Complications usually lead to misinterpretations and/or mistakes.
- Machines should be used to help staff where appropriate.

Any system must be cost-effective. The benefits should be compared with the cost of implementation and subsequent supervision costs.

The establishment of systems and procedures will ensure that organisational objectives are attained. Data and information are constantly flowing within an organisation, some being generated internally and some stemming from external sources. All of this information needs to be processed, and a system needs to be established to ensure that this is accomplished in the most effective, efficient and economical manner.

3.5 Systems and procedures manuals

Although they are not always immediately apparent, every organisation has systems that outline the operations necessary to perform a task associated with the receipt, recording, arrangement, storage, security and communication of information. These are usually referred to as 'office procedures'.

Sometimes these procedures are formalised by the preparation of an office manual. These written instructions should indicate clearly what is required to be done, when, where and how. The preparation of such a manual requires careful examination of the systems and procedures. This examination provides a benefit, in that strengths and weaknesses are revealed.

There are, however, advantages and disadvantages associated with manuals.

A list of the advantages would include the following:

- Supervision is easier.
- It helps the induction and training of new staff.
- It assists the organisation in pinpointing areas of responsibility.
- Once written down, systems and procedures are easier to adapt in response to changing circumstances.

The disadvantages would include:

- The expense in preparing manuals both in the obvious financial terms and the perhaps less obvious cost of administrative time.

- To be of continuing use an office manual must be updated periodically, again incurring additional expense.

- The instructions that are laid down in the office manual may be interpreted rather strictly and implemented too rigidly.
  Within any organisation it is often beneficial for employees to bring a degree of flexibility to their duties to cope with particular circumstances.

3.6 The review of office procedures

Systems should be kept under continuous review and altered as necessary to reflect changes in the organisation, advances in technology, or indeed suggestions from the staff for system improvement. The decision to review the office procedures could stem from weaknesses that may already have been highlighted (for instance, too much paperwork).

A review may be divided into two parts:

(i) an overview of the office and the role it plays within the organisation, which will consider:

- the purpose of the office

- what actually happens within the office

- who does what within the office

- the techniques and methods employed by staff in carrying out assigned responsibilities

- the quality of performance

(ii) a detailed step-by-step examination of the procedures themselves.

The establishment of such information is vital as a first stage. A more detailed analysis of the day-to-day routine may be attempted after this.

Changes to the environment might have an impact on the accounting function. This is considered further in later Chapters of this text.

3.7 Wider environmental factors – legislation and regulations

The law constitutes a set of environmental factors that are increasingly affecting organisations and their decision-making. They can also affect the accounting function. Most nations of the world are, or are becoming, regulated economies.

Government regulation, or self-regulation of business has four principal aims:

- **To protect business entities** – e.g. laws putting limits on market dominance by acting against monopolies and restrictive practices and providing financial assistance to selected ailing industries and companies.

- **To protect consumers** – with many consumer protection regulations covering packaging, labelling, food hygiene and advertising, and much more.

- **To protect employees** – with laws governing recruitment of staff and health and safety legislation to regulate working conditions.

- **To protect the interests of society at large against damaging business behaviour** – e.g. by acting to protect the environment.

Also at the most basic level laws are passed that enable Government to levy taxes, and company law affects the corporate structure of the business and prescribes the duties of company directors.

Managers cannot plan intelligently without a good working knowledge of the laws and regulations that affect their own companies and the businesses in which they operate. In addition to those laws that apply generally to all companies, such as laws regulating Corporation Tax or Value Added Tax, there are laws specifically used to deal with individual industries, e.g. Petroleum Revenue Tax in the offshore oil and gas industry.

There is a seemingly endless list of laws and regulations that affect business enterprises, in domestic, national or international settings.

The key point for this module is that the accounting system must make provision for the relevant regulation in place at any one time. For example if the government decided to change the VAT rate, then the accounting system must be amended to accommodate that change.

3.8 Regulations affecting accounting practice

The financial statements of limited companies must usually be prepared in accordance with the legal framework relevant to that company, for example The Companies Act 2006 (CA06) in the UK.

In addition companies are also required to comply with a generally accepted financial reporting framework, including the International Financial Reporting Standards (IFRS® Standards), issued by the International Accounting Standards Board (the Board).

3.9 The Board's Conceptual Framework (the Framework)

The Framework states that the objective of the financial statements is to provide information about the reporting entity that is useful to existing and potential investors, lenders and other creditors in making decisions about providing resources to the entity.

The Framework also suggests that financial statements should have certain qualitative characteristics.

The Framework splits qualitative characteristics into two categories:

(i)   Fundamental qualitative characteristics

- Relevance
- Faithful representation.

(ii)   Enhancing qualitative characteristics

- Comparability
- Verifiability
- Timeliness
- Understandability.

3.10 Generally Accepted Accounting Principles (GAAP)

The concept of GAAP stems from US accounting. In the UK we publish financial statements which show a 'true and fair' view. In the US the reference is to conforming to GAAP.

GAAP comprises the whole set of accounting practices which have authoritative support amongst users of financial statements.

There will be crossovers between accounting standards and GAAP where standards reflect GAAP. However, there may be a GAAP that is not represented by a standard.

UK GAAP extends further than accounting standards alone to include the requirements of The Companies Act and The Stock Exchange.

4 Further 'Test your understanding' questions

 Test your understanding 3

1 Outline the structure of your accounting function.

2 Explain quality control as a control system.

3 Outline the elements of a budgetary control system in which the financial performance of a department is compared with the budget.

4 What is the main function of an accounting system?

5 Summary

This chapter was a general introduction to systems and the accounting function in particular. It provides the theoretical background that you need to properly understand the relationships that exist within the accounting function.

Test your understanding answers

 Test your understanding 1

(a) **Direct supervision of staff**

Jersey could opt to directly monitor the activities of its staff in order to ensure their work is of appropriate quality. This could be effective at stopping the production of poor quality speakers and the associated waste that would be involved in this. The fact that Jersey only has a small number of staff would also tend to make this approach work well.

However, there would be several problems associated with this control. Firstly, each group of workers has highly specialised skills. This may make it difficult for Jersey's supervisor to understand what each group does and monitor their activities effectively. In addition, the fact that each worker may undertake the same job as their colleagues but using a different technique, will increase the complexity of the monitoring role.

While the workforce is small, there is only one supervisor. They may have insufficient time available to supervise all staff. Hiring of additional supervisors would have cost implications for Jersey.

Finally, additional supervision may have a negative impact on the motivation of employees, who are used to having autonomy over the way they perform their jobs. A sudden change to being closely monitored could cause further job dissatisfaction.

(b) **Performance targets**

Setting performance targets could be of great use to Jersey. This would likely involve offering incentives for staff (such as pay-rises and bonuses) depending on how well they perform their jobs. For Jersey, the number of defective units produced by each employee could be measured and a bonus could be offered if this was below a pre-agreed level.

This could be a very practical approach for Jersey, as it links employee rewards with the objectives of the company itself. It should be easy to implement and would prevent the production of units that were defective, reducing waste. The offer of an additional bonus or extra pay may also help to improve general motivation as workers are currently only adequately paid and have few other benefits or prospects.

Note that this may not improve the output of each worker, which is another issue for Jersey. Workers may spend longer on each unit in order to ensure the quality and thus receive their bonus, leading to a further fall in productivity.

(c)   Reliance on self-control of workers

Relying on individual staff to monitor their own activities may be problematic. It has the advantage of being cheap for Jersey, as it does not require any further staff to be hired. In addition, the staff are clearly skilled at their jobs, making it easier for them to understand the best way to approach individual tasks.

However, staff seem to be relatively de-motivated. This means that they are less likely to be concerned about the quality of their output. Unless they are offered an incentive by Jersey, there is no reason why they would focus on higher quality production.

In addition, there is no agreed 'best practice' for each of the four teams. Each worker is likely to see their method as superior to those of their colleagues, whether this is in fact correct or not. This means that they are unlikely to change their working practices to ones that would improve output and quality.

Note: this exercise is not indicative of the style of tasks in the synoptic assessment. However, it is useful to help you start thinking about how to control an organisation and what might go wrong. Tasks in the assessment will focus much more on **accounting** tasks and activities.

Test your understanding 2

The impact of the new customers on the finance function and key risks

Firstly, there will be a significant increase in the volume of transactions that will need to be processed within the finance team. There are two aspects to this that will need to be addressed:

- ensuring that there is adequate employee resource to deal with the processing of orders and invoices

- the ability of our systems to deal with the volume of data.

Secondly, there will be a potential detrimental impact on our cash flows. As we already know our small independent retailers are often taking longer to pay, which may mean paying late on occasion, it is likely that these new customers will follow the same trend.

Thirdly, there will be an increase in the recoverability risk that the business faces. By their nature small independent businesses are more likely to become insolvent or simply cease to trade than larger corporations.

Lastly, and on a positive note, one key impact will be that our brand will benefit from an increased presence in the market. This benefit might be limited if hotels and coffee shops simply sell our cakes by the slice or serve our desserts, as the end consumer will probably be unaware of the fact that it is one of our products.

Measures to mitigate any additional risk

1   **Recruit appropriate qualified people for the finance department:**

It would be sensible to recruit an appropriately experienced and qualified credit controller to ensure that all new customers are assessed as to their creditworthiness and that the receivables are monitored and chased for payment as required in a timely manner.

2   **Ensure sound credit control procedures are in place:**

All potential customers should be assessed as to their creditworthiness prior to being accepted. This might involve purchasing credit agency reports or performing an internal assessment by reviewing financial statements. In addition, there should be procedures in place for the regular monitoring of outstanding debts and for chasing up late payments through telephone calls, emails and letters.

Test your understanding 3

1   This should be based on your own business.

2   Quality control is the control system of setting quality standards, measuring performance against those standards and taking corrective action when necessary. The standard aimed for will depend on the nature of the product, the market for which the goods are produced and the standards achieved by competitors in the same market.

3   The elements of the control system are:

- standard: the budget (e.g. standard costs)

- sensor: the costing system, which records actual costs

- feedback: the actual results for the period, collected by the costing system

- comparator: the 'performance report' for the department, comparing actual with budget (e.g. variance analysis)

- effector: the manager of the department, in consultation with others, takes action to minimise future adverse variances and to exploit opportunities resulting from favourable variances.

4   The main function of an accounting function is to take inputs and convert them in to meaningful accounting information, which is useful to the various stakeholders of an organisation.

Financial information and stakeholders

2

Introduction

For your exam it is vital that you have an understanding of financial statements and management reports and their relevance to the organisation.

PERFORMANCE CRITERIA
1.2 Financial information used by stakeholders

CONTENTS
1 Introduction
2 The purpose of financial statements
3 The purpose of management reports
4 Stakeholders

1 Introduction

The accounting function in an organisation fulfils a number of important roles, least of which is the supply of information for a variety of uses and stakeholders.

Here we shall consider the purpose of key financial reports and their use.

2 The purpose of financial statements

2.1 Introduction

The main purpose of financial statements is to provide information to a wide range of users or stakeholders.

- The statement of financial position provides information on the financial position of a business (its assets and liabilities at a point in time).

- The statement of profit or loss provides information on the performance of a business (the profit or loss which results from trading over a period of time).

- The statement of other comprehensive income shows income and expenses that are not recognised in profit or loss. Note that this statement would only be presented where such income or expense existed.

- The statement of changes in equity provides information about how the equity of the company has changed over the period.

- The statement of cash flows provides information on the financial adaptability of a business (the movement of cash into and out of the business over a period of time).

2.2 Stewardship

Financial statements also show the results of the stewardship of an organisation.

Stewardship is the accountability of management for the resources entrusted to it by the owners or the Government.

This applies to the financial statements of limited companies as well as to central and local government and government-funded bodies such as the National Health Service.

2.3 Needs of users

All users of financial statements need information on financial position, performance and financial adaptability. However, many different groups of people may use financial statements and each group will need particular information. Users of financial statements may include investors, management, employees, customers, suppliers, lenders, the government and the public.

- Investors need to be able to assess the ability of a business to pay dividends and manage resources.

- Management need information with which to assess performance, take decisions, plan, and control the business.

- Employees and their unions need information to help them negotiate pay and benefits.

- Customers need to be assured that their supply will continue into the future.

- Suppliers need to be assured that they will continue to get paid on time.

- Lenders, such as banks, are interested in the ability of the business to pay interest and repay loans.

- HM Revenue and Customs uses financial statements as the basis for tax assessments.

- The public (especially pressure groups) will look at the financial reports and statements to aid their understanding of the organisation's profits derived from activities to which the pressure group is opposed.

2.4 Legal requirements

The law requires limited companies to prepare financial statements annually. These financial statements must be filed with the Registrar of Companies and are then available to all interested parties. Most businesses, whether incorporated or not, are required to produce financial statements for submission to HM Revenue and Customs.

In the UK, the form and content of limited company accounts is laid down within the Companies Act.

The preparation of limited company accounts is also subject to regulations issued by the Financial Reporting Council (FRC) if the company is still following UK standards or the Board if the company has adopted International Standards.

The financial statements of limited companies must usually be prepared within the legal framework relevant to that company.

In the case of UK companies, the Companies Act 2006 (CA06) contains guidance and rules on:

- formats for the financial statements
- fundamental accounting principles
- valuation rules.

The Companies Act has been amended to take account of the companies who have adopted International Financial Reporting Standards (IFRS Standards). It allows companies to use the format of accounts set out in IAS 1 *Presentation of Financial Statements* if they have adopted IFRS Standards or continue to use the format in the CA06 if they have not.

2.5 Evaluating financial statements

As well as looking at key figures (e.g. profit) and movements from one period to another (e.g. revenue growth), the main method of interpreting financial statements is through ratio analysis. This technique is recapped in Chapter 7.

3 The purpose of management reports

3.1 The needs of management

Management accounting provides information for planning, controlling and decision-making.

Planning

Planning involves establishing the objectives of an organisation and formulating relevant strategies that can be used to achieve those objectives.

Planning can be either short-term (tactical planning) or long-term (strategic planning).

Decision-making

Decision-making involves considering information that has been provided and making an informed decision.

Managers need reliable information to compare the different courses of action available and understand the potential consequences of choosing each of them.

Control

As discussed in Chapter 1, control is often facilitated using 'feedback'.

Managers take corrective action where appropriate, especially in the case of exceptionally bad or good performance.

3.2 Key reports

The types of management accounting reports varies considerably from one organisation to another but could include the following:

- Budget reports, detailing budgetary plans for future periods.

- Variance reports comparing actual and budget performance, to facilitate effective control.

- Reports of key performance indicators to ensure that management focus on what is important to the success of the organisation.

- One-off reports that look at individual decisions – for example a report considering a shut-down decision could examine the relevant costs associated with the different alternative courses of action.

3.3 Evaluating a management report – General issues

If you are presented with a management report and asked to discuss it, then you may need to consider some or all of the following:

The basis of preparation

It is worth considering why a report has been prepared (planning, control or decision-making) and who prepared it.

For example, suppose a manager has produced a budget for their division to help justify why that division should be given greater investment.

It would be reasonable to suggest that the manager may have been over-optimistic with future forecasts because of the personal benefit they stand to gain from the result. This is not to suggest that the manager is acting unethically but simply that they will be biased.

On a related point, it is acknowledged that participation in budgeting and target-setting can result in budget padding, as managers want to set themselves easy targets to increase their chances of gaining a bonus.

You should also consider the experience and qualifications of the person concerned in producing forecasts.

The figures used

If a report uses historic figures, then you could question whether these have been verified in any way – for example, are they drawn from audited accounts?

Most reports will include forecasts and plans, and it is important to question any assumptions made.

For example

- If revenue has grown by 3% for each of the last three years, then using future growth of 10% may be unrealistic or over-optimistic unless there are valid reasons for the increase, such as the introduction of new products.

- If sales volume is expected to grow by 7% but direct materials is only forecast to increase by 5%, this would seem strange, as direct materials is a purely variable cost so would be expected to go up in line with production volume. This could be due to optimistic budgeting, or maybe planned efficiencies due to using better quality materials for example.

- Similarly if sales volume is expected to grow by 7% and administration costs are also budgeted to grow by 7%, then this would be surprising as one would expect a significant proportion of administration costs to be fixed in nature rather than variable.

- Even with fixed costs you need to be careful. Let's say that the cost of administration for next year is the same as for last year. This might seem reasonable, given they are fixed costs, except that there is likely to be some impact from inflation, so maybe a small percentage increase would be more realistic.

- If sales are expected to increase we would probably expect to see a corresponding increase in marketing or other investment. Try to look for cause-and-effect relationships.

In all of the above you would need to look carefully at the scenario to see whether assumptions about the future are justifiable.

3.4 Evaluating a management report – specific issues relating to budgeting, performance management and control

In addition to the above points, we should also focus on the following when considering budgeting, performance management and control:

Target setting

We should establish how much pressure/incentive managers have to hit targets. If excessive, then control problems could arise.

We should determine what level of participation in target setting was involved.

If targets are being set for managers they should be viewed as fair, i.e. stretching but achievable.

With little participation and/or targets perceived as unfair, the likely result will be that staff are demotivated rather than motivated because the targets relate to factors outside the manager's control.

Assigning responsibility

Where the report involves variances, and there is an attempt to assign responsibility, we need to consider whether this has been done fairly.

Flexing

Where actual sales volumes differ from budget, the budget should be flexed to ensure a like-for-like comparison between actual and budget.

We need to check whether the figures have been flexed correctly, depending on which costs are variable and which fixed.

The impact on people concerned

The tone of the report should avoid being too aggressive.

Test your understanding 1

Good Choice Hotels runs a chain of hotels throughout the UK.

John Patel (Finance Director) has been reviewing Good Choice Hotels' systems for budgeting and control and has decided to start trying to evaluate more precisely the performance of different aspects of the business – i.e. housekeeping (room cleaning and servicing), the bar, the restaurant and so on. John has designed some performance reports comparing actual results with budget with a view to running some pilots to explore how control could be improved.

On 15th May 20X6 Jane Seagar, the Head of Housekeeping in Hotel 2, received her first quarterly performance report from John Patel, together with an explanatory memorandum. These are given below.

Jane had not been involved in setting the original budget – that was done by the hotel Manager – had never seen the budget, nor had she (or the hotel manager) been informed that there would be a performance report. Jane knew she was responsible for her department and had made every endeavour to run it as efficiently as possible, so found the report very upsetting.

Memorandum

To	Jane Seagar, Head of Housekeeping, Hotel 2
From	John Patel, Finance Director
Date	15 May 20X6

Attached is the quarterly performance report for your department for the first 3 months of 20X6.

The company has adopted a responsibility accounting system so you will be receiving one of these reports every quarter. Responsibility accounting means that you are accountable for ensuring that the expenses of running your department are kept in line with the budget.

Each report compares the actual expenses of running your department for the quarter with our budget for the same period. The difference between the actual and forecast will be highlighted so that you can identify the important variations from budget and take corrective action to get back on budget.

Any variation in excess of 5% from budget should be investigated and an explanatory memorandum sent to me giving reasons for the variations and the proposed corrective actions.

Performance Report: Housekeeping – Hotel 2

Three months to 31 March 20X6

	Actual	Original Budget	Variation (over)/ under	%
Number of guests	6,850	6,570	(280)	4.3
Housekeeping expenses	£	£	£	%
Cleaning materials	2,730	2,628	(102)	3.9
Room consumables – soap, shampoo, tea bags, sugar, milk	20,750	19,710	(1,040)	5.3
Cleaning staff wages	76,000	75,000	(1,000)	1.3
Head of Housekeeping's wages	8,750	9,000	250	2.8
Equipment depreciation	750	750	–	–
Laundry costs	27,300	26,280	(1,020)	3.9
Allocated hotel costs	5,200	5,000	(200)	4.0
Total cost	141,480	138,368	(3,112)	2.2

Comment: We need to have an urgent discussion about your over-spending!

Task

Evaluate the performance report by looking at

- the way it was prepared and who was involved,
- its contents and tone, and
- the effect it had (and could have going forwards) on staff.

3.5 Evaluating a management report – specific issues relating to decision-making

In addition to the above points in section 3.3, we should also focus on the following when looking at decision-making.

The method used

A key concept when making decisions is the use of relevant costing – i.e. decisions should be based on future, incremental cash flows.

This means that we should ignore sunk costs, costs such as depreciation that are not cash flows, and costs that will be incurred anyway, such as apportioned overheads.

Many scenarios may be simplified with a set selling price, simple variable costs and simple fixed costs. In such a scenario, changing the level of output, say, would impact revenue and variable costs but not fixed costs, meaning that we should be focussing on contribution as our relevant cash flow.

For example, break-even discussions are best addressed by looking at contribution, not profit.

Similarly, if given a report that looks at how best to deal with a scarce resources, you should rank options by looking at the contribution per unit of that scarce resource. However, if a director in the scenario suggests that we should look at gross profit rather than contribution, then their opinion can be criticised on that basis.

4 Stakeholders

4.1 The purpose of accounting

The purpose of accounting is to provide information to users of financial statements. Legally, company financial statements are drawn up for the benefit of the shareholders, so they can assess the performance of their Board of Directors. However, in practice many other stakeholder groups will use these financial statements. These groups, and their needs, are described below.

4.2 External and internal stakeholders

Stakeholders may be divided between those involved in the day-to-day running of the business, or internal stakeholders, and the remainder, known as external stakeholders. The information required by, and available to, these types of stakeholders will obviously vary.

4.3 Management

Management, as an internal stakeholder, will be interested in an analysis of revenues and expenses that will provide information that is useful when plans are formulated and decisions made.

Once the budget for a business is complete, the accountant can produce figures for what actually happens as the budget period unfolds, so that they can be compared with the budget. Management will also need to know the cost consequences of a particular course of action to aid their decision-making.

One key area of difference between external stakeholders and management is the need for management to monitor Key Performance Indicators (KPIs). KPIs vary from business to business and, because they are used internally like management accounts, are not in any way regulated.

For example a motor trader might feel that a KPI should be the volume of cars or the number of service hours sold. These would then be measured as KPIs, and the accounting function would need to accommodate the recording of them as needed.

4.4 Employees and their trade union representatives

Employees and their trade union representatives are also internal stakeholders. These use accounting information to assess the potential performance of the business. This information is relevant to employees, who wish to discover whether the company can offer them safe employment and promotion through growth over a period of years. The information is also useful to trade unions, who use past profits and potential profits in their calculations and claims for higher wages or better conditions. The viability of different divisions of a company is also of interest to this group.

4.5 Shareholders and potential shareholders

This stakeholder group can be split between current shareholders (internal) and potential shareholders or investors (external) and includes the investing public at large and the stockbrokers and commentators who advise them. The shareholders should be informed of the manner in which management has used their funds that have been invested in the business. This is a matter of reporting on past events. However, both shareholders and potential shareholders are also interested in the future performance of the business and use past figures as a guide to the future if they have to vote on proposals or decide whether to sell their shares.

Financial analysts advising investors such as insurance companies, pension funds, unit trusts and investment trusts are among the most sophisticated users of accounting information. The company contemplating a takeover bid is yet another type of potential shareholder.

4.6 Lenders

This external stakeholder group includes those who have financed the business over a long period by lending money to be repaid at the end of a number of years, as well as short-term payables such as a bank which allows a company to overdraw its bank account for a number of months.

Lenders are interested in the security of their loan, so they will look at an accounting statement to ensure that the company will be able to make payments of interest and capital on the due dates. The amount of cash available and the value of assets, which form a security for the debt, are of importance to this group.

4.7 Government agencies

The government is an external stakeholder and uses accounting information, either when collecting statistical information to reveal trends within the economy as a whole or, in the case of HMRC, to assess the profit on which the company's tax liability is to be computed.

4.8 Customers

Customers of a business will clearly be external stakeholders. They may use accounting data to assess the viability of a company if a long-term contract is soon to be placed, or may wish to reassure themselves about security of future goods supply.

4.9 Suppliers

Another external stakeholder is suppliers, particularly those who permit a company to buy goods or services on credit from them. In this case the financial information is used by suppliers to establish creditworthiness. Credit rating agencies are interested in financial statements for similar reasons.

4.10 The public

From time to time other groups not included above may have an external interest in the company e.g. members of a community local to where the company operates, environmental pressure groups and so on.

5 Additional 'Test your understanding' questions

 Test your understanding 2

1   What are the four main statements that would be seen in a set of financial statements?

2   What is meant by the term 'stewardship'?

3   Why would a bank look at a set of financial statements?

6 Summary

This chapter demonstrated the role of accounting within the organisation and considered the purpose and evaluation of financial statements by the stakeholders concerned.

Test your understanding answers

 Test your understanding 1

The way the report was prepared

A lack of participation in target setting

The first problem with the report was the fact that, while the hotel manager was involved in setting hotel budget, the targets involved no participation by the Housekeeping Head. Jane will feel that this has been imposed upon her.

It is generally agreed that participation in target setting by the Head of Housekeeping would have resulted in targets being seen as more reasonable, targets potentially being more realistic and greater ownership of the targets in the process.

There is a risk that participation may result in staff trying to get easier targets for themselves and budget "padding" but is generally the case that the advantages outlined above outweigh such concerns.

Communication

The second problem with the way the report was prepared is that nothing was communicated to the Head of Housekeeping in advance, resulting in the nasty surprise seen. At the very least the idea of a pilot should have been discussed with the Hotel Manager.

Greater communication would also have resulted in greater buy-in from the Hotel Manager, vital if variances are supposed to be subsequently investigated and action taken.

The report contents and tone

Flexing budgets

The first problem with the figures is that the budget has not been flexed before calculating variances.

To make a meaningful "like for like" comparison the budget figures should be adjusted to reflect the actual number of guests that stayed in the hotel over the period.

Given the actual number of guests was 4% higher than expected it is no surprise that many costs were also higher. Flexing budgets allows you to effectively separate out the volume difference and see what other differences still remain.

For example, looking at cleaning materials, a revised (flexed) target would be

$$£2,628 × 6,850/6,570 = £2,740$$

Compared to this figure the actual cost of £2,730 shows an underspend of £10 rather than an overspend of £102.

However, when flexing one needs to be careful to distinguish between fixed and variable costs – for example, equipment depreciation will be a fixed cost so does not need adjusting before making a comparison.

Controllable factors

The second main problem with the content of the report is that it includes many costs that are uncontrollable.

A key principle with responsibility accounting is that people should only be assessed with respect to factors that they can control and/or are responsible for. Being assessed on uncontrollable factors may result in demotivation as someone may fail to reach a target despite performing better than expected.

With the report used for housekeeping, the following costs are uncontrollable:

- Head of Housekeeping's wages – Jane cannot set her own salary!
- Equipment depreciation – this will be determined by accounting policies.
- Laundry costs – while the housekeeping team sort what needs to be to the laundry, the Head of Housekeeping cannot control either the amount of washing or the prices charged by the laundry.
- Allocated hotel costs – this will be determined by overall hotel cost control (not just housekeeping) and the method of allocating costs. Neither can be controlled by the Head of Housekeeping.

Emphasis on financial figures only

If Good Choice Hotels really wants to evaluate the performance of housekeeping, then reports should also incorporate measures of quality, such as feedback from customer satisfaction surveys.

Which variances to investigate

A fixed percentage of 5% has been set for investigation – this may not be an ideal system for deciding which variances should be investigated and which should not.

It seems an arbitrary figure and is being applied to all costs.

The tone of the report

The memorandum has been presented in a somewhat authoritarian style based solely on accounting information and the tone of the final comment is particularly aggressive, implying that the Head of Housekeeping is being blamed for the variances.

Impact on staff

The lack of participation may result in staff feeling resentment towards what they consider to be unfair targets.

This will be compounded if budgets are not flexed as targets will definitely be seen as unrealistic and unachievable.

If the tone and implied pressure to hit results continues, then staff may put more effort into finding excuses for poor cost control or even attempting to falsify data where possible, rather than focussing on doing a quality job.

The emphasis on financial aspects only may mean that the quality of cleaning falls as staff try to hit cost targets, undermining the customer experience.

Preliminary recommendations

Before developing the pilot further, you should arrange meetings with relevant managers and staff to explain the concept, its benefits and how it will work going forwards.

If possible, heads should be included in the budget setting process to give greater buy-in and ownership.

The report should have controllable costs only and these should be flexed before variances are calculated. This will make it clearer what the Head of Housekeeping (and other heads) can be held responsible for.

The report should include non-financial data, especially customer feedback, as well to give a more balanced perspective.

Test your understanding 2

1   Statement of financial position, statement of profit or loss, statement of changes in equity and statement of cash flow.

2   Stewardship is the accountability of management for the resources entrusted to it by the owners or the Government.

3   A bank is normally, in this context, a lender. Consequently they will tend to be interested in the financial statements to check the business's ability to repay any loans outstanding and that assets on which they depend for security are still recorded at good value.

Internal control systems

3

Introduction

In this chapter we look at specific examples of controls within different accounting systems.

This chapter needs to be studied carefully. You need to be able to suggest good controls and spot weaknesses caused by the absence of those controls.

PERFORMANCE CRITERIA
2.1 Internal controls
3.1 An organisation's accounting system and its effectiveness

1   Internal control systems

1.1   Internal control

 Definition of internal control

'The process designed and effected by those charged with governance, management and other personnel to provide reasonable assurance about the achievement of the entity's objectives with regard to reliability of financial reporting, effectiveness and efficiency of operations and compliance with applicable laws and regulations.' (ISA 315)

 Examples

The following examples show some of the ways that internal controls could help a company achieve its objectives and mitigate risk:

- Quality control/management can prevent the production of poor quality goods

- Credit control can limit the level of irrecoverable debts

- Controls over inventory ordering can prevent stock-outs and ensure an optimal level of inventory to minimise holding costs

- A compliance department can implement policies to ensure the business complies with relevant laws and regulations

- Controls over payroll can ensure employees are paid the correct amount, avoiding disputes with staff and incorrect payment of payroll taxes which could result in penalties from HMRC.

 Test your understanding 1

For the risks below, list some controls which may help minimize these risks.

- Non-payment by customers
- Producing damaged/poor quality products
- Paying too much for supplies

   KAPLAN PUBLISHING

Internal control consists of the following components:

- the control environment
- the entity's risk assessment process
- the information system, including the related business processes, relevant to financial reporting, and communication
- control activities; and
- monitoring of controls.

1.2 The control environment

The control environment includes the governance and management function of an organisation.

It focuses largely on the attitude, awareness and actions of those responsible for designing, implementing and monitoring internal controls.

Elements of the control environment include the following:

- communication and enforcement of integrity and ethical values
- commitment to competence
- participation by those charged with governance
- management's philosophy and operating style.

1.3 The entity's risk assessment process

The risk assessment process forms the basis for how management determines the business risks to be managed, i.e. threats to the achievement of ongoing business objectives.

These processes will vary hugely depending upon the nature, size and complexity of the organisation.

Threats to business objectives can lead to misstatement in the financial statements, e.g. non-compliance with laws and regulations may lead to fines and penalties, which require disclosure or provision in the financial statements.

If the company has robust procedures for assessing the business risks it faces, the risk of misstatement will be lower.

1.4 The information system

The information system is all of the business processes relevant to financial reporting and communication. It includes the procedures within both information technology and manual systems.

The information system includes all of the procedures and records which are designed to:

- initiate, record, process and report transactions

- maintain accountability for assets, liabilities and equity

- resolve incorrect processing of transactions

- transfer information to the general/nominal ledger

- ensure information required to be disclosed is appropriately reported.

1.5 Control activities

Control activities are policies and procedures that help ensure that management directives are carried out. Control activities are a component of internal control.

For the purposes of this module it is possible to identify eight categories of internal controls that are relevant and that will be useful whilst carrying out a review of an accounting function. These controls are applicable to both computerised and non-computerised environments.

Here is a list of typical internal controls. You should learn this list and you may find **SPAM SOAP** a useful mnemonic to remember these eight categories.

Later the text applies these controls to specific systems. Computer-based controls are equally important and are discussed in the following Chapter.

(i) **Segregation of duties** – a fundamental form of control in any enterprise is the separation of responsibilities so that no one person can fully record and process a transaction.

This can be achieved by ensuring that the **C**ustodial function, the **A**uthorisation function, the **R**ecording function and the **E**xecution function are kept separate.

(The mnemonic CARE might be useful to you in remembering these four functions.)

For example, warehouse staff should not be responsible for the inventory count, as this would not detect if goods were being stolen by staff throughout the year.

(ii) **Physical controls** – these are concerned with the custody of assets and records and are concerned with ensuring that access to assets and records is only permitted to authorised personnel.

For example, keeping cash in a safe to prevent theft.

(iii) **Authorisation and approval** – all transactions require authorisation or approval by a responsible person. Limits on authorisations should be set down in writing/documented.

For example, a manager signing off an employee's timesheet to confirm that the hours stated have been worked and can be paid. This should ensure the employee is not claiming for hours not worked.

(iv) **Management** – these are controls exercised by the management outside the day-to-day routine of the system.

Examples are the use of monitoring procedures through the use of budgetary control and other management accounting techniques as well as the provision of internal audit procedures.

(v) **Supervision** – an important aspect of any control system is the existence of supervisory procedures by the management.

(vi) **Organisation** – there must be a well-defined organisational structure showing how responsibility and authority are delegated. This was discussed in Chapter 1.

(vii) **Arithmetical and accounting** – these controls include those that check the arithmetical accuracy of records such as control accounts, cross totals, reconciliations and sequential controls over documents.

For example, sequence checks on sales invoices ensure the number sequence is complete and no invoices are missing.

(viii) **Personnel** – the proper functioning of the system depends upon the employment of well-motivated, competent personnel who possess the necessary integrity for their tasks.

For example, performing background checks on potential applicants to see if they have a criminal record.

1.6   Monitoring of controls

This is the process of assessing the effectiveness of controls over time and taking necessary remedial action. Clearly if a control is not implemented properly (or is simply considered ineffective), then misstatements may pass undetected into the financial statements and/or adversely affect management decision making.

Monitoring can be either ongoing or performed on a separate evaluation basis (or a combination of both). Either way, it needs to be effective for the system to work. Monitoring of internal controls is often the key role of internal auditors.

1.7 Limitations of internal controls

No system of internal controls will ever mitigate risks entirely due to the inherent limitation of controls. These limitations could be:

- Human error – mistakes made by those responsible for performing controls
- Unusual transactions tend to be outside the scope of control systems
- Collusion – staff work together to bypass segregation of duties
- Special considerations in small companies
- Informal nature/lack of documentation
- Limited numbers of staff make segregation of duties difficult.

1.8 Overall supervisory controls

If an internal control system is to work satisfactorily, there must be certain overall disciplines which enable the framework of controls to be maintained.

In particular, there must be segregation of duties and appropriate supervision.

- Segregation of duties means that the individuals who raise orders should be independent of the ledger keeping function, the inventory recording/control sub-system and the cheque drawing/approval/signing functions.
- Supervision means that there must be overall systems of review by a responsible official.

1.9 Internal audit

Internal audit is not specifically in the syllabus, but some knowledge of it is useful as one of its key roles is the testing of internal controls and the methods that an internal auditor uses will help you spot system weaknesses.

There are two types of test that are used by auditors in the course of their work:

- **Compliance tests** are tests of controls and provide evidence as to whether or not the controls on which the auditor wishes to rely were functioning adequately during the period under review.
- **Substantive tests** are tests of transactions, account balances and the existence of assets and liabilities and their valuation (e.g. inventories, non-current assets and receivables) and other procedures such as analytical review, which seek to provide audit evidence as to the completeness, accuracy and validity of the information contained in the accounting records or in the financial statements.

1.10   Internal control questionnaires (ICQs)

As their name suggests, internal control questionnaires (ICQs) are a set of questions designed to discover the existence of internal controls and to identify any possible areas of weakness.

The questions are framed with yes/no answers to identify any situation where there is no sub-division of duties between essential functions, where controls do not exist, or where aspects of managerial supervision are deficient.

In most assessment tasks the weaknesses are fairly standard (e.g. lack of authorisation). Examples of ICQs for sales, purchases and payroll are shown below, and if you can remember as many of the typical ICQ questions as possible, they will help you to quickly spot system weaknesses.

2   Sales system

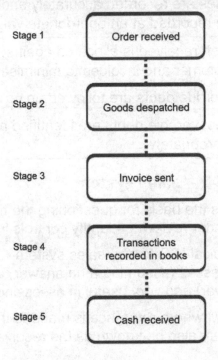

Stage 1 — Order received

Stage 2 — Goods despatched

Stage 3 — Invoice sent

Stage 4 — Transactions recorded in books

Stage 5 — Cash received

2.1   Internal control objectives within the sales system

The objectives of controls in the sales system are to ensure that:

Stage	Objective
Ordering	All orders are processed.
	All orders can be fulfilled.
	Orders only accepted from creditworthy customers
Despatch	All orders are despatched promptly and in full to the correct customer.
Invoicing	All goods despatched are invoiced.
	Invoices are raised accurately.
Recording	Only valid sales are recorded.
	All sales and related receivables are recorded and in the correct accounts.
	Revenue is recorded in the period to which it relates.
	Sales are recorded accurately and related receivables are recorded at an appropriate value.
Cash received	Cash received is allocated against the correct customer and invoices to minimise disputes.
	Overdue debts are followed up on a timely basis.
	Irrecoverable debts are identified and written off appropriately.

2.2   Specimen ICQ – sales system

An ICQ will be used as the basis for questioning the members of staff who operate the system under review to identify controls in place.

Below we outline a typical ICQ for the sales system. This is an excellent list of potential weaknesses (assuming a no answer) and strengths (assuming a yes answer) and very useful in assessing internal controls.

Note: In the ICQ below, where reference is made to the sales ledger control account, this can also be known as the receivables ledger control account.

Client:	Normanton Ltd		
Year end:	30 September 20X6	Prepared by: B E Mignano	
Cycle:	Sales	Date: 7.9.X6	
			Yes/No or N/A
1	**To ensure that all orders received are processed in such a way that keeps errors to a minimum**		
	Are persons responsible for preparation of sales orders independent of credit control, custody of inventory and recording sales transactions?		
	Are standard forms used to record orders?		
	Are sales orders pre-numbered?		
	Do sales order clerks check that the goods ordered are available in the quantity and quality required?		
	Are standard prices, delivery and payment terms in written form for the use of sales order clerks?		
	Are special orders (special qualities, quantities, prices) authorised by a responsible official?		
2	**To ensure that sales orders are not accepted in respect of a bad credit risk**		
	Is the credit controller independent of the sales order clerks?		
	Are new credit customers vetted for creditworthiness by reference to independent persons or organisations?		
	Are orders from existing customers checked for payment record, sales ledger balance and credit limit?		
	Are credit limits set by responsible officials for all credit customers?		
	Is the credit approval evidenced on the sales order by the signature of a responsible official?		
	Is the work of a credit control clerk independently checked?		
3	**To ensure that goods are only despatched to customers after proper authorisation**		
	Is warehouse/despatch department independent of sales order preparation, credit control and invoicing?		
	Do warehouse personnel release goods from the warehouse on the basis of sales orders signed by authorised sales order and credit control personnel?		
	Is the despatch of goods evidenced by the preparation of a goods despatch note?		
	Are goods despatch notes pre-numbered?		

	Are two copies of the goods despatch notes sent to the customer for one to be returned as evidence of receipt?	
	Is a copy of the despatch note sent to a stock/inventory control department to update stock/inventory records?	
	Is stock/inventory counted periodically and compared with stock/inventory records?	
4	**To ensure that all goods despatched are invoiced at authorised prices and terms**	
	Is sales invoicing independent of sales order preparation, credit control, warehouse and despatch departments?	
	Are copies of sales orders received by sales invoicing?	
	Is a sequence check carried out on sales orders?	
	Is a sequence check carried out on goods despatch notes?	
	Are goods despatch notes matched with sales orders and unmatched orders followed up?	
	Do invoicing clerks have details of current prices, terms and conditions, including special agreements with particular customers?	
	Are sales invoices independently checked before despatch?	
5	**To ensure that all sales invoices are properly recorded in individual customers' accounts in the sales ledger**	
	Is the sales ledger clerk independent of sales order preparation, credit control, warehouse, despatch and sales invoicing?	
	Is a sales ledger control account maintained independent of the sales ledger clerk?	
	Are differences between extracted list of sales ledger balances and control account balances investigated by a responsible official?	
	Are monthly statements of amounts outstanding prepared and despatched to customers?	
	Is an aged receivables listing prepared and reviewed by a responsible official?	
	Are sales ledger balances made up of identifiable sales invoices and other items?	
	Are irrecoverable write-offs and discounts authorised by a responsible official other than the sales ledger clerk?	

 KAPLAN PUBLISHING

Test your understanding 2 – Sales system

Gustavus plc

Gustavus plc sell a variety of electrical equipment on a wholesale basis to some 1,500 credit customers. No cash sales are made.

Sales orders are received by telephone and are recorded on a pre-numbered order form in two parts. Part 1 is sent to the customer as acknowledgement of the order. Part 2 is used by the manager of the sales office as an action copy, in order to record the sales order. The Manager then authorises the order after checking the account balance with the accounts department to ensure that the credit limit is not exceeded. The order is then passed to the warehouse where the goods are picked and sent to despatch.

The order form is then passed to the invoice typing section in the sales office and three-part invoice sets are typed. Each set is numbered by reference to a number register and the top copy is given to the customer with the goods at the collection point. The second copy is an accounts copy and the third is filed in the customer file in the sales office. There are no other procedures in relation to sales order processing.

Required:

Comment on the weaknesses inherent in the sales system.

3 Purchase system

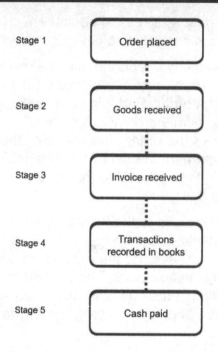

Stage 1 — Order placed

Stage 2 — Goods received

Stage 3 — Invoice received

Stage 4 — Transactions recorded in books

Stage 5 — Cash paid

3.1 Internal control objectives within the purchase system

The objectives of controls in the purchases system are to ensure that:

Stage	Objective
Ordering	All purchases are made with suppliers who have been checked for quality, reliability and pricing. Purchases are only made for a valid business use. Orders are placed taking consideration of delivery lead times to avoid disruption to the business.
Goods received	Only goods ordered by the company are accepted. Goods received are recorded promptly.
Invoice received	Invoices received relate to goods actually received. Invoices received relate to the company. Invoices received are correct in terms of quantities, prices, discounts.
Recording	All purchases and related payables are recorded. Purchases are recorded accurately and related payables are recorded at an appropriate value. Purchases are recorded in the period to which they relate. Purchases and payables are recorded in the correct accounts.
Cash payments	Payments are only made for goods received. Payments are only made once.

3.2 Specimen ICQ – purchase system

The ICQ below gives a comprehensive range of the types of controls that could be used within the purchase system.

Purchases and payments to suppliers	
Client: Normanton Ltd Year end: 30 September 20X6 Prepared by: B E Mignano Cycle: Purchases Date: 7.9.X6	
	Yes/No or N/A
1 To ensure that all orders are raised to minimise errors	
Are the orders raised in the order/purchasing department which is independent of all other departments?	
Are the orders requisitioned by a user department which is separate from the ordering department and stores?	
Are orders raised on authorised order forms which are pre-numbered serially and sequentially controlled?	
Is the supplier's price list checked to ensure that the correct quality and quantity of goods are being ordered at the correct price?	
Is a supplier's file maintained which will confirm details of discounts?	
Are all orders issued checked regularly to ensure that they have been fulfilled?	
Are unfulfilled orders checked to ensure that they are being satisfactorily progressed by the supplier?	
Is the official order signed by a responsible official?	
2 To ensure that goods received are correctly controlled	
Are goods received in a stores department that is independent of the user and purchasing departments?	
Does the organisation use official goods received notes?	
Is the goods received note correctly filled in when an order is received and signed off by a responsible official?	
Are the goods received notes sequentially pre-numbered and is there control over them?	
Is the delivery note which accompanies the goods from the supplier signed and returned to the supplier?	
Is a copy of the delivery note sent by the supplier retained and filed?	

	Is the goods received note raised by the company matched and filed with the delivery note sent by the supplier?	
3	**To ensure that invoices received are valid and agree with the goods delivered**	
	Are the invoices arithmetically checked?	
	Is the invoice compared to the purchase order and quantities, qualities and prices checked?	
	Is the invoice compared to the goods received note and supplier's delivery note to ensure that the correct quantities and quality were received?	
	Is the invoice stamped with a 'grid' so that the above checks are correctly evidenced on the face/electronic copy of the invoice?	
	Is the invoice correctly coded so that goods received are allocated to the correct nominal ledger code?	
	Are the invoices received allocated an internal sequential number and filed sequentially?	
4	**To ensure that payments to suppliers are correctly made**	
	Are the persons who sign the cheques different from those who handle the authorisation of the invoices?	
	Are there two responsible officials who act as cheque signatories?	
	Is close control maintained over the custody of the cheques?	
	Are all cheques issued in sequential order?	
	Are spoilt or cancelled cheques retained?	
	Are all cheques stamped 'A/C payee'?	
	Are cheques presented for signature with relevant authorising documentation, e.g. an authorised invoice?	
	Is the number of the cheque used to pay the invoice written on the face of the invoice?	
	If BACS are used to pay suppliers, do two responsible officials sign the BACS authorisation?	
	Does company policy forbid the use of cash to pay suppliers' invoices?	

Note that the internal control questionnaire outlined above is a fairly detailed questionnaire which is designed to assess a fairly 'advanced/ideal' system. In many smaller organisations, it will not be possible or even necessary to have a system which contains many of these features.

Test your understanding 3 – Purchases

Miller Ltd

Miller Ltd is a company engaged in pharmaceutical manufacturing. The purchasing department is managed by Mr Wurm, the buyer, and the buying assistant Walter Green. The value of purchase contracts placed annually is about £3 million. When goods are required the stock/inventory records clerk (Frederica) sends a purchase requisition to Mr Wurm, who gets Walter to type out an order form. Walter enters a serial number, sequentially-numbered after the last purchase order, and photocopies the order. The original is sent to the supplier and the copy is kept in a file.

When the goods arrive, they are taken into stock/inventory and the supplier's despatch note is sent to Walter from the goods inwards supervisor. Walter then marks off the items received on the order and sends the despatch note to the stock/inventory records section. They then use it to write up the stock/inventory ledger and file it in chronological sequence.

(a) Identify the weaknesses in the system and briefly indicate the effect of that weakness.

(b) What outline recommendations would you make to improve the system? You may assume that the company has adequate resources to implement your recommendations.

 Test your understanding 4 – Payments to suppliers

Melchior Manufacturing Supplies Ltd

At monthly intervals the purchase ledger clerk of Melchior Manufacturing Supplies Ltd, Mrs Thorborg, lists the ledger balances. She then compares them with a file of suppliers' statements. Those statements that agree with the list of balances are extracted and placed in another file. Those that do not agree with the listed balances are left in the original file.

Mrs Thorborg then prepares a list of payments for all the suppliers who have sent statements as follows.

(1) Where the statement agrees with the balance, the statement is attached to the list.

(2) Where there is a disagreement, Mrs Thorborg computes a 'round sum amount' (which is generally slightly less than the balance on the ledger) and enters this amount on the list of payments. She leaves these statements in the file.

(3)   The list of payments is then passed to Mr Lehmann, the assistant accountant, who writes out the cheques.

(4)   The cheques, list and statements are then sent to Mrs Turner, the commercial director, who signs them after checking against the statements (where these are attached) and the list.

(5)   The cheques are then passed to the managing director, Mr Widdop, the other signatory, who signs the cheques and sends them back to Mr Lehmann, who then posts them to the parties concerned.

Required:

The internal auditors have made various comments regarding the poor quality of the accounting controls. Identify those areas that you think would have been likely to attract adverse comment from the internal auditors.

Note: You are not required to make recommendations.

3.3   Non-current assets – internal controls

Expenditure on non-current assets should be controlled in a similar way to other purchases. However, because of the significant amounts involved, additional controls should be in place.

3.4   Non-current assets – control objectives

The additional objectives of controls in the purchases system related to non-current assets are to ensure that:

*   Assets are only purchased if there is a business need.

*   Assets are purchased at an appropriate price.

*   The company can afford the capital expenditure proposed.

*   Capital expenditure is appropriately treated in the accounting records.

*   Capital expenditure is completely and accurately recorded in the accounting records.

*   Assets are covered by adequate insurance to prevent loss to the company.

*   Documents relating to assets are safeguarded from theft or damage.

3.5 Non-current assets – controls

Additional types of controls that could be used for non-current assets would include the following:

- Requisitions for capital expenditure should be made by an appropriate person.

- Authorisation for purchases of non-current assets should be at a more senior level.

- Several quotations should be obtained before purchase in order to obtain the best price.

- An annual capital expenditure budget for each department should be prepared and authorisation should only be given for purchases which have been budgeted.

- Regular review of revenue expenditure should be performed to ensure capital items have not been expensed in error.

- A regular reconciliation of the asset register to the physical assets held should be performed.

- An asset register should be maintained which includes cost, depreciation, location, insurance details, etc.

- Adequate insurance cover should be purchased.

- Documentation such as title deeds, vehicle registration documents, insurance policies, etc. should be stored in a secure, fire-proof location.

4 Payroll system

Stage 1 — Clock cards submitted and input

Stage 2 — Gross pay, deductions and net pay calculated

Stage 3 — Other amendments input

Stage 4 — Final payroll calculated and payslips produced

Stage 5 — Payments to employees and tax authorities

Stage 6 — Payroll costs and payments recorded

4.1   Internal control objectives within the payroll system

The objectives of controls in the payroll system are to ensure that:

Stage	Objective
Clock cards (or timesheets) submitted.	Employees are only paid for work actually done.
Payroll calculation	Only genuine employees are paid. Employees are paid at the correct rates of pay. Gross pay is calculated and recorded accurately. Net pay is calculated and recorded accurately.
Standing data amendments	Standing data is kept up to date. Access to standing data is restricted to prevent fraud or error occurring.
Recording	All payroll amounts are recorded. Payroll amounts are recorded accurately. Payroll costs are recorded in the period to which they relate.
Payments to employees and tax authorities	Correct amounts are paid to the employees and taxation authorities. Payments are made on time. Payments are only made to valid employees.

4.2   Internal control questionnaire – payroll

The ICQ below gives a comprehensive range of the types of controls that could be used within the payroll system.

	Yes/No or N/A
1 **Fundamental controls of a payroll system**	
Is a permanent record kept for each employee containing details of engagement, dismissal, changes in rates of pay, etc?	
Are these details and any changes in details evidenced in writing by a responsible official?	
Are timesheets kept for each employee giving details for each payment period of normal hours and overtime hours worked?	
For piecework employees, are details kept of amounts produced as a basis for payment?	
For each payment period, are the calculations which make up gross pay checked for each employee against the timesheets and records of rates, etc?	
Is the calculation for the total amount of the payroll checked for each payment period?	
Are all payments for overtime approved by a responsible official?	
2 **To ensure the correct preparation and payment of the payroll**	
Does a responsible official formally approve the total payroll by signing it?	
Where employees are paid by cheque or BACS, does a responsible official check the total amount being paid to each employee?	
Where wages are paid by cash, do two responsible officials authorise and sign the cheque to raise the cash?	
Is the cash securely transported from the bank and securely held on the premises?	
Does a responsible official oversee the correct cash being placed into each wages packet?	
Are unclaimed wages securely held in the company's premises until collected?	

Client: Normanton Ltd
Year end: 30 September 20X6 Prepared by: B E Mignano
Cycle: Payroll Date: 7.9.X6

3	Controls over accounting for payroll	
	Are payroll liabilities reconciled with the source total payroll (i.e. PAYE and NIC deductions included)?	
	Is PAYE and NIC paid on the due date?	
	Do adequate procedures exist to ensure that payroll is analysed and entered in the appropriate nominal ledger accounts?	

 Test your understanding 5 – Payroll

Bingham

Employees of Bingham Manufacturing are paid on the basis of hours worked and quantities produced. The hours worked are recorded on clock cards and the quantities produced are confirmed by the foreman. Wages are paid in cash each Friday for the previous week's work. Appointment of employees is authorised by the managing director, and the personnel department maintains employees' records and their rates of pay. The cashier is separate from the wages department.

Required:

State the principal controls you would expect to exist in a wages system and explain their purpose.

 Test your understanding 6 – Payroll

Burnden Limited

Burnden Limited manufactures a range of components and spare parts for the textile industry. The company employs 150 hourly-paid workers and 20 administrative staff, including the three directors of the company. There are two wages clerks who deal with the weekly payroll of the hourly-paid employees. They are directly responsible to the assistant accountant.

The company uses a computerised time clock at the factory gate to record the hours worked by the production employees. Each employee has a card with a magnetic strip with their own identification code on it. This card is inserted in the computerised time clock on the arrival and departure of each worker, whereupon it records on the card the hours worked. The cards are collected weekly by the wages clerks, who simply insert them individually into the microcomputer, which then reads them and prepares the payroll. The production manager keeps the unused clock cards in a locked cabinet in their own office.

Wages are paid one week in arrears. The wages clerks compile the payroll by means of the microcomputer system, and pass the payroll to the assistant accountant who scrutinises it before drawing the wages cheque, which is passed to one of the directors for signature. Any pay increases are negotiated locally by representatives of the employees. If any alterations are required to the standing data on the microcomputer, then the wages clerks amend the records. For example, when a wage increase has been negotiated, the rates of pay are changed by the wages clerks.

The cheque is drawn to cover net wages and the cashier makes arrangements for collecting the cash from the bank.

The wages clerks then make up the wages envelopes.

Whenever there is assistance required on preparing wages, the assistant accountant helps the wages clerks. The payment of wages is carried out by the production manager who returns any unclaimed wages to the wages clerks who keep them in a locked filing cabinet. Each employee is expected to collect any unclaimed wages personally.

New production employees are notified to the wages department verbally by the production manager and when employees leave, a note to that effect is sent to the wages department by the production manager. All statutory deductions are paid to the appropriate authorities by the chief accountant.

Administrative staff are paid monthly by credit transfer to their bank account. The payroll is prepared by the assistant accountant and the bank credit transfers are authorised by a director. Any increases in the salaries of the administrative staff are notified to the assistant accountant verbally by the chief accountant. The employment of administrative staff is authorised by the financial director.

Required:

Assuming that the only controls are those set out above, describe the weaknesses in the present payroll system, and suggest, with reasons, improvements which could be made to the system.

5 Inventory system

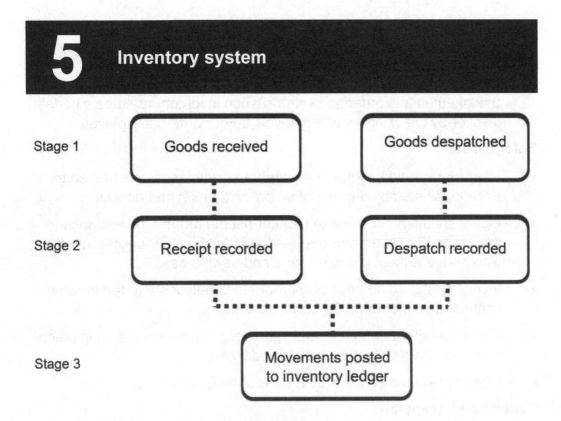

5.1 Internal control objectives

The objectives of controls in the inventory system are to ensure that:

Stage	Objective
General	Inventory levels meet the needs of production (raw materials and components) and customer demand (finished goods).
	Inventory levels are not excessive, preventing obsolescence and unnecessary storage costs.
	Inventory is safeguarded from theft, loss or damage.
Receipt and despatch	Inventory received and despatched is correctly recorded on a timely basis.
Recording	All inventory is recorded.
	Inventory should be recorded at the appropriate value.
	Only inventory owned by the company is recorded.

5.2   Controls

Levels

- Inventory should be maintained at an appropriate level through the use of automatic ordering systems when inventory reaches a certain level or by checking inventory levels before orders are placed.

Safeguards

- Inventory should be kept in a warehouse with access restricted to warehouse staff by the use of swipe card or keypad access.

- CCTV should be in place to monitor people around the entrance to the warehouse to ensure people do not follow other people into the warehouse without the need for a code/swipe card.

- Inventory should be kept in appropriate conditions e.g. temperature controlled environment for perishable items.

- Fire/smoke/heat detectors and sprinkler systems should be in place to reduce the risk of damage caused by fire.

- Inventory should be insured in case of theft or damage.

Receipt and despatch

- Inventory movements should be recorded in the system promptly using Goods Received Notes (GRNs) and Goods Delivered Notes (GDNs). The GRNs and GDNs should be stamped to confirm they have been input and the system is up to date.

Inventory counts

- Inventory counts should take place on a regular basis so that physical inventory quantities can be reconciled with the accounting system on a regular basis to ensure the records are accurate and up to date.

- Inventory should be reviewed during the count for damage or obsolescence and valued separately from the other inventory by making an allowance to write the inventory down to net realisable value.

6   Bank and cash system

Stage 1 — Request for payment

Stage 2 — Payment authorisation

Stage 3 — Payment made   Receipts

Stage 4 — Payments and receipts recorded

6.1   Internal control objectives

The objectives of controls in the cash system are to ensure that:

Stage	Objective
General	Petty cash levels are kept to a minimum, preventing theft. Cash is safeguarded to prevent theft.
Authorisation	Payments can only be made for legitimate business expenditure. Cash can only be withdrawn for business purposes.
Receipts	Receipts are banked on a timely basis to prevent theft.
Recording	Cash movements are recorded on a timely basis.

6.2 Internal controls: bank payments

Payments are an important part of the system for incurring expenditure and so we need to consider the internal controls in this specific context.

It is necessary to remember the fundamental principle of internal control: the need for a division of duties between **C**ustodial, **A**uthorisation, **R**ecording and **E**xecution functions. This principle should be applied to all payments, whether by cheque or electronic transfer. Electronic transfers will usually either be BACS (Bankers' Automated Clearing System) or FPS (Faster Payments Service) payments.

Cheques

(a) **Division of duties**

  (i) The persons who sign cheques should be different from the authorisation, recording and custodial functions.

  (ii) There must be two responsible officials who act as cheque signatories. If pre-printed cheques are in use, or a cheque signing machine is installed, the control over the issue and custody of cheques must be closely supervised by a responsible official who is different from the recording or custodial function.

(b) **Custody**

  (i) All cheques should be issued in sequential order and their sequence should be controlled.

  (ii) Unused stocks of cheque books must be kept under lock and key.

  (iii) Spoilt or cancelled cheques must be retained.

  (iv) All cheques should be crossed 'A/c payee only' to minimise the chance of fraud if the cheque is lost.

(c) **Authorisation**

  (i) No cheque should be prepared without supporting documentation, e.g. an approved invoice, a signed payroll or an authorised cheque requisition.

  (ii) The cheque signatories' authority should be laid down in writing and be in accordance with the bank mandate.

  (iii) The system of cheque payments must be supervised by a responsible official who will oversee the preparation of regular bank reconciliations and carry out spot checks thereon.

Electronic transfer

Although the principles will be the same, the precise controls necessary for electronic transfers will differ from those for cheques due to the nature of the payments.

(a) **Division of duties**

    (i)   The people who process the bank transfer should be separate from the authorisation and recording functions.

    (ii)   Many banks allow electronic transfers to be performed by an individual. This is equivalent to allowing cheques to have a single signatory, so extra vigilance is necessary.

(b) **Authorisation**

    (i)   No transfer should be processed without supporting documentation, e.g. an approved invoice, a signed payroll or an authorised transfer requisition.

    (ii)   The system of electronic transfers must be supervised by a responsible official who will oversee the preparation of regular bank reconciliations and carry out spot checks thereon.

6.3 Internal controls: bank and cash receipts

The cash receipts system is an important part of the income cycle, so it is necessary to consider the internal control aspects of this part of the system. As with cash payments, one should consider the importance of a proper subdivision of duties between Custodial, Authorisation, Recording and Execution functions.

(a) **Custodial procedures**

    (i)   All post should be opened by at least two responsible officials.

    (ii)   All cheques and postal orders should be crossed restrictively to the company's bankers.

    (iii) A cash diary should be maintained of daily amounts of cash received.

    (iv) All monies received should be banked intact on the same business day.

(b) **Separation of duties**

    (i)   Different members of staff should be responsible for opening the post, preparing the paying-in details and controlling the sales ledger.

    (ii)   There should be an independent check on cash receipts by a suitable official who can spot-check the details in the cash diary with the paying in records.

(c) **Recording controls**

    (i)   The entries in the cash receipts book should be proved by regular bank reconciliations.

    (ii)   The bank reconciliations should be reviewed and spot-checked on a regular basis by a responsible official remote from the recording functions.

7 The effect of weaknesses

7.1 Introduction

Clearly you need to be able to go further than simply spot weaknesses in accounting systems. You are also likely to be required to be able to describe what the effect of those weaknesses might be on the organisation.

7.2 A wide perspective

The effect that a weakness might have should be considered widely. You could consider the effect on:

- Assets
- Liabilities
- Income
- Expenses
- Theft or fraud
- Morale
- Efficiency of system
- Business reputation
- Time taken to produce information.

8 Additional 'Test your understanding' questions

 Test your understanding 7

1   Can you identify four of the eight categories of internal control?

2   Internal checks are a feature of internal control. What are they designed to ensure?

3   Describe the essence of an internal check.

4   Briefly explain the two types of test that are used by internal auditors in the course of their work.

5   What are ICQs?

9 Summary

This has been a very important chapter and in some ways goes to the heart of the analysis of the accounting systems.

The division of responsibilities is a key element to internal control and you should always be aware of any shortcomings in this respect when analysing a system.

The internal control questionnaire is a very good way of gaining information about a system and its shortcomings.

Test your understanding answers

Test your understanding 1

Non-payment by customers

- Credit checks on all new customers
- Credit limits set for all customers
- Regular review of balances against credit limits to ensure not breached
- Reducing/altering payment terms for poor payers

Producing damaged/poor quality products

- Choose suppliers with good market reputation (create an approved supplier list)
- Regularly review level of returns/credit notes issued to determine whether a problem exists
- Instigate appropriate training techniques for production staff
- Implement adequate quality control/management procedures

Paying too much for supplies

- Check taking advantage of any prompt payment/bulk discounts
- Compare all invoices received to goods received note (GRN) prior to payment
- Marking paid invoices as such to avoid duplicate payments being made.

Test your understanding 2 – Sales system

Weaknesses in the system

- There is no separation of duties between the functions of recording and authorisation of sales orders.

- The validation procedures appear to be inadequate as there is no evidence of formal procedures such as validation of prices and stock/inventory availability.

- There are no procedures to ensure that the customer signs for the goods collected which would serve as proof of delivery.

- Invoices are not pre-numbered; this is a serious control weakness as transactions can be suppressed without trace.

- Invoices are not checked for arithmetical accuracy before being despatched.

- There are no procedures for dealing with unsatisfied orders.

- There are no procedures to update the order file with details of orders despatched to customers.

 Test your understanding 3 – Purchase system

(a) **Weaknesses in the system**

(i) The purchase orders are not multipart, pre-numbered documents (the numbers are added manually). As a result of this weakness, unauthorised orders can be placed. The lack of original documentation makes the system susceptible to loss or irregular alteration.

(ii) The orders are neither priced, nor are they checked by Mr Wurm before they are processed.

This could lead to incorrect pricing being committed to or incorrect goods being ordered.

(iii) Mr Wurm does not sign the orders as the company's authorised signatory. The effect of this is as for (ii) above.

(iv) There is no goods received note system to evidence the arrival of goods. Goods could be invoiced for but not received and we could not prove otherwise.

(v) The acceptance of goods in the goods inwards section is done without reference to the purchase order; Walter only matches them up later. Goods that have not been ordered could be accepted and potentially subsequently paid for.

(vi) There is no review of outstanding purchase orders in order to chase up unfulfilled orders. Production delays could occur.

(b) **Recommendations**

(i) The purchase orders should be a three-part document and sequentially-controlled. Unissued order pads should be kept under lock and key. Sequential control should then be maintained over books of purchase orders in issue. Spoilt and unused copies should be retained and the completeness of the sequential numbering monitored frequently.

(ii) The purchase orders should be priced by reference to suppliers' catalogues before ordering. This enables the amount eventually invoiced by the supplier to be checked.

(iii) Purchase requisitions should be checked before being processed. Similarly, purchase orders should be signed by Mr Wurm as evidence of authority before being despatched.

This ensures that unauthorised purchases cannot be made.

(iv) A copy of the purchase order should be sent to the goods inwards department in order to provide authority for the acceptance of the goods.

(v) When goods arrive they should be checked against the copy purchase order and evidenced on a pre-numbered, three-part goods received note (GRN). One part (top) of the GRN should be used to update the order file i.e. to indicate which orders have been fulfilled and which are still outstanding. The second part can be used to write up the stock/inventory ledger. The third part can be kept as a master copy in serial number order.

(vi) Mr Wurm should review the order file weekly and check on the position of outstanding orders.

Test your understanding 4 – Payments to suppliers

Matters likely to cause adverse comment from the auditors:

(a) Mrs Thorborg appears to operate in a careless and uninterested fashion in that she:

    (i) does not appear to claim cash discounts for early payment

    (ii) makes no attempt to reconcile bought ledger accounts

    (iii) makes round sum payments and is therefore likely to increase the problem of account balances that disagree

    (iv) does not attach invoices for payment; thus there is no attempt to identify specifically the transactions that are being settled and the same invoice could therefore be paid twice.

(b) There is a lack of evidence for the first cheque signatory, as Mrs Turner does not see the statements for balances that disagree.

(c) Mr Widdop does not receive supporting evidence for payment. Consequently Mr Widdop may not notice errors or be aware of any lapses in control.

(d) The signed cheques are sent to Mr Lehmann who could suppress or alter them for Mr Lehmann's own benefit.

(e) The payment of invoices or statements does not alert the company to errors made by the supplier. Thus it is possible to pay for items not ordered and charged to the company in error.

Test your understanding 5 – Payroll

Controls

The principal controls in a wages system would include the following.

There should be a proper division of duties in the payroll system. For example, employees who calculate wages should not be responsible for making up the wage packets.

Any unclaimed wages should be stored securely until they are claimed.

Deductions should be calculated using software to reduce the risk of errors, or reviewed by someone more senior to check the calculation has been performed correctly.

New employee details, authorised by a senior manager should be provided to the personnel department. No new employee should be created in the payroll system without an authorised form.

The payroll journal should be authorised prior to posting to the general ledger.

Purpose

The purpose of these controls is to ensure that employees are paid at authorised rates for work done, that the transactions are recorded accurately in the accounting records, that the employees and other authorities are paid the correct sums and that the risk of fraud and error is minimised.

Test your understanding 6 – Payroll

Weaknesses and improvements

The weaknesses in the company's present wages and salaries system and suggestions for improvements are as follows:

- W: There are two wages clerks dealing with the production payroll.

  I: To improve control within the wages department, the duties of these clerks should be rotated during the year. Neither of the clerks should be responsible for all functions in the department.

- W: No personnel records currently kept for each employee.

  I: These should be kept for each employee giving details of engagement, retirement, dismissal or resignation, rates of pay, holidays etc, with a specimen signature for the employee. They would be essential in the event of failure or corruption of the computer system.

- W: The production manager verbally notifies the wages department of new employees.

  I: It is important that there is written authorisation from the chief accountant for the appointment and removal of all employees.

- W: The production manager also controls the unused clock cards and pays out the wage, so could introduce a fictitious employee.

  I:The unused clock cards should also be kept in a secure place by someone other than the production manager. They should be issued weekly by a responsible official.

- W: The wages clerks appear to amend pay rates without any authorisation.

  I: Changes in rates of pay should be authorised in writing by an official outside the wages department.

- W: The clocking-in and out procedures do not seem to be supervised.

  I: There should be supervision of the cards and timing devices.

- W: The production manager pays out wages alone.

  I: It would be preferable if the two wages clerks paid out the wages. A surprise attendance at the payout should be made periodically by an independent official. It would also be preferable that an employee should not be allowed to take the wages of another employee without written authorisation. Unclaimed wages should be recorded immediately in a register and held by someone outside the wages department until claimed or until a predefined period after which the money should be re-banked.

- W: The payroll is not authorised.

  I: It should be signed by the person preparing it. The director should check that it has been authorised before signing the wages cheque. They should also sign the payroll. Further, the payroll should be carefully scrutinised by the assistant accountant who should carry out random checks on rates of pay, amendments to employees etc.

- W: Access to the computer payroll system does not appear to be restricted.

  I: Access should be controlled by passwords which should be changed regularly.

- W: There is a security risk in drawing large amounts of cash from the bank and keeping this on the premises.

  I: If possible, the company should transfer the employees onto a bank giro transfer system (i.e: transfer the payment of wages onto an electronic system).

- W: There are weaknesses in the monthly payroll. The assistant accountant does not sign the payroll as preparer and the director should authorise the bank credit transfer only after checking an authorised payroll.

  I: Ensure that the assistant accountant signs as the preparer and the director completes the relevant authorisation.

- W: No director authorisation of salary increases.

  I: Salary increases should be notified in writing by the chief accountant after authorisation by a director. Personnel records should be kept as for production staff and appointments and dismissals should be authorised only by directors.

- W: No overtime authorisation is completed.

  I: If any overtime is worked it should be authorised by the production manager.

- W: Director does not check authorised payroll prior to bank transfer authorisation.

  I: Director should authorise the bank credit transfer only after checking on authorised payroll.

- Note: A manual back-up system should be available in the event of computer failure.

❋ Test your understanding 7

1   You could choose any four of the following types of internal control: organisation, segregation of duties, supervision, management, physical controls, authorisation and approval and personnel. The proper functioning of the system depends upon the employment of well-motivated, competent personnel who possess the necessary integrity for their tasks.

2   Internal checks are designed to ensure that all transactions and other accounting information that should be recorded have been recorded, any errors or irregularities in processing accounting information are highlighted and assets and liabilities recorded in the accounts do actually exist and are recorded at their correct amount.

3   The essence of an internal check is to ensure that no one person carries too much responsibility and that each person's work is reviewed or checked by another. This is achieved by a division of responsibilities. The absence of internal checks leads to errors remaining undiscovered and can also lead to fraudulent acts, which are committed because the fraudster feels free of any form of supervision.

4   There are two types of test that are used by auditors in the course of their work:

Tests of controls (compliance tests) provide evidence as to whether or not the controls on which the auditor wishes to rely were functioning adequately during the period under review.

Substantive procedures (or substantive tests) are those tests of transactions, account balances and the existence of assets and liabilities and their valuation (e.g. inventories, non-current assets and receivables) and other procedures such as analytical review, which seek to provide audit evidence as to the completeness, accuracy and validity of the information contained in the accounting records or in the financial statements.

5   As their name suggests, internal control questionnaires (ICQs) are checklists of questions that are designed to discover the existence of internal controls and to identify any possible areas of weakness. An important feature of the ICQ is the way in which questions are phrased; an affirmative answer indicates a strength and a negative answer a weakness.

Internal controls in a computerised environment

Introduction

Most businesses have accounting systems within a computerised environment. In principle there is little difference in the accounting function but some different internal controls are necessary.

When considering scenarios in a computerised environment, the approach will essentially be the same as in the previous Chapter. You will still have to spot weaknesses and make recommendations.

PERFORMANCE CRITERIA	
2.1	Internal controls
3.2	Risk of fraud
3.3	Operating practice

CONTENTS	
1	Information systems controls
2	Integrity controls
3	Contingency controls
4	Assessing and managing risk

1 Information systems controls

1.1 Risks to information systems

Q Definition

The British Computer Society defines security as 'the establishment and application of safeguards to protect data, software and computer hardware from accidental or malicious modification, destruction or disclosure'. Security is the protection of the system from harm. It relates to all elements of the system, including hardware, software, data and the system users themselves.

There are three basic concerns relevant to the computerised information system. Security should maintain:

(i)   the availability of the computerised service itself

(ii)   the integrity of the data that it processes and stores, and

(iii) the confidentiality of the data before, during and after processing.

Controls are procedures or system features that help to ensure that the system operates in accordance with the requirements of the organisation and the user. The issue of the information system's security is based on the following three elements:

* **physical** – the operation of computer equipment can be severely impaired where it is subject to events such as fire, flooding and improper environmental conditions, e.g. heat

* **people** as a threat, and

* the **data/information** that might be lost or damaged.

The security measures adopted should perform the following functions:

* the avoidance or prevention of loss

* the deterrence of as many threats as possible

* easy recovery after any loss

* identification of the cause of any loss after the event, and

* the correction of vulnerable areas to reduce the risk of repeated loss.

1.2 General controls

General controls relate to the environment within which computer-based systems are developed, maintained and operated and are generally applicable to all the applications running on the system. You should memorise as much of this list as possible:

- **Personnel recruitment** policies to ensure honesty and competence.

- **Segregation** of duties between different types of job, to minimise tampering with programs or data.

- Proper **training** programmes for new staff and for new systems developments.

- **Physical** security of hardware and software against accidental or malicious damage or natural disasters.

- **Authorisation** procedures for program amendments and testing.

- **Back-up procedures** (maintaining copies of files off-site, back-up facilities).

- **Access** controls. (e.g. firewalls and anti-virus checkers).

- Measures to ensure the system is not accessed during data **transmission** (hacking).

- Controls to ensure that the computing resources are used **efficiently**.

1.3 Data security

A critical element of effective data protection is the need for security. There is a range of issues that should be considered:

- the nature of the personal data and the harm that would result from access, alteration, disclosure, loss or destruction

- the place where the personal data is stored

- reliability of staff having access to the data.

Data security measures involve different aspects:

- **Physical security**, such as the security of data storage facilities, from flood as well as unauthorised access

- **Software security**, such as maintaining a log of all failed access requests, and

- **Operational security**, with regard to such things as work data being taken home by employees, and periodic data protection audits of the computer systems.

Under the terms of the **Data Protection Act 2018**, the need for privacy is recognised by the requirements that all personal data on individuals should be held only for specified explicit purposes. There is stronger legal protection for more sensitive information, such as race, ethnic background, political opinions and religious beliefs.

The Act states that data must be:

- accurate and, where necessary, kept up to date

- kept for no longer than is necessary

- handled in a way that ensures appropriate security, including protection against unlawful or unauthorised processing, access, loss, destruction or damage.

1.4 Physical security

Computer systems consist of a mixture of electronic and mechanical devices that can be severely impaired when they are subject to events such as fire, flooding, and improper environmental conditions. As well as covering these threats, physical security also covers the prevention of theft and accidental or malicious damage caused by external parties or internal staff.

The organisation must assess the physical risks applicable to them, and put in place appropriate controls. These controls may be designed to detect the risk or may be designed to prevent it, and might include the following:

- **Fire systems and procedures** – systems of fire alarms, heat and smoke detectors can alert staff to the risk or presence of fire in time for preventive action to be taken. The fire control system might also trigger automatic fire extinguishing equipment, though the use of water sprinkler systems in offices with computer hardware is inappropriate due to the damage they can cause to electrical equipment.

- **Location of hardware** away from sources of risk – not siting computer facilities in areas susceptible to flooding or natural disasters is common sense, but there are other controls that may be less obvious e.g. locating equipment where it cannot be seen through windows from a public area may reduce the risk of theft.

- **Regular building maintenance** – attention to roofs, windows and doors will reduce the risk of water penetration and make forcible entry more difficult. Training – staff should be given copies of relevant policies and procedures, and trained in the implementation of them. Specific training should cover evacuation drills, fire control and fighting, safe behaviour, first aid, how to deal with a bomb threat and general risk identification and management.

- **Physical access controls** – there are a number of steps that can be taken to prevent the access of unauthorised persons to computer facilities.

  Examples include security guards to check identification and authorisation, CCTV, using badge readers or coded locks on access doors from public areas and electronic tagging of hardware.

Environmental threats can come from extremes of temperature, excessive humidity and interruptions or inconsistencies in the power supply. The mechanisms that can be used to control the computer environment include heating and air-conditioning systems, smoothed power supplies and uninterruptable power supplies (UPS).

1.5 Individual staff controls

No matter what the size of organisation, or the type of hardware involved, where activities are undertaken that are important to the commercial fabric of the organisation, individual staff functions must be specifically defined and documented where they involve data processing of any form.

This is vital, as it may be the only control in smaller organisations that will prevent, minimise or lead to the detection of fraudulent manipulation of data during processing, destruction of data, the accidental incorrect processing of data and unauthorised access to personal or confidential data that may be in contravention of the Data Protection Act 2018, or may be otherwise unlawful.

It is necessary to restrict access to the system, to protect the confidentiality of the software and data. Access must be limited to those with the proper authority, and a number of controls are available. These include the physical access controls that we have already outlined as well as the following:

- **Logical access system** – unauthorised people can get around physical access controls and gain access to data and program files unless different controls are used to deter them. Measures such as identification of the user, authentication of user identity and checks on user authority are alternative ways of achieving control.

- **Personal identification** – the most common form of personal identification is the PIN (personal identification number), which acts as a form of password. Users should be required to log in to the system using a unique user name and a password that is kept secret and changed frequently. Other, more sophisticated personal identification techniques include fingerprint recognition, eye retina 'prints' and voice 'prints'.

- **Usage logs** – the system should be designed to automatically record the log-in and log-off times of each user, and the applications accessed. Periodic checks should be made for unusual patterns, such as a day-shift worker accessing the system at night.

- **Storage of CDs, removable data storage devices in secure locations** – given that one of the risks that the organisation is trying to counteract is the physical destruction of the installation, it is sensible to put in place controls to ensure that back-up data is stored in a fire-proof environment on-site, and occasionally some form of master back-up is removed from the installation site completely.

 Test your understanding 1

You are a trainee management accountant in a small manufacturing company. Your head of department is going to a meeting and has asked you to provide some information for him.

Write a briefing report for the head of department which:

(a) examines the factors that you consider most affect the security of an organisation's computer systems

(b) identifies ways in which the risks associated with computer security might be successfully managed.

2 Integrity controls

2.1 Sources of error

It is important to identify how errors might occur during the operation of a system other than as a result of failing to establish proper administrative controls. Errors will fall into the following classes:

1   **Data capture/classification errors** – these occur before data is ready for input to a system and arise because of:

- incorrect classification of data (e.g. allocating a production cost as an administrative cost)

- measuring mistakes (e.g. recording the arrival of ten tons of raw material when only nine tons was delivered)

- incorrect spelling (e.g. of a customer's name)

- transposition (e.g. recording a receipt as £50,690 instead of the actual figure of £50,960).

2   **Transcription errors** – these arise during the preparation of data for processing.

For example, data which has been written down previously or which is passed on orally may be incorrectly recorded on data input forms.

3   **Data communication faults** – if the system operates over a wide area network (WAN) then the original input at the terminal/PC may become corrupted during transmission either during online processing or where the information is stored in a batch file and transmitted over the WAN later for processing. Similar issues need to be considered for local area networks (LANs) but far fewer problems arise due to the greater level of resilience inherent in LANs.

4   **Data processing errors** – these can arise due to programming error, system design and/or data corruption on the system itself.

Because the above errors are likely to occur throughout the life of a system, with varying degrees of seriousness, we must take specific measures to identify when they occur and to ensure that corrections are made to the data, either before or after processing has occurred.

2.2   System activities

The purpose of the controls is to ensure as far as possible that:

- the data being processed is complete
- the data being processed is authorised
- the results are accurate
- a complete audit trail of activity is available.

The areas in which we would expect controls to be assigned to provide protection to the system are concerned with input, file processing and output.

Input activities	File processing activities	Output activities
• data collection and preparation • data authorisation • data conversion (if appropriate) • data transmission • data correction • corrected data re-input	• data validation and edit • data manipulation, sorting/merging • master file updating	• output control and reconciliation with predetermined data • information distribution

Controls in these areas are vital and must deal with errors or problems as they arise instead of delaying their resolution to a later processing stage. Inaccurate data represents a waste of both computer time and human effort and may lead to further unforeseen errors occurring and misleading final results.

2.3 Data integrity

Data integrity means completeness and accuracy of data. For decisions to be made consistently throughout the organisation, it is necessary for the system to contain controls over the input, processing and output of data to maintain its integrity.

While computer systems are made up of physical items, the input of data and the output of information is designed for the benefit of human beings and is subject to their interpretation. Security risks arise where input and output occurs. Risks may arise due to innocent events such as running the wrong program, or inadvertently deleting data that is still of value to the organisation.

More importantly, as more and more systems consist of networks of computers either in the form of Local Area Networks and/or Wide Area Networks, the risks of unauthorised users accessing those systems increase significantly.

This type of activity is referred to as 'hacking' and encompasses anything from the unauthorised accessing of personnel information to the manipulation of important accounting or other financial information.

Many of the security controls described in the previous section will have some effect on data integrity. Data controls should ensure that data is:

- collected in full and with accuracy

- generated at the appropriate times

- kept up-to-date and accurate on file, and

- processed properly and accurately to provide meaningful and useful output.

Information can only be reliable if the underlying data is also reliable. Controls should be exercised to ensure that data could only be derived in the first instance from properly identified and responsible data providers. In order to remain reliable, such data must subsequently be processed and maintained in an adequately controlled environment.

Input data can get lost or contain errors. Human error is usually the biggest security weakness in the system. Controls should be applied to reduce the risk of this occurring.

The extensiveness of the input controls will depend on the method used to process the input data and the cost of making an error.

If the consequences of input errors would be costly, the system should include more extensive controls than it would if the cost of making an error was insignificant.

2.4 Input controls

Input controls

Input controls will be designed with a view to completeness, authorisation, accuracy and compliance with audit needs. The controls will use the following techniques:

Verification

Verification determines whether the data has been properly conveyed to the system from the source (unlike validation which is concerned with whether the data is correct or not).This procedure is normally carried out by a system user to check the completeness and accuracy of data. The main types of error found in data verification are transcription (copying) errors and transposition errors, e.g. where a value of £369,500 might have been entered as £365,900. Similarly, transposition errors in the text might be found where a customer's name might have been entered wrongly (Smtih instead of Smith).Various checks are used including:

- **Type checks** – every entry must comply with the prescribed format, e.g. dates may be defined as consisting of 2 digits, 3 alphabetic characters and 2 further digits such as 04DEC04. Any other form of input will result in an error.

- **Non-existence checks** – data fields requiring entry may have a separate validation table behind them such that the data being input must exist on that table, e.g. a supplier account number must already exist on the system before the system will accept that number when inputting an invoice.

- **Checks for consistency** – where data is initially entered and does not require ongoing maintenance, the fact that it is still consistent with the original data input should be checked within an appropriate timescale, e.g. batch totals should not be altered once input, payee codes for suppliers paid by BACS should be confirmed by print-out against source data on a half-yearly basis.

- **Duplication checks** – the system may check, for example, that the supplier's invoice number currently being input has not previously been entered.

- **Range checks** – a minimum and maximum value could be established against which input can be checked.

- **Input comparison** between document and screen.

- **Checking batch and hash totals**. A batch total is the total of e.g. invoice values, which are to be processed in a batch. The operator manually calculates the total value prior to input and enters that figure onto the batch header document. The total actually processed is then checked against that calculated figure to confirm the accuracy of the input. A hash total is the same as a batch total except it lacks inherent meaning. For example it could be the total of the account numbers. The purpose of these two controls is to enable the operator to e.g. verify that all invoices were processed at the right amount and to the right accounts.

- **One-for-one** checks between data lists.

Validation

Validation is the application, normally by the computer software, of a series of rules or tests designed to check the reasonableness of the data. Computers are unable to check the completeness and accuracy of data, as they are unable to see or read the source data. Instead, they must be programmed with rules and tests to apply to data to check its reasonableness.

Techniques used in validation include:

- **Comparison of totals**, e.g. checking that the total of debits equals the total of credits on a journal voucher.

- **Comparison of data sets**, e.g. a one-for-one check between two computerised files of data to identify and reject any differences.

- **Check digits** – are commonly used in supplier, customer and account numbers. The final digit in the account number will be a check digit, calculated using the previous digits. The computer would perform the calculation on the input account number, and compare the check digit calculated with the check digit input. If the number has been entered incorrectly then the check digit would be different and so the transaction would be rejected by the computer.

- **Sequence numbers** – often documents such as invoices, orders and credit notes have sequential numbers to avoid omission or duplication of a document. The software can be programmed to reject any document that is out of order, or to periodically report any missing documents.

- **Range checks** – the computer might be programmed with an acceptable range for each piece of data, e.g. if products have a sales price between £3.49 and £12.99, the sales system might be told to reject unit prices lower than £3 and higher than £20.

- **Format checks** – the software might be programmed to expect certain data to be alphabetic, numeric or a combination of the two. A numeric field would then reject the letter O being input instead of the number 0, or the letter l (lower case L) instead of the number 1.

- **File controls** – should be applied to make sure that:
  - correct data files are used for processing
  - whole files or data on a file are not lost or corrupted
  - unauthorised access to data on files is prevented
  - if data is lost or corrupted, it can be re-created.

Data communication/transmission controls

If a system operates over a WAN, then the original input at the terminal/PC may become corrupted during transmission, either during on-line processing or where the information is stored in a batch file and transmitted over the WAN later for processing. Similar issues need to be considered for LANs but far fewer problems arise due to the greater level of resilience inherent in LANs.

Controls are necessary where data is transmitted in any form. The less sophisticated the techniques used for transmitting data, the higher the level of separate controls that need to be designed to identify errors and ensure that incorrect data is not processed.

2.5 Processing controls

These should ensure the accuracy and completeness of processing. Data processing errors can arise due to programming error, system design and/or data corruption on the system itself. Because these errors are likely to occur throughout the life of a system, with varying degrees of seriousness, specific measures should be taken to identify when they occur and to ensure that corrections are made to the data, either before or after processing has occurred.

Programs should be subject to development controls and to rigorous testing. Periodic running of test data is also recommended. Other processing controls include the following:

- **standardisation** – structured procedures for processing activities

- **batch control** documents – information about the batch that is entered prior to processing

- **double processing** – repeat of processing with comparison of individual reports.

2.6 Output controls

These are controls to ensure that the produced output is checked against the input controls to ensure completeness and accuracy of processing.

The system output, particularly in hard copy form, must be controlled so that the recipient receives complete and accurate information. There are a number of features that can be built into each report to ensure this:

- Batch control totals – the totals of accepted and rejected data.

- Exception reports – reporting abnormal transactions that may require further investigation (e.g. a report of all employees paid more than £3,000 in a particular payroll run).

- Markers showing the start and end of the report and page numbers – it should be impossible for a user to receive a report with pages missing without realising immediately. This is often used in error reports, where careless staff might 'lose' some pages from a report of the errors they have made.

- Nil return reports – if there is nothing to report, a report should be produced that says so. This is particularly important for error, exception and security control reports. A person committing a fraud might steal the report that showed evidence of their action, then claim there was no report produced because there were no items to report.

- Distribution lists – the header of each report should show the distribution list for the report, the number of copies, the copy number and the planned recipient of the report.

2.7 Application controls

These can be incorporated in the software of the system to ensure that applications preserve the integrity of data. These controls include the following:

- **Passwords** – are a set of characters that may be allocated to a person, a terminal or a room, which have to be keyed into the system before access is permitted. They may be built in to the system to allow individual users access to certain parts of the system but not to others. This will prevent accidental or deliberate changes to data.

- **Authorisation levels** – certain actions may require a user to have authorisation attached to their user-name. This type of control is commonly used for the production of cheques. Authorisation is also often necessary when rolling forward the system defaults at the end of a month or year, due to the complicated nature of correcting any errors relating to the process.

- **Training and supervision** – staff should receive adequate training to prevent them from making common mistakes. They should also be made aware of any tasks that they should not attempt.

- **Audit trails** – software should be written in such a way that a clear logic exists in the sequence of tasks performed, and data at different stages of processing is retained rather than being over-written. In this way the sequence of events can be evidenced by any observer trying to check that the system works correctly.

 Test your understanding 2

Controls are invariably incorporated into the input, processing and output stages of a computer-based system.

(a) State the guidelines which should normally be followed in determining what controls should be built into a system.

(b) Identify and briefly describe one type of control which might be used to detect each of the following input data errors:

    (i) Errors of transcription resulting in an incorrect customer account code.

    (ii) Quantity of raw material normally written in kilograms weight but entered in error as tonnes.

    (iii) Entry on a despatch note for a product to be despatched from a warehouse which does not stock that particular product.

    (iv) A five-digit product code used instead of a six-digit salesman code.

    (v) Invalid expenditure code entered on an invoice.

2.8 Systems integrity

Systems integrity relates to the controlling and monitoring of the system in order to ensure that it does exactly what it was designed to do. Factors include:

- project management
- operations management
- systems design
- personnel
- procedure control
- hardware configuration.

These factors are all relevant to the system operating as intended.

Some of the controls discussed in earlier Chapters are applicable to the integrity of the system.

There is an overlap with control measures that apply to system security and system integrity because the loss of security to a system will obviously also result in the loss of integrity of the system.

(a) Administrative systems

Administrative controls relate to personnel and support functions. For some positions, segregation of duties is a security requirement involving division of responsibility into separate roles. The selection process for personnel (both for new staff and movement of existing staff within an organisation) should reflect the nature of the work. If sensitive information is to be handled, positive vetting might be applied. All staff should all have detailed job descriptions, clearly identifying those responsible for control. Other controls include job rotation, enforced vacations, system logs and supervision.

Administrative procedures should be clearly documented and adhered to. These include health and safety procedures, especially fire drills, the operation of a 'clean desk' policy, logging document movements and the filing or shredding of documents.

The physical security of the site is vital. Visitors need to be authorised and accompanied while on site. Access to more sensitive facilities can be controlled by devices such as electronic key fobs. The location of hardware should ensure that screens and documents are not visible to any passers-by. Access to specific terminals can be restricted by the use of devices such as passwords.

Procedures to be followed in the event of interruptions to processing should be documented and observed. Computer-based information should be backed up frequently, with copies stored in fire-proof safes in separate locations. Recovery plans should identify procedures for all eventualities, from the retrieval of a corrupt file through to complete system failure. These plans should clearly identify the people responsible for carrying out the procedures.

(b) **On-line and real time systems**

In this kind of processing, transactions are input as and when they arise. There is no attempt to accumulate and batch similar transactions. This gives rise to particular control problems. Traditional batch controls are not normally applicable, while the number of people inputting transactions from widely scattered terminals makes security difficult to ensure.

The following controls may be used in on-line and real time systems.

- **Passwords** with a logical access system.

- **Transaction log** – the totals of data on the transaction log (which may be a daily or weekly log) can be matched to movements on master file control accounts.

- **Supervisory controls** i.e. regular physical supervision by management. This is particularly important for situations where there is a lack of segregation of computer operator duties.

- **Physical restriction** of access to terminals – terminals may be located in separate locked buildings or offices. The terminals themselves may require a key to be inserted before the terminal can be used.

- **Documentation of transactions** All transaction or input documents should be recorded and signed by appropriate personnel within the user department. Pre-numbering of documents is also important so that sequence checks can be performed and reports of duplicated or missing data can be produced.

- **Matching transactions** to master file data. An on-line system enables full matching of transaction data to master file data.

(c) Systems integrity in a network environment

The complexity of local and wide area networks (LANs and WANs) allows for many more breaches of security than a single computer and each breach can, of course, involve many computers. The main risks on a networked system are:

- **Hardware/software disruption or malfunction**.

- **Computer viruses** – usually unwittingly distributed by opening an infected e-mail message, but also sourced from infected CDs and USB devices. Once the virus comes into contact with a system it replicates itself onto the system and lies dormant until either the use of the system, some defined event or transaction, or a certain date activates it. The replication of the virus makes it very difficult to find its original source.

- **Unauthorised access** to the system – hacking is usually associated with people who are not employees of the organisation, but who gain access to an organisation's data for mischievous or malicious intent. However, in its widest term – a person who gains access to a computer without permission – it can also be applied to company employees themselves. Hacking has been made possible by organisations using always-on broadband telecommunications networks that are accessible to the hacker via powerful workstations and modems.

- **Electronic eavesdropping** – which has become more of a risk as more organisations implement wireless network configurations. Possible controls include many that we have already discussed and some that are specific for the risks outlined above. They include:

  - **Physical access controls** – the use of strict controls over the locking of the rooms in which the computers are located and the distribution of keys to authorised personnel only. This is vital where the computers are used either to access sensitive data files or to alter or develop programs. Secondly, machine access – the restriction of access to and use of computers by keys, cards and badges.

  - **User identification** – this includes the positive confirmation of the identity of the user and the proof of his/her/their identification (authentication). The former includes the input of the name, employee number and account number. The latter includes the input of something that is known (e.g. passwords, question-and-answer sequences), or something that is possessed (badges, cards), or something personal to the user (e.g. fingerprint, hand or voice features, signature).

- **Data and program access authorisation** – after identification of the user, the type of privileges are checked to ensure that the user has the necessary authority. Privileges cover the type of files and programs that can be accessed, and the activities allowed during access. The user is denied access if he/she/they are not specifically authorised.

- **Program integrity controls** – ensure that unauthorised access and alterations cannot be made to programs.

- **Database integrity controls** – controls and audit techniques that protect database management systems software and data against unauthorised access, modification, disclosure and destruction.

- **Anti-virus software** – (regularly updated with new releases) detects known viruses and destroys them. Each common virus will be known and identifiable by the anti-virus software. However, it must be recognised that such software only protects against known viruses. All emails, removable disks and CDs should be checked before they can be used internally. Most organisations implement stringent internal procedures to make sure that unauthorised disks and CDs are not used within the organisation. Failure to comply with these requirements usually leads to disciplinary action, including dismissal.

- **Surveillance** – the detection of security violations by direct observation, by review of computer logs or by use of the operator's console to display current program and data usage.

- **Communication lines safeguards** – while impossible to fully protect communication lines, controls such as encryption, phone tap and bug checks should go a long way to prevent penetration of the system via the communication lines.

- **Encryption** – is a control to translate a message into coded form using a code key that is only known to the sender and recipient of the message. This is a useful control for preventing eavesdropping, particularly in a wireless network.

- **Firewalls** – are security devices that effectively isolate the sensitive parts of an organisation's system from those areas available to external users.

- **Administrative considerations** – procedures that ensure that controls and safeguards are effective in preventing, deterring and detecting unauthorised or fraudulent systems data and program access and modification.

3 Contingency controls

3.1 Disasters affecting the computer system

In computing terms, a disaster might mean the loss or unavailability of some of the computer systems. In a modern business there are few areas unaffected by computing and consequently few that will not suffer if its performance is impaired. Also, risks are increasing. An organisation now has to cope with the risks of hacking, virus infection and industrial action aimed at the computing staff.

Losses that can be expected due to the non-availability of computer systems increase with time. It is therefore important to make plans to keep downtime to a minimum.

Management commitment is an essential component of any contingency plan because it will almost certainly involve considerable expense. Various stand-by plans must be considered, the choice of which will depend on the amount of time that the installation can reasonably expect to survive without computing.

The key feature of any disaster recovery plan is the regular back-up of data and software. If, at the time of disaster, there are no back-up copies, then no amount of stand-by provision will replace them.

The contingency plan must specify what actions are to be taken during a disaster and also during the time that computer systems are unavailable until full operations are restored. The plan must be as detailed as possible, should state who is responsible at each stage, when it should be invoked, and where copies may be found. The more care that is taken with a contingency plan, the better the organisation will be able to survive a computing disaster. It also concentrates the mind on computer security and the risks faced, with an increased likelihood that counter measures will be installed which will reduce the risks.

3.2 Contingency controls

Contingency controls are those which correct the consequences of a risk occurring, rather than preventing or reducing the risk. Within the computing environment it is the process of planning for the potential breakdown of the computer system. For organisations that rely upon their computer systems to carry on their business, the loss of those systems, even for a short period, can be disastrous, therefore good contingency plans should be put in place.

The plan should include:

- standby procedures – so that essential operations can be performed while normal services are disrupted

- recovery procedures – to return to normal working once the breakdown is fixed

- management policies to ensure that the plan is implemented.

The effectiveness of the contingency plan is dependent on comprehensive back-up procedures for both data and software. The contingency plan must identify initial responses and clearly delineate responsibility at each stage of the exercise, from damage limitation through to full recovery.

3.3 Backing up

Information on your computer is vulnerable: hard disks can fail, computer systems can fail, viruses can wipe a disk, careless operators can delete files, and very careless operators can delete whole areas of hard disks by mistake. Computers can also be damaged or stolen. For these reasons backing up your data is essential. This involves making copies of essential files, together with necessary update transactions and keeping them on another computer, or on some form of storage media so that copies can be recreated. Your organisation will have procedures and you will have been taught how to do this.

To ensure that you can back up easily you will probably have your own 'workspace' – an area of a disk that contains your work. This helps segregate your unique work from files or information that are held by a number of people.

It is important to get into the habit of backing up in different ways for different reasons to increase the reliability of your backed-up data. You should consider backing-up:

- when you have done a large amount of work over a short period – in which case you should back up all the contents of your 'workspace'

- when you have completed a major body of work – you should clean up the directory containing the files (to get rid of files that are not needed) and just back up that directory

- on a regular basis, back up your whole 'workspace' and the essential system files.

Where the data is maintained by batch processing, the Grandfather/ Father/Son method of backing-up will be used. The principle of this method is that at any point in time the last two back-ups made should be available plus all of the batches that have been processed since the older of the back-ups was made. These would be in the form of master and data discs that would be separately labelled and stored. Once the Grandfather disc becomes older than that, it can be re-used as the latest disc for back-up purposes and becomes the Son.

These days, where it is more likely that the data is maintained on-line, data will be backed-up each day, so that if the normal storage medium fails, the information is available for the system to be restored to the last point of data entry prior to the back-up being taken. Copies of all data files should be taken on a frequent and regular basis and kept off-site or in a fireproof safe. The data can then be restored in case of data loss or corruption.

Software backup – copies of system software and applications should also be taken and stored off-site. Thus the computer system can be re-created on new hardware in case the building is damaged or destroyed. Software can also be restored in case it becomes corrupted or accidentally deleted.

Procedures to be followed in the event of interruptions to processing should be documented and observed. Computer-based information should be backed up frequently, with the copies stored in separate locations, in fireproof safes. Recovery plans should identify procedures for all eventualities from the retrieval of a corrupt file through to complete system failure due to, for example, fire. These plans should clearly identify the people responsible to effect the procedures.

 Test your understanding 3

List and give a brief explanation of the control techniques and safeguards to protect a system where multiple users have access to centralised data through terminal devices at remote locations linked to a central computer system via telephone lines or other communication links.

3.4 Advantages and disadvantages of contingency planning

The main argument in favour of contingency planning is that it places the management team in a better position to cope with the change by eliminating or at least reducing the time delay (and hence lost profits) in making a response to an emergency. The emergency may be a lost opportunity or a definite threat. Specific reserve plans help managers to respond more rationally to the event. A crisis can lead to decisions being made within a very short time span and without full information. Early evaluation of the demands of low probability events and the alternative remedies allows more detailed consideration and consequently should reduce the likelihood of panic measures.

Although contingency planning does force managers to consider unlikely events that can result in beneficial spin-offs, it can also result in negative attitudes. Events with low probabilities may be threats and focusing attention on these threats could be demoralising and demotivating.

4 Assessing and managing risk

4.1 Managing risk

In general terms, risk would be taken as meaning anything that could cause the organisation to make a financial loss. The types of risk include disasters outside the control of the organisation, poor trading, mismanagement, errors due to human or machine problems and misappropriation of resources, physical assets or intangible assets.

You must understand the concept of risk and how it may be assessed in the planning of controls within an organisation.

The following step-by-step process is a useful framework for the risk assessment process:

- Identify risks.
- Quantify risks.
- Identify counter measures (some of the possibilities are listed below).
- Cost counter measures.
- Choose which counter measures are required.
- Draw up contingency plans.
- Implement the plan to manage the risk.
- Monitor, review and update the plan.
- Constantly watch for new risks – encourage all staff to report situations where they feel there might be a risk.

Counter measures that an organisation can adopt include the following possibilities:

- Transfer the risks (by means of an insurance policy) – limited liability is another way of transferring risk.
- Decide to live with the risks, if the counter measures cannot be justified.
- Modify a system so as to eliminate the risks.
- Reduce the probability of risk by introducing controls e.g. two signatures on payments.
- Reduce the exposure to risk by removing the organisation from risky situations.
- Adopt measures that reduce the cost associated with a risk (e.g. by ensuring an adequate back-up system).
- Enable recovery by implementing recovery procedures appropriate to the situation e.g. relocation plans and computer disaster recovery plans.

5 Additional 'Test your understanding' questions

Test your understanding 4

1   Why do organisations adopt security measures?

2   Describe the three elements of the information system's security.

3   Outline the terms of the Data Protection Act.

4   What are usage logs?

5   Identify four of the techniques used in data validation.

6   What do you understand by the term 'data integrity'?

7   What sort of documents need sequence controls?

8   To maintain systems integrity, what types of control may be used in on-line and real time systems?

9   What type of control is encryption?

6 Summary

Computer systems require special attention in any organisation for two reasons. Firstly, the fact that the audit trail through a computer system is not visible as in a manual system may lead to problems of control. Secondly, any errors in a computer system of a systematic nature can have a very serious impact on the accuracy of the records, whereas in a manual system the damage is likely to be far more localised to one specific area.

You should therefore ensure that the computer systems of an organisation are very well controlled with tight security over all the key functions.

Test your understanding answers

 Test your understanding 1

BRIEFING REPORT

To: Head of Department

From: Trainee management accountant

Date: 2 November 20X7

Security of an organisation's computer system

The factors, which most affect the security of an organisation's computer system, can be divided into three groups – physical, systems and human.

Physical aspects – these relate to the security risks to which the computer hardware is exposed. These risks mainly come from outside the system and include theft, fire, dust, humidity, flooding and wind and earth movement damage to the building housing the computer.

Systems aspects – these relate to risks, which are inherent in the system itself and include loss of data, loss of software and possibly damage to equipment, all caused by system malfunctioning brought about by either hardware or software failure or errors.

Human aspects – these include risks from inside and outside the organisation and risks arising from both intentional and unintentional actions. For example a large multi-user networked computer system is at risk from outside 'hacking' as well as from employees within the organisation. Unintentional damage to equipment, data and software etc may be caused by accidents e.g. spilling drinks into equipment, accidental changes to data e.g. correcting the wrong file or deleting a file, running the wrong software, forgetting to run a particular process etc. Intentional aspects include setting up fake accounts, causing unauthorised payments either as credit or cheques to be made, allowing favourable discount terms to particular clients and damage such as the deletion or corruption of data files and software.

Managing the risks associated with computer security

Managing the risks associated with computer security involves reducing the risks and the effects to the lowest possible levels. Three stages are necessary.

Risk assessment – a full examination of all the risks in the three groups above is made. Particular types of computer systems and particular locations and environments each have their own problems. The risks are, of course, different for a centralised system as against a distributed computing system.

Another factor is the importance of the work being done on the computer. For example if a personnel department computer went down, it would not be as serious as if the computer monitoring a production line failed and there would not be such a need to get the personnel computer up and running again quickly.

Risk minimisation – this comprises the actions, which may be taken when the risks to a computer system have been assessed. These actions include both taking physical and system precautions and providing fall-back and remedial measures. The list of actions includes:

- securing the building(s) housing equipment with bars, strong doors, locks, monitoring systems, access control, etc.

- provision of an environment suitable for reliable computer operation, having clean air at the correct temperature and humidity and an electrical power supply that is both continuous and smooth

- strict control of the quality of new software and on any modifications required to existing software

- vetting of all computer staff appointments and the taking out of 'fidelity guarantees' with suitable insurance companies

- access control for the system from terminals, etc. This will normally involve a system of passwords changed on a regular basis

- a high level of training and education of computer staff

- automated operating procedures with built in checks (probably utilising job control language 'programs') so that operators do not have to trust to memory and are given minimum scope for error

- fully documented systems and procedure manuals including precise statements of actions to be taken for system recovery after breakdowns

- provision of standby facilities and a reciprocal processing agreement with another organisation.

(If the computer failed and it was expected that it would not be repairable for quite some time, then back-up disks would be transferred and processing carried out on the other organisation's computer, overnight or at the weekend – and vice versa.)

Risk transference – it is impossible to eliminate all risks, but it is possible to transfer the element of uncovered risk to another party through the medium of insurance i.e. in the event of a computer catastrophe, the losses caused would be covered by insurance.

 Test your understanding 2

(a) **Systems controls should be designed according to the following guidelines:**

- All transactions should be processed.

- All errors in transactions should be reported. Errors should be corrected and re-input. Fraud should be prevented.

- The likelihood of error should be estimated. This will depend partly on the location in which the source document is prepared and the type of person originating it.

- The importance of errors should be assessed. In accounting systems, 100% accuracy may be required. In other systems (e.g. market surveys), a degree of error may be acceptable.

- The cost of control should be considered in relation to the cost of an error. The cost of 100% accuracy is, in practice, usually too high. The controls should not interfere unduly with the progress of work. The controls should be as simple as possible, and acceptable to users. Auditors should be consulted and the system designed to meet their requirements.

(b) **Incorrect customer account code**

This should be detected by a check digit. The account code would include an extra digit derived by calculation from other digits. On input to the computer, the program would perform the calculations and, if the digit derived was not the check digit, an error would be reported. The system selected should minimise the possibility of undetected error.

Raw material quantity

This should be detected by a reasonableness check. Upper and lower limits would be set, outside which a quantity should not lie. Since the entry of kilograms instead of tonnes would result in a value 1000 times as big as the correct one, it would be detected.

Product not stocked

This would be detected by an on-file check. On input, the despatch note details would be referred to the stock/inventory master files, which would indicate that the product was not held in the warehouse shown.

Five-digit product code

This would be detected by a format check. The validation program would have parameters for the size of fields, and would report the product code as being a digit short.

Invalid expenditure code

This would be detected by a range check. The validation program would have parameters showing the upper and lower values of expenditure codes. Comparison of the code with the parameters would reveal that it was not in the permissible range.

Test your understanding 3

The control techniques and safeguards used to protect a system where multiple users have access to centralised data through terminal devices at remote locations linked to a central computer system via telephone lines or other communication links are as follows.

- **Terminal physical security** – this covers two aspects. Firstly, terminal room access – the use of strict controls over the locking of the rooms in which the terminals are located and the distribution of keys to authorised personnel only. This is vital where the terminals are used either to access sensitive data files or to alter or develop programs. Secondly, terminal machine access – the restriction of access to and use of terminals by keys, cards and badges.

- **User identification** – this includes the positive confirmation of the identity of the user and the proof of his/her/their identification (authentication). The former includes the input of his/her/their name, employee number and account number. The latter includes the input of something that is known (e.g. passwords, question-and-answer sequences), or something that is possessed (badges, cards), or something personal to the user (e.g. fingerprint, hand or voice features, signature).

- **Data and program access authorisation** – after identification of the user (above), the privileges the user has as to what can be accessed (files and programs) and what can be done during access have to be checked to ensure that the necessary authority is in place. The user must be denied access if not specifically authorised.

- **Surveillance** – the detection of security violations by direct observation, by review of computer logs or by use of the operator's console to display current program and data usage.

- **Communication lines safeguards** – while impossible to fully protect communication lines controls such as encryption, phone tap and bug checks should go a long way to prevent penetration of the system via the communication lines.

- **Encryption** – the transformation of a message or of data for the purpose of rendering it unintelligible to everyone but the correct users who are able to translate the message back to its original form. Program integrity controls – controls, which ensure that unauthorised access and alterations cannot be made to programs.

- **Database integrity controls** – controls and audit techniques, which protect database management systems software and data against unauthorised access, modification, disclosure and destruction.

- **Administrative considerations** – procedures, which ensure that controls and safeguards are effective in preventing, deterring and detecting unauthorised or fraudulent systems data and program access and modification.

Test your understanding 4

1 They adopt security measures:

    i.   to avoid or prevent loss

    ii.   to deter as many threats as possible

    iii. for easy recovery after any loss

    iv.   to identify the cause of any loss after the event

    v.   to correct vulnerable areas to reduce the risk of repeated loss.

2 The information systems security is based on three elements. The people, the data/information elements and the physical elements, which acknowledge that the operation of computer equipment can be severely impaired where it is subject to events such as fire, flooding and improper environmental conditions, e.g. heat.

3 Under the terms of the Data Protection Act 2018, the need for privacy is recognised by the requirements that all personal data on individuals should be held only for clearly designated purposes. Accuracy and integrity must be maintained and the data must be open to inspection. Only legitimate parties can access data and information must be secured against alteration, accidental loss or deliberate damage. Furthermore, the Act states that data must be obtained fairly, to precise specifications and must not be kept for longer than required.

4 Usage logs are part of the system, which is designed to automatically record the log-in and log-off times of each user, the applications accessed and any applications or files where access has been denied. Periodic checks are made for unusual patterns, such as a day-shift worker accessing the system at night.

5   The techniques used in data validation include comparison of totals, comparison of data sets, check digits, sequence, range checks and format checks.

6   Data integrity means completeness and accuracy of data. For decisions to be made consistently throughout the organisation, it is necessary for the system to contain controls over the input, processing and output of data to maintain its integrity.

7   Documents such as invoices, orders, petty cash vouchers and credit notes need sequential numbers to avoid omission of a document.

8   The following controls may be used in on-line and real time systems.

   • Using passwords with a logical access system.

   • Transaction log – the totals of data on the transaction log (which may be a daily or weekly log) can be matched to movements on master file control accounts.

   • Supervisory controls, i.e. regular physical supervision by management. This is particularly important for situations where there is a lack of segregation of computer operator duties.

   • Physical restriction of access to terminals – terminals may be kept in separate locked buildings or offices. The terminals themselves may require a key to be inserted before the terminal can be used.

   • Documentation of transactions. All transaction or input documents should be recorded and signed or initialled by appropriate personnel within the user department. Pre-numbering of documents is also important so that sequence checks can be performed, and reports of duplicated or missing data can be produced.

9   Encryption is a control to translate a message into coded form using a code key that is only known to the sender and recipient of the message. This is a useful control for preventing eavesdropping, particularly in a wireless network.

Information and technology

5

Introduction

Technology is changing the way that accountancy information is processed, and this unit requires knowledge of the fundamental principles of data analytics and artificial intelligence (AI), which may be used as an alternative way to gather and analyse information. Cloud accounting is changing the way accountants work and visualisation, including dashboards, is increasingly used to present information in a way that is easier for stakeholders to understand. Data security and breaches are regularly reported in the press, and therefore it is imperative that learners are aware of the importance of keeping all data secure and consider the confidential nature of the data that they will be processing as part of their everyday role.

PERFORMANCE CRITERIA	CONTENTS
4.1 Reporting information using technology	1 Introduction
4.2 Using technology within the accounting system	2 Information technology and information systems
	3 Cloud computing
	4 Artificial Intelligence (AI)
	5 Big Data and data analytics
	6 Cyber security

1 Introduction

1.1 Data and information

 Definitions

Data consists of numbers, letters, symbols, raw facts, events and transactions, which have been recorded but not yet processed into a form that is suitable for making decisions.

Information is data that has been processed in such a way that it has meaning to the person that receives it, who may then use it to improve the quality of their decision-making.

Information is vital to an organisation and is required both internally and externally. Management requires information:

- to provide records, both current and historical

- to analyse what is happening in the business

- to provide the basis for decision-making in the short and long-term

- to monitor the performance of the business by comparing actual results with plans and forecasts.

This information will also be used by various external stakeholders, as covered in Chapter 2.

 Example – Turning data into information

Twenty five employees from the finance department of a large organisation took an introductory course in Computing. The test at the end of the course resulted in the marks shown below. The marks were out of 50 and the pass mark was 20 out of 50.

12	19	8	21	32
25	34	22	30	20
43	21	16	45	32
27	38	39	21	18
33	11	28	26	27

At the moment, this data is simply not useful. To give it meaning, we need to process it and turn it into information. There are actually many ways that this data can be turned into information. For example, we could simply calculate the percentage of students who passed the assessment. In this case, 19 employees out of 25 passed – or 76%.

Alternatively, for more detail we could create a frequency distribution.

Marks obtained	Frequency
0–9	1
10–19	5
20–29	10
30–39	7
40+	2

This shows that the 19 employees that pass the test (achieve 20+) are in the top 3 class intervals and those that fail – 6 employees – are in the bottom two intervals.

However the data is processed, we can use it to make key decisions. For instance, we could compare these results to those of other classes and identify whether there were any problems with it.

2 Information technology and information systems

2.1 Introduction

In the modern business world, many organisations hold and process vast amounts of data and information. This would not be practical to do manually, so they rely on automated systems to perform the handling and storage required.

Information systems (IS) refer to the management and provision of information to support the running of the organisation.

Information technology (IT) describes any equipment concerned with the capture, storage, transmission or presentation of data.

Put simply, IT is the hardware infrastructure that runs the information systems. This will include desktop computers, laptops, servers, printers and hard drives used by the organisation.

2.2 Types of information system

There are three levels of management – strategic, tactical and operational.

Each level needs different types of information:

- The **strategic level** of management requires information from internal and external sources in order to plan the long-term strategies of the organisation. Internal information – both quantitative and qualitative – is usually supplied in a summarised form, often on an ad-hoc basis.

- The **tactical level** of management requires information and instructions from the strategic level of management, together with routine and regular quantitative information from the operational level of management. The information would be in a summarised form, but detailed enough to allow tactical planning of resources and staffing.

- The **operational level** of management requires information and instructions from the tactical level of management. The operational level is primarily concerned with the day-to-day performance of tasks and most of the information is obtained from internal sources. The information must be detailed and precise.

Example – Management structure and information

This example refers to plant and machinery used in an organisation:

Operational information would include a current week's report for a cost centre on the percentage capacity of the plant and machinery used in the period.

Tactical information could include the short-term budget for 12 months and would show the budgeted machine use in terms of machine hours for each item of plant. The total machine hours being predetermined from the production budget for the period.

Strategic information would relate to the longer-term strategy on the company's market share, which in turn informs the production plan. This plan would be used to predetermine the level of investment required in plant and machinery in the longer term. This process would also lead to investigating new methods and technology.

Test your understanding 1

Operational level managers need information that is _____ term and comes mainly from _____ sources.

Which words correctly complete the sentence above?

(1) Long

(2) Short

(3) Internal

(4) External

A   (1) and (4)

B   (2) and (3)

C   (1) and (3)

D   (2) and (4)

As each level of manager needs different types of information, they will need different information systems to provide them with this.

Transaction processing system (TPS)

A TPS records all the daily transactions of the organisation and summarises them so they can be reported on a routine basis.

Transaction processing systems are used mainly by operational managers to make basic decisions, and would include:

Sales/marketing systems – recording sales transactions and providing details on marketing and promotional activities

Manufacturing production systems – recording details of purchases, production and shipping of goods

Finance and accounting systems – maintenance of financial data in an organisation.

 Example – Transaction Processing System

A TPS could be used to record the sales for a bookstore. At the end of each day, it will produce a summary of how many of each type of book has been sold.

This will allow the operational managers to decide which books they need to order from their suppliers and how many books they need to buy in order to replenish their stocks/inventory.

Management information system (MIS)

Management information systems convert data from the TPS into information for tactical managers. This information will be designed to help them monitor performance, maintain co-ordination and provide background information about the organisation's operations.

The MIS will be used for both historic and current analysis of business performance, as well as to make predictions about future operations.

 Example – Management Information System

A company that operates a national chain of car showrooms could use a MIS for performance measurement.

The MIS could use the information from the sales TPS to generate reports such as:

- total sales for each type of car

- total sales made by each salesperson

- total sales by showroom or by geographic area.

This information could be extremely useful for control and performance appraisal purposes.

Executive information system (EIS)

These systems provide strategic managers with flexible access to information from the entire business, as well as relevant information from the external environment.

The EIS enables senior management to easily model the entire business by turning its data into useful, summarised reports. These reports are often presented as '**dashboards**', combining multiple pieces of useful information onto a single screen or page, in the same way that the dashboard on a car presents the driver with all the information necessary (speed, fuel, time, temperature etc.) to drive the car.

This information can then easily be distributed to key staff members.

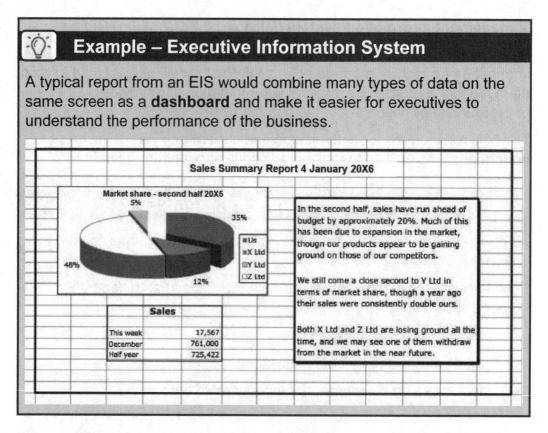

Example – Executive Information System

A typical report from an EIS would combine many types of data on the same screen as a **dashboard** and make it easier for executives to understand the performance of the business.

2.3 Advantages of computerisation

Most aspects of the economy, from the music industry to manufacturing, banking, retailing and defence, are now totally dependent on modern information processing systems. Developments in information technology provide companies with new opportunities. For example:

- internet
- access to corporate databases
- mobile computing
- improved telecommunication structure.

The value of computer systems in handling and processing business data cannot be underestimated.

The advantages of computerisation include the following:

Speed Computers are ideal for dealing with repetitive processes. The limiting factors, for example, in processing a payroll by computer are not the speed of calculation by the computer, but the speed with which data can be input and the speed of the printer at the output.

Accuracy In general, computers do not suffer from errors, or lapses of concentration but process data perfectly. Any mistakes within computer systems nowadays are not caused by electronic error, but by human error, for example at the input stage, or in designing and programming software.

Volume Not only do computers work quickly, but they do not need to take breaks. They can work twenty-four hours a day when required. They are therefore able to handle vast volumes of data.

Complexity Once subsystems are computerised they can generally function more reliably than human beings. This makes it easier to integrate various subsystems. Computers are therefore able to handle complex information systems efficiently. However, one of the problems with this is that when the computer does fail, there is often a major breakdown in the system, with many personnel unable to perform their work functions.

Cost All the above advantages mean that computers have become highly cost-effective providers of information. The process of substituting computers for human beings has revolutionised information-oriented industries such as accountancy, banking and insurance, and this process is continuing.

Presentation More recently, emphasis has been placed on displaying information in as 'user-friendly' a way as possible. Modern packages containing sophisticated word processors, spreadsheets and graphics combined with the development of colour printers now enable potentially boring reports to be attractively presented. This is particularly helpful when presenting complex financial information to non-financial managers.

It should however be borne in mind that people have advantages as providers of information. Chief amongst these is interpretation and judgement of reasonableness. People can usually see when an item of information looks unreasonable. Although it is possible to program limited reasonableness tests into computer systems, it is still very difficult to program judgement. The computer's 'judgement' will be based on however it has been programmed, which is particularly apparent when a programming error is made or it is subject to a computer virus.

3 Cloud computing

3.1 Introduction

Cloud computing is computing based on the internet. It avoids the need for software, applications, servers and services stored on physical computers. Instead, it stores these with cloud service providers who store these things on the internet and grant access to authorised users.

3.2 Cloud computing accounting software

Cloud computing accounting software is accounting software that is hosted on remote servers. Cloud based accounting software works in essentially the same way as all other cloud-based software. Due to the information being stored in such a way that it is always accessible, users can log in and perform accounting processes on any computer on the planet with an Internet connection.

Using cloud computing accounting software means that the business does not have to pay for, install, manage or protect software on individual machines.

3.3 Benefits of cloud computing to the organisation

- **Store and share data** Cloud services can often store more data than traditional, local physical drives, and the data can be shared more easily (regardless of physical location).

- **On-demand self-service** Users can gain access to technology on demand. For example, every time you download an app from iTunes or the Play store you are downloading it from a cloud service where it is stored.

- **Flexibility** Work can be performed more flexibly as employees no longer need to be 'plugged into' work networks or facilities to access the data they need.

- **Collaboration** The cloud facilitates better workforce collaboration – documents, plans etc. can be worked on by many different users simultaneously.

- **More competitive** Without the need for significant financial investment, smaller firms can gain access to technology and services that may otherwise only be available to the largest organisations. This can allow small organisations to compete better with larger rivals.

- **Easier scaling** Cloud services provide high levels of flexibility in terms of size, number of authorised users etc. This means that the service can grow as the business grows, and allows businesses to scale up much more easily.

- **Reduced maintenance** There is no longer a need on the part of the organisation for regular maintenance and updates of IT security or software services. The cloud provider will take care of this.

- **Back-ups** The cloud can be used to back up data. This adds an extra layer of security and removes the need for physical devices to store backed-up data.

- **Disaster recovery** The lack of need for physical devices to store backed-up data can also aid disaster recovery. Using cloud technology makes this faster and cheaper.

- **Better security** The cloud can increase security of data. For example, if in the past an employee were to lose a laptop containing sensitive data, this would be a high-risk security event for the organisation. Cloud storage should reduce such hardware-associated risks.

- **Improved sustainability** Cloud computing reduces the use of paper within an office environment. Invoices, statements and accounting documents can be sent electronically. You will cover this further in Chapter 9.

 Test your understanding 2

Which of the following scenarios are best suited to maximise the benefits of using cloud technology?

A   An organisation that does not want to sacrifice security or make changes to their management practices but needs additional resources for test and development of new solutions.

B   An organisation that requires minimal security over their data and has a large existing infrastructure that is capable of handling future needs.

C   A small start-up business focused primarily on short-term projects and has minimal security policies.

D   An organisation whose IT infrastructure is under-utilised on average and the system load is fairly consistent.

3.4   Disadvantages of cloud computing

Reliance on the cloud service provider

If the service provider suffers a cyber-attack or its servers go down for any reason then it can put a halt to a company's business until service is resumed. This can lead to significant disruption and costs. A good internet connection is also essential to avoid disruption to day-to day business activities.

Regulatory risks

A company needs to ensure that the service provider is acting responsibly and following regulations over data protection and cyber security.

Unauthorised access to data

There is the risk that service provider staff could access a company's customer and business data without authorisation, or that anyone could log in to the data if they managed to steal passwords.

4   Artificial intelligence (AI)

4.1   What is artificial intelligence (AI)?

Artificial Intelligence is an area of computer science that emphasises the creation of intelligent machines that work and react like human beings.

Some of the activities that computers with artificial intelligence are designed for include:

- Voice recognition
- Planning
- Learning
- Problem solving

Example – Artificial Intelligence

Companies such as Apple and Amazon have developed and marketed voice recognition systems, either to be built into an existing product (such as Apple with its Siri system) or developed into new products whose main function is voice recognition (such as Amazon and Alexa).

A further simple example is that of Facebook, and its process of recommending new friends for users to connect with.

There are many, more complex examples of Artificial Intelligence, but a common factor to both the simple and the more involved is machine learning.

Machine learning

Most recent advances in AI have been achieved by applying machine learning to very large data sets. Machine learning algorithms detect patterns and learn how to make predictions and recommendations by processing data and experiences, rather than by explicit programming instruction. The algorithms themselves then adapt to new data and experiences to improve their function over time.

4.2   Artificial intelligence and accountancy

Despite the dramatic recent evolution in artificial intelligence techniques such as machine learning, and the fast pace of its development, widespread adoption of the concept in the financial world is still in its relatively early stages.

It is evident that, in many cases, systems can carry out tasks that result in far more accurate and consistent outputs than could be achieved by humans.

AI brings many opportunities for accountants to improve their efficiency and deliver more value to businesses. In the longer term, AI brings opportunities for more extensive developments, as systems increasingly carry out decision-making tasks that would otherwise be carried out by humans, potentially reducing staffing levels.

There is no doubt that AI will contribute to significant beneficial changes across all areas of accounting. It will equip accountants with powerful new capabilities, as well as enabling machines to deal with an increasing amount of tasks and judgements.

Examples include using machine learning to:

- code accounting entries

- recognise what constitutes 'normal' activities in order to improve fraud detection

- forecast revenues with the use of predictive models

- improving access to, and analysis of, unstructured data, such as contracts, emails and multimedia content.

Having identified many of the opportunities that AI can bring to the accountancy profession, we must appreciate that machines will never act as a direct replacement for human intelligence. The ways in which humans and computers can work together in the most efficient way is therefore a key consideration.

 Test your understanding 3

What is artificial intelligence?

A   Programming with your own intelligence

B   Making a machine intelligent

C   Putting more memory into a computer

D   Backing up data, enabling more efficient data recovery

KAPLAN PUBLISHING

5 Big Data and data analytics

5.1 What is Big Data?

Big Data is a term for a collection of data which is so large that it becomes difficult to store and process using traditional databases and data-processing applications.

Big Data often also includes more than simply financial information and can involve other organisational data (both internal and external) which is often unstructured.

Examples of data that inputs into Big Data systems can include:

- social network traffic
- web server logs
- streamed audio content
- banking transactions
- web page histories and content
- government documentation
- financial market data.

5.2 Data stored electronically

Traditionally, businesses gathered structured information on relevant issues from a variety of sources and placed them into a database, or data warehouse.

As the world has increasingly moved towards digitisation (and especially through the growth of the internet), almost all information relating to the organisation and its environment can be stored electronically. The amount of unstructured data generated by electronic interactions has increased significantly – through emails, online shopping, text messages, social media sites as well as various electronic devices (such as smartphones) which gather and transmit data. In fact, it is estimated that around 90% of the information in the world today has been created in the last few years.

The amount of data which businesses have to store and interrogate has therefore increased at an exponential rate, requiring new tools and techniques to make the most of them.

 Example – Big Data

Ford's modern hybrid Fusion model (which has a hybrid petrol/electric engine) generates up to 25 GB of data per hour and the company is experimenting with vehicles that produce ten times that amount. This data can be used for many purposes, including:

- A computer model has been developed that projects CO2 emissions generated by the fleet of vehicles on roads worldwide for the next 50 years. This helps Ford to balance fuel economy requirements and environmental considerations.

- Mathematical models have analysed millions of possible vehicle combinations to assist in the construction of a technology roadmap which has resulted in the development of new features such as Ford Auto Start-Stop.

- Ford researchers have developed specific tools such as the Ford Fleet Purchase Planner, which analyses fleet customers' needs and identifies their optimal vehicle choice.

5.3   The features of Big Data

According to Gartner, Big Data has features that can be described using the '3Vs':

- **Volume** This refers to the significant amount of data that the organisation needs to store and process. Match.com (an online dating company) estimates that it has 70 terabytes of data about its customers and this may continue to grow.

- **Variety** Big Data can come from numerous sources. For example, Match.com (with user permission) also gathers data on users' browser and search histories, viewing habits and purchase histories to build an accurate view of the sort of person the customer might like to date.

- **Velocity** Data is likely to change on a regular basis and needs to be continually updated. For Match.com, new customers will join the service, or existing customers will change the type of partner that they are seeking. Match.com needs to continually gather data to ensure that they are able to deal with this.

Another V which is sometimes added by organisations to the above list is:

- **Veracity** (truthfulness) It is vital that the organisation gathers data that is accurate. Failure to do so will make analysis meaningless. Match.com has found that when gathering customer data, customers may lie to present themselves in the most positive light possible to prospective partners. This will lead to inaccurate matches. Using non-biased sources of information (such as purchasing or web browser histories) rather than relying on customer feedback is therefore important.

 Test your understanding 4

The Managing Director of Ajda Co has recently started looking at ways of gathering Big Data for their business. They are concerned that some of the sources of data they have chosen are unreliable, and may therefore lead them to inaccurate conclusions.

Which features may be missing for Ajda's Big Data?

A   Variety

B   Velocity

C   Veracity

D   Volume

Example – Big Data

Netflix has over 120 million users worldwide who watch billions of hours of programmes a month. The company uses information gathered from the analysis of viewing habits to inform decisions on which shows to invest in. Analysing past viewing figures and understanding viewer populations and the shows they are likely to watch allows the analysts to predict likely viewing figures before a show has even aired. This can help determine if the show is viable.

5.4 Benefits of Big Data

Big Data has several stated benefits to the organisation, including:

- **Driving innovation** by reducing the time taken to answer key business questions and therefore make decisions.

- **Gaining competitive advantage** by identifying trends or information that has not been identified by rivals.

- **Improving productivity** by identifying waste and inefficiency, or identifying improvements to working procedures.

 Example – Big Data

Delivery company UPS equips its delivery vehicles with sensors which monitor data on speed, direction, braking performance and other mechanical aspects of the vehicle.

Using this data to optimise performance and routes has led to significant improvements, including:

- Over 15 million minutes of idling time were eliminated in one year, saving 103,000 gallons of fuel.

- 1.7 million miles of driving were also eliminated in the same year, saving a further 183,000 gallons of fuel.

5.5   Data analytics

We've seen that many organisations analyse data to help them make business decisions, converting the data into information that they can use. Data analytics provides a way of converting that data into usable information. There are different types of analytics, including descriptive, diagnostic, predictive, and prescriptive analytics. They are all forms of data analytics, but each use the data to provide different information.

- **Descriptive Analytics** tells us what happened in the past.

- **Diagnostic Analytics** helps us to understand why something happened in the past.

- **Predictive Analytics** predicts what is most likely to happen in the future, based on the current data.

- **Prescriptive Analytics** recommends actions we can take to affect those outcomes.

Let's consider each in more detail.

Descriptive analytics looks at data statistically to tell us what happened in the past. Descriptive analytics helps a business understand how it is performing by providing context to help stakeholders interpret information, perhaps in the form of data visualisations (see below) like graphs, charts, reports, and dashboards. This form of presentation can enable non-financial managers to interpret information more easily, and can often highlight areas of anomaly, possibly indicating fraud or error.

In a sales environment, for example, say that an unusually high number of sales occurred in the final quarter. Descriptive analytics tells us that this is happening and provides real-time data with all the corresponding statistics (dates, units sold, customer details, etc.).

Diagnostic analytics takes descriptive data and provides deeper analysis to help understand why things happened. Diagnostic analysis is sometimes referred to as root cause analysis. This includes using processes such as data mining and drill down.

In the sales example, diagnostic analytics would explore the data and make correlations. For instance, it may help us determine that a large proportion of the sales were made on certain days of the week, corresponding to particular advertising activity. We now have an explanation for the increase in sales.

Predictive analytics takes historical data and feeds it into a machine learning model that considers key trends and patterns. The model is then applied to current data to predict what will happen next.

In our sales example, predictive analytics may forecast a continuing high level of sales due to ongoing advertising activity.

Prescriptive analytics takes predictive data to the next level. Now that we have an idea of what is likely to happen in the future, it suggests various courses of action and outlines what the potential implications would be for each.

With our sales example the prescriptive analytics tool may suggest increased advertising spends with related increases in production to cope with the anticipated demand.

In summary then, both descriptive and diagnostic analytics look at past data to explain what happened and why it happened. Predictive and prescriptive analytics use this past data to forecast what will happen in the future and what actions we could take to affect those outcomes. Many organisations use a variety of analytics together to help them identify business opportunities to work smarter, focus and prioritise their resources.

5.6 Data visualisation

This area of technology is of particular significance to the finance function of an organisation. The provision of information to help support the efficient and effective running of all functions within a business and the business overall is the fundamental purpose of the finance function.

Big Data and data analytics are now mainstream in business. This growth in data and the need to communicate the information and insights to be found within the data makes data visualisation critically important to the finance function. The ability to make data relevant, accessible and easy for all end-users is vital.

Key benefits of data visualisation include:

Accessibility – traditional spreadsheets and financial reports can be both difficult to understand and unappealing to look at. Modern data visualisation graphics and dashboards are designed to be user friendly and intuitive.

Real-time synchronising – real time data with data visualisation tools gives live up-to-date numbers in a clear, informative style. This allows a quicker response to business changes rather than waiting for weekly or monthly reports.

Performance optimisation – the immediacy and clarity of the information being displayed supports better decision-making and proactive, efficient utilisation of resources as problems are identified promptly.

Insight and understanding – combining data and visualising it in a new way can lead to improved understanding and fresh insights about the cause and effect relationships that underpin performance.

 KAPLAN PUBLISHING

Example – Visualisation

Key performance indicators (KPIs) are a set of metrics used by a business to monitor performance in areas where things must go according to plan for the business to be successful. These critical areas must first be identified, and then suitable metrics established to monitor performance, before finally setting targets for the desired performance.

Companies are increasingly using dashboards (a collection of key infographics displayed together) to display KPIs to staff in real time and to flag areas requiring improvement in order to hit the pre-determined targets and drive success. This instant feedback allows for action to be taken quickly to highlight and fix potential problems.

For instance, an IT service desk within a business will use KPI dashboards to monitor and display performance for all staff and the department as a whole.

Metrics such as the number of support tickets logged, time taken to open support tickets, time taken to resolve support tickets and customer satisfaction would all be displayed clearly using graphics.

If performance in any of the areas is falling below target levels the graphics will clearly display this, prompting action to resolve the poor performance.

6 Cyber security

6.1 What is cyber security?

Cyber security is the protection of internet-connected systems, including hardware, software and data, from cyber attacks.

A cyber attack is a malicious and deliberate attempt by an individual or organisation to breach the information system of another individual or organisation. Usually, the attacker seeks some type of benefit from disrupting the victim's network.

In a computing context, security comprises cyber security and physical security – both are used by organisations to protect against unauthorised access to data and systems.

6.2   Key risks to data of cyber attacks

If the data on an organisation's computer system is accessed without authorisation or damaged, lost or stolen, it can lead to disaster.

A number of different technical methods are deployed by cybercriminals. There are always new methods proliferating, and some of these categories overlap, but these are the terms that you are most likely to hear discussed.

- **Malware** – short for malicious software. It is software designed to cause damage to a single computer, server or computer network. Worms, viruses and trojans are all varieties of malware, distinguished from one another by the means by which they reproduce and spread. These attacks may render a computer or network inoperable, or grant the attacker access so that they can control the system remotely.

- **Phishing** – a technique by which cybercriminals craft emails to fool a target into taking some harmful action. The recipient might be tricked into downloading malware that is disguised as an important document, for example, or urged to click on a link that takes them to a fake website where they will be asked for sensitive information like usernames and passwords.

- **Denial of service attacks** – a brute force method to try stop an online service from working properly. For example, attackers might send so much traffic to a website or so many requests to a database that it overwhelms the system's ability to function, making it unavailable to anybody.

- **Man in the middle attacks** – a method by which attackers manage to interpose themselves secretly between the user and a web service that they are trying to access. For example, an attacker might set up a Wi-Fi network with a login screen designed to mimic a hotel network. Once a user logs in, the attacker can harvest any information that user sends, including passwords.

Example – Marriott International cyber attack

What happened?

On 30 November 2018, Marriott International announced that the records of up to 500 million customers had been compromised in what may be one of the largest data breaches in history.

The global chain revealed that hackers accessed the guest reservation database at Marriott-owned Starwood hotels as early as 2014.

The company said it received an alert on 8 September that warned of an attempt by an 'unauthorised party' to access the Starwood guest reservation database in the US. That discovery prompted further investigation, which uncovered the long-term unauthorised access across the Starwood network.

The hacker copied and secured the data with encryption, making it more difficult for authorities to determine the contents. The categories of data exposed included:

Name

Mailing address

Phone number

Email address

Passport number

Date of birth

Gender

Test your understanding 5

Which of the following is a common example of a 'phishing' attack?

A   You receive an email from an acquaintance with whom you are rarely in contact that contains only a web link.

B   You receive an email that appears to be from your bank asking you to enter your account number and password, but the web address looks unfamiliar.

C   You receive a text message claiming that you won a contest and asking you to click on a link.

D   All of the above.

6.3 Protection of IT systems and software within business

There are various methods that can be used to keep data secure.

Potential threat	Solution
Natural disasters – e.g. fire, flood.	Fire procedures – fire alarms, extinguishers, fire doors, staff training and insurance cover.
	Location e.g. not in a basement area prone to flooding.
	Physical environment e.g. air conditioning, dust controls.
	Back-up procedures – data should be backed up on a regular basis to allow recovery.
Malfunction – of computer hardware or software.	Network design – to cope with periods of high volumes.
	Back-up procedures (as above).
Viruses – a small program that once introduced into the system spreads extensively. Can affect the whole computer system.	Virus software should be run and updated regularly to prevent corruption of the system by viruses.
	Formal security policy and procedures.
	Regular audits to check for unauthorised software.

KAPLAN PUBLISHING

Hackers – deliberate access to systems by unauthorised persons.	Firewall software – should provide protection from unauthorised access to the system from the Internet. Passwords and usernames – limit unauthorised access to the system.
Electronic eavesdropping, e.g. users accessing private information not intended for them.	Data encryption – data is scrambled prior to transmission and is recovered in a readable format once transmission is complete. Passwords and usernames (as above).
Human errors – unintentional errors from using computers and networks, e.g. data issued in error.	Training – adequate staff training and operating procedures.

7 Summary

In this chapter we have seen the significance of technology in processing and reporting information within the accounting system, and how advances in technology can affect, and hopefully enhance, the accounting system. We looked at the impact of cloud accounting, artificial intelligence and data analytics.

It is important to note that technology represents a useful tool for the presentation of data in a way that is more easily understandable to users, especially non-financial users, enhancing their financial understanding through visualisation.

Test your understanding answers

 ## Test your understanding 1

The correct answer is **B** – they need short-term information from internal sources.

 ## Test your understanding 2

The correct answer is **A** – the question asks you to select the 'best suited option. Therefore you need to pick the option which has a core focus on the importance of security, requires extra resource and is looking to further develop new solutions.

 ## Test your understanding 3

The correct answer is **B** – Artificial intelligence is the development of computer systems able to perform tasks normally requiring human intelligence.

 ## Test your understanding 4

The correct answer is **C**. Veracity refers to the accuracy and truthfulness of the data. If this is missing, it can lead to inaccurate conclusions being drawn.

 ## Test your understanding 5

The correct answer is **D** – all options given are common examples of phishing attacks/attempts.

KAPLAN PUBLISHING

Preventing and detecting fraud

Introduction

Fraud can take many forms. It is management's responsibility to prevent fraud, and if it does happen to detect it quickly in order to mitigate the situation.

The risk of fraud needs to be assessed and then appropriate steps taken.

PERFORMANCE CRITERIA
2.2 Prevent and detect fraud and systemic weaknesses
3.2 Risk of fraud

CONTENTS	
1	Introduction
2	Types of fraud
3	Implications of fraud
4	Detecting fraud
5	Preventing fraud
6	Fraud policy and contingency plans

1 Introduction

1.1 What is fraud?

 Definition

Fraud is an intentional act involving the use of deception to obtain an unjust or illegal advantage – essentially 'theft by deception'.

Fraud (intentional) should be contrasted with error (unintentional).

 Example – Fraud or error

If a purchase ledger clerk deliberately enters a false invoice from a friend into the purchase ledger, in order for it to be paid so that the clerk and the friend can split the proceeds, this is a fraud. However if the clerk accidentally enters an invoice twice into the ledger, this is an error.

Note that fraud may be carried out by management, employees or third parties. For example:

- Managers may deliberately select inappropriate accounting policies.

- Employees may omit to enter a cash sale into the accounting records and steal the cash received.

- Third parties may send bogus invoices to the company, hoping that they will be paid in error.

Fraud is a criminal offence, punishable by a fine or imprisonment.

 Test your understanding 1

A safety inspector has found several safety violations in the manufacturing plant where you work. Correcting these will cost £30,000.

The inspector has offered to ignore the violations in return for a secret payment of £5,000, which your boss has asked you to organise. The workers will never be told about the safety violations and the inspector will file a report stating that the plant passes all the safety regulations.

What would you do?

1.2   Different types of fraud

Examples of fraud include:

- Employee crimes against employers, e.g. payroll fraud, falsifying expense claims, theft of cash.

- Crimes against investors, consumers and employees, e.g. financial statement fraud.

- Crimes by professional criminals, e.g. money laundering.

- E-crime by people using computers, e.g. spamming, copyright crimes, hacking.

Types of fraud are discussed in greater detail below.

1.3   The Fraud Act (2006)

Fraud is a criminal act and can be broken down into three distinct offences.

- Fraud by false representation is defined by Section 2 of the Act as a case where a person makes 'any representation as to fact or law... express or implied' which they know to be untrue or misleading.

- Fraud by failing to disclose information is defined by Section 3 of the Act as a case where a person fails to disclose any information to a third party when they are under a legal duty to disclose such information.

- Fraud by abuse of position is defined by Section 4 of the Act as a case where a person occupies a position where they are expected to safeguard the financial interests of another person, and abuses that position.

In all three classes of fraud, it requires that for an offence to have occurred, the person must have **acted dishonestly**, and that they had to have acted with the intent of **making a gain** for themselves or anyone else, or **inflicting a loss** (or a risk of loss) on another.

1.4 Prerequisites for fraud

Fraud generally occurs when someone has identified an opportunity, a weakness in the company's systems, and believes that the potential rewards will outweigh the risk of being caught.

There are thus three prerequisites for fraud to occur: rationalisation (could also be seen as dishonesty), opportunity and motivation. All three are usually required – for example an honest employee is unlikely to commit fraud even if given opportunity and motive.

The three elements are known as the fraud triangle and can be summarised in the image below.

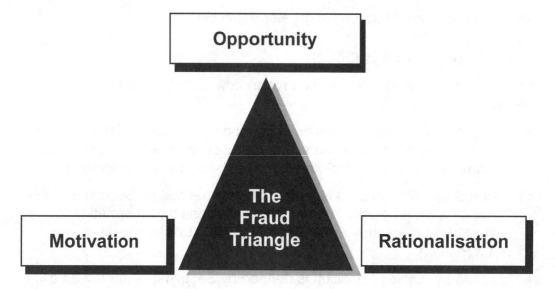

1.5 Fraud prevention

The aim of preventative controls is to reduce opportunity and remove temptation from potential offenders. Prevention techniques include the introduction of policies, procedures and controls, and activities such as training and fraud awareness to stop fraud from occurring.

The existence of a fraud strategy is itself a deterrent. This can be achieved through:

- **An anti-fraud culture** Where minor unethical practices are overlooked regarding, for example, expenses or time recording, this may lead to a culture in which larger frauds occur. High ethical standards bring long-term benefits as customers, suppliers, employees and the community realise they are dealing with a trustworthy organisation.

KAPLAN PUBLISHING

- **Risk awareness** Fraud should never be discounted, and there should be awareness among all staff that there is always the possibility that fraud is taking place. It is important to raise awareness through training programmes. Particular attention should be given to training and awareness among those people involved in receiving cash, purchasing and paying suppliers.

- **Publicity** can also be given to fraud that has been exposed. This serves as a reminder to those who may be tempted to commit fraud and a warning to those responsible for the management of controls.

- **Whistle-blowing** Fraud may be suspected by those who are not personally involved. People must be encouraged to raise the alarm about fraud.

- **Sound internal control systems** Sound systems of internal control should monitor fraud by identifying risks and then putting into place procedures to monitor and report on those risks.

2 Types of fraud

2.1 Introduction

There are two main types of irregularity which are of concern when considering fraud:

- Theft – dishonestly appropriating the property of another with the intention of permanently depriving them of it. This may include the removal or misuse of funds, assets or cash.

- Some theft, particularly of tangible assets such as computer or telephone equipment, can be opportunistic and may not always involve deception. A theft does not therefore necessarily fit into the general perception of 'fraud'.

- False accounting – dishonestly destroying, defacing, concealing or falsifying any account, record or document required for any accounting purpose, with a view to personal gain or gain for another, or with the intent to cause loss to another or furnishing information which is or may be misleading, false or deceptive.

2.2   Theft

Any business assets can be stolen, whether by employees or management, acting alone or in collusion with third parties.

This may involve the theft of inventory, euphemistically known as 'shrinkage'. Computer equipment is particularly vulnerable here.

Small scale theft

There are incidences of theft that will go unnoticed because of the scale of the crime.

- Small amounts of cash taken from the till of a retailer or the petty cash box in an office might not be noticed because the sums involved are not significant enough to have any impact on the organisation.

- Many employees think nothing of taking pens and paper from the stationery cupboard to stock up their home supply.

Larger scale theft

There are thefts that are for significant amounts. For example:

- The last cheques in the company's cheque book could be removed and the thief could forge authorised signatures, clear the funds, withdraw and disappear. This may not be detected until the bank statement arrived, by which time it would be too late.

- The theft of intellectual property, perhaps in the form of customer or price lists, also falls into this category.

- Staff who are confident of not being challenged may submit false expense claims, covering anything from private entertainment to large-scale projects.

- Theft from a company may also take the form of payroll fraud where payments to former or fictitious employees are diverted to the fraudster's own bank account.

Collusion

Collusion is a common element in frauds whereby individuals pool their resources to achieve their aims – specialist skills might not be available to the individual acting independently.

- Employees can collude with customers, other employees or friends. Customers may act in collusion with the employee to share any benefits generated, such as excessive discounts or uninvoiced deliveries.

- There may be kickbacks or commission paid from a supplier directly to an employee as a reward for being awarded a contract. These are particularly difficult to detect since the kickback does not go through the company's books/accounting records.

- Sometimes an employee has an undisclosed interest in a business transaction, resulting in harm to the business because the contract price is not the best that the company could have negotiated.

Computer fraud

There is a great deal of talk about computer fraud but in fact it could be argued that the fraud is carried out using a computer rather than traditional methods of paper and pen. The computer is simply the mechanism for perpetrating the fraud.

Computers may be used to disguise the true nature of a transaction by manipulating the date records and programs, to hack into an organisation's computer system to steal or manipulate information or for the unauthorised electronic transfer of funds.

On the Internet, fraudsters may pose as a legitimate business to obtain payment for goods that are either not delivered or are of significantly lower quality.

Computer fraud may be summarised as the use of information technology resources to commit or conceal a criminal offence or civil wrong.

Computer fraud typically includes:

- financial fraud

- sabotage of data and/or networks

- theft of proprietary information

- system penetration from the outside, including denial of service attacks

- unauthorised access by insiders, including employee misuse of Internet access privileges as well as malicious software.

2.3 False accounting

The main aim of false accounting is to present the results and affairs of the organisation in a better light than the reality.

Frequently, there are commercial pressures to report an unrealistic level of earnings, which can take precedence over controls designed to prevent fraud.

Management may occasionally wish to '**window-dress**' their statement of financial position (i.e. present either a better or worse picture than that which can be fairly presented) by a variety of devices.

For example

- Payments are entered before the year end but are not sent to suppliers until after the year end, so that the level of payables in the financial statements is reduced.

- The cashbook is kept open for receipts for some days after the year end so that money received after the year end is included in the cashbook balance.

This will give an incorrect impression of the company's creditworthiness to a reader of the accounts.

The owners or managers of the business could commit fraud through:

- a misuse of pension funds

- overvaluing assets

- not writing off irrecoverable debts and avoiding the effects on profits and assets

- understating depreciation

- understating expenses

Whatever the purpose of the fraud, the feature common to all cases is the need to falsify records, alter figures, and perhaps keep two sets of books/records. In every instance, it is only a matter of time before the fraud is exposed.

Some of the most dramatic corporate collapses and high-profile fraud trials have been characterised by false accounting used to cover up extensive fraud or theft within the business. The early 21st century saw the end of huge multinationals Enron and WorldCom, both of which fraudulently inflated their profits by deliberately misstating revenues to disguise mounting losses.

Although the aim is always to present the business in a flattering light, the reasons for doing it can vary. In some cases the purpose is to deceive the bank into providing more finance. The target of the deception may be a customer, who is more likely to be attracted by a successful company, or it may be a regulator whose intervention can be prevented or delayed.

False accounting is obviously carried out by insiders – either employees or management who are in a position to override the normal controls and to present figures that are simply not true.

 Test your understanding 2

Can you think of three ways that inventory can be used to show a false increase in the value of the assets in the company?

2.4 Types of fraud – further examples

The following table outlines some of the various types of fraud.

Type of fraud	Examples
False accounting	• Obtaining external financing by falsely improving the results. • Obtaining performance bonuses for managers by inflating profits. • Covering up internal theft by altering, adding, falsifying or deleting bank/inventory/purchase or other records. • A fictitious customer can be created. Orders can be sent, goods despatched on credit and the 'customer' never pays. The debt is written off. • Hiding losses in the hopes that fortunes may reverse.
Theft	• Direct theft of cash, inventory or assets – theft of inventory, commonly known as inventory shrinkage, can be significant. Computer equipment is particularly vulnerable. • Employees can falsify their time sheets and claim for overtime hours they did not work or claim a higher rate for the job. • False expense claims e.g. claiming for private entertainment expenses • Rolling customer receipts – misappropriating cash received from customers then allocating subsequent receipts against those earlier customers. This is known as teeming and lading and takings appear to be banked permanently behind the date on which they are actually received.

Third-party	• Customers ordering goods on credit with no intention of paying – includes some credit card frauds.
	• Commission (or kickbacks) paid by a supplier to an employee as a reward for awarding the contract to that supplier. These are particularly difficult to detect, since the kickback is paid directly to the employee and does not go through the company's books/records.
	• Collusion with customers to charge lower prices or raise spurious credit notes, with the benefit shared between customer and employee.
	• Collusion with suppliers to accept under-deliveries of inventory.
Computer fraud	• Hacking/unauthorised access to bank accounts to transfer funds.
	• Setting up as a legitimate Internet business and obtaining payment for goods that are either never delivered or are of lower quality than advertised.
	• Disguising the true nature of a transaction by manipulation of date records and programs held on a computer.
	• Hacking into an organisation's computer system to steal or manipulate information.

3 Implications of fraud

3.1 Typical elements of fraud

Fraud investigations often reveal one or more of the following:

- Credit notes given to customers for undisclosed or inadequate reasons.

- High level of inventory losses accepted without investigation.

- Suppliers insist on dealing with only one employee in the department.

- Discrepancies in petty cash are not investigated or are written off to 'sundry' expenses.

- Payroll summaries are not checked by department heads or by the HR department.

- Company assets are not checked against a non-current asset register or inventory listing.

- Inadequate reconciliation of statement of financial position accounts.

- Unusually high levels of despatches or purchases just prior to the period end.

- Employees' expense claims are not checked and authorised by departmental managers.

- Management appears to condone petty fraud because 'everybody knows about it but never does anything about it'.

- Invoices from some suppliers seem high in relation to the goods or services rendered.

- Amounts are written off the sales ledger without authorisation or investigation.

- Management and supervision are remote from those they control.

 Test your understanding 3

There are a number of ways that an expenses system could be abused. Make a list of the ways that an employee could defraud their employer.

3.2 The impact of fraud

The way the organisation is affected by the fraud depends on the type of fraud perpetrated.

Type of fraud	Implications
Any fraud that is discovered and addressed.	• Negative publicity can damage the organisation irrevocably by affecting public perception and consumer confidence.
	• Whilst publicity will certainly deter other frauds within the company, its effects on outsiders must be managed. If the case goes to court the facts cannot be prevented from getting out. We need to consider what effect any publicity would have on suppliers and customers. Will suppliers withdraw credit? Will customers look elsewhere for their supplies?
	• Fraudsters may be arrested and, depending on the scale and seriousness of the fraud, may face a custodial sentence.
Theft of funds or assets from the organisation.	• Profits are lower than they should be. Because there is less cash or fewer assets the net asset position is weakened. Returns to shareholders are likely to be reduced as a result.
	• If the working capital is reduced it can be difficult for the organisation to operate effectively. In the most serious cases of fraud, otherwise successful businesses can collapse e.g. Barings Bank.
Misrepresentation of the financial position of the organisation – results artificially enhanced.	• Too much of the organisation's profits may be distributed to shareholders.
	• Investors making decisions based on inaccurate information may not achieve the expected returns.
	• Suppliers may extend credit while being misled about the financial position of the organisation.

Misrepresentation of the financial position of the organisation – results under-stated.	• Access to loans may be restricted where assets are under reported. • If the organisation is a listed company and quoted on the Stock Exchange, the share price might fall and market strength might be eroded. • Returns to investors may be reduced unnecessarily.

4 Detecting fraud

4.1 Conditions for fraud

Fraud is found to be more frequent in organisations with some or all of the following characteristics:

- Domineering management with no effective overseeing board or committee.

- High staff turnover rates in key controlling functions.

- Long-service staff in stores/purchasing departments.

- Chronic understaffing in key control areas.

- Frequent changes of legal advisers, auditors or professional advisers.

- Remuneration based very significantly on financial performance.

- Inadequate segregation of duties – e.g. where an individual orders goods, approves the invoices and then authorises the payments.

- Lack of effective procedures in HR, credit control, inventory control, purchasing or accounts departments. Consistent failure to correct major weaknesses in internal control.

- Management frequently override internal controls.

- Frequent transactions with related parties/no checking that suppliers are appropriate.

- Mismatch between profitability and cash flow.

- Excessive pressure to meet budgets, targets or forecast earnings.

- Personnel not required to take their holiday entitlement.

- When an employee is on holiday leave, the work is left until the employee returns.

- Inadequate responses to queries from management, suppliers, auditors or bankers.

- Lack of common-sense controls such as changing passwords frequently, requiring two signatures on cheques or restricting access to sensitive areas.

Effective fraud detection requires management to be sufficiently knowledgeable about the mechanics of the business and constantly aware of the need to be vigilant against fraud.

4.2 Uncovering fraud

Discovering fraud can be exceptionally difficult and the majority of frauds, whether computer-based or not, are found by accident. Well-operated controls should prevent fraud taking place but, as one of the ways fraud is committed is by circumventing controls, these controls may be inadequate to discover the fraud.

Key ways of uncovering fraud include performing regular control checks, e.g. inventory counts, cash counts. Often computers are used to cover up non-computer frauds. All frauds have a weak point in having to remove what has been taken (cash or other assets).

Look out for signs that there may be a problem, e.g. late customer payments or an ageing list of customer balances, incomplete audit trails.

4.3 Risk management

Risk management is a tool for helping to tackle potential fraud. It comprises risk assessment (identifying and analysing risk) and risk control (taking steps to reduce risk, provide contingency plans and monitor improvements). Risk management can be seen as a series of steps:

- **Risk identification** – producing lists of risk items.

- **Risk analysis** – assessing the loss probability and magnitude for each item. No matter what process is used, the risk analysis method is always the same: identify the asset, ascertain the risk, determine the vulnerability. Clearly, stronger internal controls reduce the risk here.

  A useful tool for risk analysis is a risk or fraud matrix (see below).

- **Risk prioritisation** – producing a ranked ordering of risk items.

- **Risk-management planning** – deciding how to address each risk item, perhaps by avoiding, transferring, absorbing or reducing the risk (see below).

- **Risk resolution** – producing a situation in which risk items are eliminated or resolved.

- **Risk monitoring** – tracking progress toward resolving risk items and taking corrective action.

Threats

As well as the risk of fraud, there are other types of risks a business may be exposed to, such as:

- malicious attacks

- user error

- natural disasters

- systems/applications supporting the organisation's operations interrupted

- customer loss of confidence

- sensitive information disclosed

- assets lost

- integrity of data compromised

4.4 Grading the risk level

You might be expected to be able to grade the risk from low, through medium to high, or possibly using numerical values where a higher number indicates a higher risk. This requires a degree of judgement.

It is difficult to provide precise guidance here but:

- the more desirable the asset the more likely it could be stolen. Cash, high value items or household goods are more prone to theft and hence would be rated as higher risk.

- the level of past incidence. If frauds have occurred in the past then they are more likely to reoccur.

- cash-based businesses are high-risk areas as it's relatively easy to steal and any controls are highly dependent on the integrity of individuals.

- complex accounting environments are more prone to fraud as fewer people understand what is happening.

- weak control environments can encourage more fraud as there is a reduced chance of discovery.

Example – risk of fraud

Consider the following taxi businesses

1   **Taxi business A**. Customers can flag down a taxi and almost always pay cash for the journey. The taxis do not have a GPS system attached so no record is kept of the mileage covered. Petrol is bought by the driver using cash received from customers.

This is clearly very high risk. It is cash-based and no verification is possible of mileage or the petrol consumed from which an estimate of fares could be made.

2   **Taxi business B**. Customers can only book using an application on their smart phones. Payment is made by bank transfer automatically. All petrol is bought at one location owned by the business where a record of miles covered and fuel used is kept.

This is low risk. The extra controls and the method of payment have improved the risk profile considerably. If petrol were being bought elsewhere then a calculation of the miles per gallon figures would reveal that.

You can see here that the type of business may not be relevant. The methods followed and the level of control is also a factor.

Risk matrix

When performing risk analysis, a common qualitative way of assessing the significance of risk is to produce a risk matrix.

The matrix identifies whether a risk will have a significant impact on the organisation and links that into the likelihood of the risk occurring.

The approach can provide a framework for prioritising risks in the business.

Risks with a significant impact and a high likelihood of occurrence need more urgent attention than risks with a low impact and low likelihood of occurrence.

Risks can be plotted onto a risk matrix, as shown below. The matrix can provide a useful framework to determine an appropriate risk response. Likelihoods and impacts are graded low, medium or high. Low grade is scored 1, medium 2 and high 3. The grid is completed by multiplying the likelihood score by the corresponding impact score to give a risk score.

		Impact		
		Low (1)	Medium (2)	High (3)
Likelihood / probability	High (3)	3	6	9
	Medium (2)	2	4	6
	Low (1)	1	2	3

Thus a threat with a high probability and high impact would score 9, indicating the severest risk requiring urgent attention, whereas a high impact threat that had a low probability would only score 3.

A simpler form of matrix may be used, in this case the probability and impact may just be identified as either high or low. The response to the risk (transfer, avoid, reduce, accept) is then indicated on the matrix as shown below:

		Impact / Consequence	
		Low	High
Probability / Likelihood	High	Reduce	Avoid
	Low	Accept	Transfer

Transfer In some circumstances, risk can be transferred wholly or in part to a third party, so that if an adverse event occurs, the third party suffers all or most of the loss. This would be appropriate for a high-impact event with low-probability. A common example of risk transfer is insurance. Businesses arrange a wide range of insurance policies for protection against possible losses. This strategy is also sometimes referred to as sharing.

Avoid For a high-impact high-probability event an organisation might choose to avoid a risk altogether. However, since risks are unavoidable in business ventures, they can be avoided only by not investing (or withdrawing from the business area completely). The same applies to not-for-profit organisations: risk is unavoidable in the activities they undertake.

Reduce/mitigate A third strategy is to reduce the risk, either by limiting exposure in a particular area or attempting to decrease the adverse effects should that risk actually crystallise. This may be appropriate for events with low impact but high probability. For example, risk of inventory theft will be reduced by implementing controls such as CCTV, security guard, security tags etc.

Accept The final strategy is to simply accept that the risk may occur and decide to deal with the consequences in that particular situation. The strategy is appropriate normally where the adverse effect is minimal, so low impact and low probability. For example, there is nearly always a risk of rain. Unless the business activity cannot take place when it rains (e.g. certain sporting events) then the risk of rain occurring is not normally insured against.

This type of risk matrix is sometimes referred to as a TARA matrix, based on the initial letters of the response actions.

5 Preventing fraud

5.1 Prerequisites for fraud

As with any crime prevention strategy, the key to minimising the risk of fraud lies in understanding why it occurs, identifying business areas that are at risk and implementing procedures to address vulnerable areas.

As mentioned above, there are three prerequisites for fraud to occur: rationalisation (or dishonesty), opportunity and motivation.

One approach for reducing fraud is to target these three prerequisites.

Motivation (or Motive)

The motive for fraud is often simply dissatisfaction, based on being passed over for promotion, inadequate pay or a feeling of carrying more than a fair workload. Just giving employees the opportunity to air their grievances and discuss aspirations could be sufficient to reduce this problem. Employees may also be aware of other problems within the organisation and would welcome some forum where they could come forward.

Motivation to commit fraud will thus normally be prevented by:

* good employment conditions (e.g. pay, working hours)

* instant dismissal where appropriate

* sympathetic grievance procedures.

KAPLAN PUBLISHING

Rationalisation (or dishonesty)

Rationalisation relates to an individual's own personal justification/reason for committing the fraud. This can be linked to the individual being dishonest. Dishonesty will be prevented by careful scrutiny of staff. The fight against fraud should start even before a new employee joins the company. References must be checked thoroughly. Fraud will be reduced in a culture of:

- severe disciplinary procedures for offenders
- moral leadership by management.

Opportunity

Opportunity relates to the circumstances that are in place, that allow the fraud to happen. This is the one element of the entire fraud triangle, which a business will have full control over.

Opportunity will be prevented by:

- separation of duties
- input and output controls on computer processing
- control over and testing of new computer programs
- physical security of assets and computer hardware
- controls over forms and documentation, e.g. cheques.

Most of the above controls are standard internal controls on preventing fraud. In addition to controls to prevent fraud it is important to have a system for detecting fraud covering such areas as:

- an audit trail
- logging of access to files, terminals, books and records
- good documentation of accounting procedures and programs.

Employees and third parties should be encouraged to report their suspicions of fraud or other irregular activity without fear of reprisal.

In fact, where the report is made in good faith, the whistle-blower is now protected by law.

5.2 Prevention and deterrence

Prevention of fraud is a two-stage process:

1 ensure that opportunities for fraud are minimised (fraud prevention), and

2 ensure that potential fraudsters believe they will be caught (fraud deterrence).

Prevention

Fraud prevention – means examining all the key company systems and viewing them with the mind-set of a potential fraudster. The review will bring to light a number of weaknesses in the current systems that could be exploited by a fraudster. Having identified the weaknesses in the current systems, the company must then change those systems by introducing new or different controls.

Simple controls are often the most effective and frequently require little management time or effort. For example:

- Credit notes above a threshold amount must be authorised by a senior independent manager before issue.

- Inventory write-downs must be investigated before authorisation by an independent manager.

- Key statement of financial position accounts must be reconciled monthly and the reconciliation reviewed regularly by senior managers.

- Non-current assets must be labelled and checked periodically – this can often be combined with the regular testing of electrical and lifting equipment.

- Ensure that no goods or assets leave a site without a despatch note or other documentation.

- Sickness absence must be monitored and controlled.

- Wherever practical, duties must be segregated so that no one person is responsible for both approving expenditure and authorising payment. Physical and electronic access to sensitive areas and procedures must be restricted.

- Employees must take their vacation entitlement and the work of those employees on vacation must be covered by others.

- All employees' expense claims must be authorised by their immediate managers before payment.

- New employees must be screened and their references must be checked.

The introduction and enforcement of controls like these will reduce the opportunities for fraudsters. The controls themselves warn potential fraudsters that management is actively monitoring the business and that in itself will deter fraud.

KAPLAN PUBLISHING

Deterrence

Fraud deterrence – only when potential fraudsters believe fraud will be detected and when whistle-blowers believe they will be protected will there be an effective deterrence of fraud. The most effective ways of detecting fraud have been found to be:

- Internal controls and internal audit.
- Management review or change of management.
- Whistle-blowers or anonymous tip-offs.
- External audit.
- Access/exit controls – operating effective access controls within the premises is obviously essential. Never underestimate the role of security tags, CCTV cameras or other surveillance equipment.

Fraud is difficult to prevent and detect, but all organisations should institute basic controls. These include:

- segregation of duties (often lost with computerised systems) employment of honest staff
- a control log or audit trail of all transactions carried out.

5.3 Fraud matrix

We saw the use of risk matrices in the previous section. Organisations sometimes use a matrix to assess the extent of fraud risk in an accounting system. Generally speaking, frauds that are likely (disappearing stationery) have a lower impact than those with remote risk (removal of assets from a pension fund). The impact of a fraud can therefore be graded:

- high – the effects of fraud are very serious for the organisation, affecting its profit and/or liquidity
- moderate – the effects of the fraud are significant but can be dealt with internally, or in some cases by the police (theft, collusion)
- low – the impact of the fraud is insignificant (petty pilfering)

The areas of the system in which the fraud might occur must first be identified, for example:

- cash payments
- cash receipts
- sales/receivables ledger
- purchases/payables ledger
- expenses

- inventory control

- payroll

- non-current asset purchase

A matrix (or a section of a matrix) will then be drawn up for each of the areas identified. An example of entries in a typical matrix is illustrated below. The matrix might display:

- the identified risk area of the organisation

- the details of the type of fraud

- the role of the employee who may become involved in it

- any third party who may become involved through collusion

- the likelihood of the fraud (high, moderate, low)

- the impact of the fraud (high, moderate, low)

This matrix will then become a valuable tool which will enable management to assess the risks and establish an appropriate strategy for minimising them.

Note that the format of the matrices you will encounter is likely to vary, but the example below for a payroll department is fairly typical.

Details of risk	Employees	Collusion	Likelihood	Impact
Stationery pilferage	Payroll staff	None	high	low
Theft of cash	Payroll staff	None	moderate	moderate
Payment to fictitious employees	Payroll staff	Third party recipient	moderate	moderate

You may also see a simpler fraud matrix which simply lists the details of the fraud risk with a numerical value rating the fraud, typically from 1 to 5:

5	Very high
4	High
3	Medium
2	Low
1	Very low

Note that if a slightly different numbering system is provided in exam questions, you must apply the one provided to the question set.

So the payroll department matrix above becomes:

Details of risk	Rating
Stationery pilferage	1
Theft of cash	3
Payment to fictitious employees	3

Test your understanding 4

Steve works for Sciss Ltd, a manufacturer of cardboard boxes, as Head of the Production Department. Steve is awarded a bonus each year if profits exceed budget. Steve is able to view the accounts each month to see whether the department is exceeding the budget.

In the final month of the year, to maintain production, Steve had to order glue which cost £1,000. Within Sciss Ltd glue is not capitalised and recorded in inventory but is simply written off as an expense. Unfortunately this extra bill will be sufficient to reduce the year-end profit so that the department will not receive their bonus.

The employees have started using the glue, but Steve has hidden the invoice in his desk until the year-end accounts have been finalised.

For each of the following controls, identify which may have deterred Steve from acting in this way:

	Yes/No
The matching of all orders to goods received notes.	
A year-end inventory count.	
The use of sequentially numbered orders.	
The use of sequentially numbered goods received notes.	
The matching of goods received notes to invoices.	
The use of sequentially numbered invoices.	
A sequence check on all orders and goods received notes.	

6 Fraud policy and contingency plans

6.1 Fraud ethics policy

A fraud ethics policy is intended to show the company's desire to be open and honest in all its dealings, internally and externally. It should be clear that the company values integrity and effort, not merely financial performance, in all dealings with staff, customers and suppliers. It is important to emphasise that the policy applies consistently to all staff, whatever their level. Failure to comply with the policy will be considered a disciplinary offence.

Values and behaviour

What is considered acceptable and unacceptable behaviour may vary between countries and cultures, therefore specific guidance should be given on this, with reference to the core values of the organisation. The company should give its definition of fraud and provide a detailed list of examples of actions that it considers to be fraud.

Employee responsibilities

The company should explain that unless authorised, personal interests in outside organisations should be avoided. Employees may not act as a director, officer, employee or partner of any other organisation outside the group. Relationships with parties of another organisation should be disclosed to management, who should then ensure that the individual is not involved in any activity in the area of the conflict of interest.

If employees find themselves in a position where there is a conflict of interest, this must be disclosed immediately.

Reporting

The company must make it clear that employees may not accept gifts to a value in excess of what is laid down in the ethics policy. Employees should be advised to use discretion and common sense if accepting modest gifts. All gifts received must be reported and recorded by the company. A similar policy should exist for giving gifts to customers and for entertainment.

Confidentiality

The policy should state that employees have a duty of confidentiality to the company and its clients. Information received in the course of employment must not be disclosed to persons outside the group. Information received must not be used for an employee's own benefit or the benefit of others. The policy should make it clear that employees are obliged to report suspicions of fraud or irregular activity.

Response

Finally, the fraud ethics policy must state that all suspicions and reports of fraud will be treated seriously and investigated. If necessary, the fraud contingency plan (see below) will be implemented and appropriate action taken, which could include police involvement.

6.2 Fraud consequences

When faced with the suggestion that fraud has been perpetrated against them, companies react in different ways. For some, it is critical that no hint of the matter ever comes to light. They only want to recover the lost funds. Others believe that to maximise the impact of their corporate code of ethics, action should be taken and should be seen to be taken against the perpetrator and that this is more important than recovering the money.

Few companies have established and agreed procedures for handling suspected fraud. Yet, if the suspicion and supporting evidence are handled in the wrong way, considerable damage can be done to the organisation's finances and reputation.

6.3 Fraud contingency plan

Many organisations have disaster recovery procedures in place in the event of fire, bomb explosion or major computer failure. Few have established and agreed procedures for handling suspected fraud. Yet, if the suspicion and supporting evidence are handled in the wrong way, considerable damage can be done to both the organisation's finances and reputation.

A fraud contingency plan provides the route map that enables the company to undertake an investigation that meets its objectives and protects its interests. This plan:

- identifies fraud risks in each area from management, employees, third parties or through collusion

- implements appropriate controls

- determines who will lead the investigation as well as the objectives and powers of the investigation team and

- decides on how to work with the police and handle publicity.

In the initial stages, an investigation is likely to be undertaken by company personnel and/or external investigators, perhaps forensic accountants.

At a later stage it is of particular benefit to use private organisations and forensic specialists to establish and assess the facts, which can then be handed over to the police in the event of a criminal prosecution.

No matter how suspicion was aroused, it is essential to ascertain as soon as possible who is implicated. Where the suspect is an employee, the designation and position of the suspect may determine the financial damage that could be caused, the reputation damage that could result if the matter became known publicly, the parties to be informed and the action to be taken.

Fundamental to any investigation is the documentary information, which may be what first aroused suspicion, and will subsequently provide the evidence that an irregularity has occurred. It is essential to ensure that this information cannot be destroyed, altered or removed from the company's control.

Internal and external publicity must be managed in order to avoid scaremongering, while those who need to know are kept informed. A carefully managed media strategy can help to deflect criticism and concerns about the organisation's stability.

 Test your understanding 5

NL is a qualified accountant. NL works for the treasury department at B Bank. NL manages a small department of six staff who specialise in foreign exchange transactions. Their work is very complex and only the best people are recruited to the department.

Many managers of other departments do not understand the workings of the foreign exchange employees and leave NL to supervise all of their activities. NL started as a junior in the foreign exchange department ten years ago and has rapidly worked his way to the top.

NL reports to the board of B Bank at each board meeting. Reported profits by NL increase slightly each year, enough to warrant the bonus available according to the department's employment contracts – up to 200% of their salaries.

One Board member has become suspicious that reported profits have been manipulated.

Which THREE of the following controls would allay the board members suspicions?

The department's reported profits should be independently scrutinized.	
The reported profit should be recalculated.	
NL should be supervised by at least one other Board member with foreign exchange experience.	
Reviewing other bank's foreign exchange profits to see if they too are generally rising each year.	
Verifying that NL is a qualified accountant and able to produce financial statements.	

7 Additional Test your understanding questions

Test your understanding 6

1   Explain the term 'window dressing'.
2   Identify five types of false accounting.
3   Give an example of collusion.
4   List as many types of computer fraud that you can.
5   How would you go about uncovering fraud?
6   Outline the four ways that risks can be handled.
7   What are the three prerequisites for fraud to occur?
8   What areas would be covered in a fraud policy statement?

8 Summary

This chapter has identified the risks and common indicators of fraud. You should understand how to evaluate a system and identify potential risk areas and be able to suggest ways of detecting and avoiding incidences of fraud.

Test your understanding answers

Test your understanding 1

You should refuse to accept the £5,000 and explain to the boss why you are unable to do this.

If the boss still then insists, then the businesses whistle-blowing policy should be considered.

If such a policy does not exist, then the details should be passed to another senior manager to review.

You could also contact the AAT ethics helpline for advice.

Test your understanding 2

The ways of artificially inflating the value of inventory include the following:

- Instead of being written-off, obsolete or damaged inventory may be shown at cost on the statement of financial position.

- Records can be falsified at the inventory count, i.e. generating inventory that does not actually exist.

- Returns to suppliers may not be recorded or suppressed until after the year-end inventory count.

- Similarly with deliveries to customers – the reduction in inventory may not be recorded or suppressed until after the year-end inventory count.

KAPLAN PUBLISHING

163

Test your understanding 3

This list could be really long, but here are a few to start you off:

- Claim for a meal that you did not have.

- Take someone with you on a business trip and both stay at the hotel at the company's expense.

- Use the free 'park and ride' service but claim for parking the car in the city centre.

- Travel in a group and share petrol costs but claim individually for mileage allowance.

- Claim for restaurant tips that you did not give.

Test your understanding 4

	Yes/No
The matching of all orders to goods received notes.	Y
A year-end inventory count.	N
The use of sequentially numbered orders.	Y
The use of sequentially numbered goods received notes.	Y
The matching of goods received notes to invoices.	Y
The use of sequentially numbered invoices.	N
A sequence check on all orders and goods received notes.	Y

All paperwork issued should be sequentially numbered. An order will be raised initially which should be matched to the GRN when the goods arrive. These two documents should be matched to the invoice when it arrives, but if it doesn't arrive before the year end (hidden in Steve's desk) then the estimated cost of the goods (stated on the order or a quote, etc.) should be used to account.

Glue is not recorded in the year-end inventory count.

Sequentially numbered invoices would not help as invoices received from suppliers will have their own numbering and not be in sequence according to Sciss.

Test your understanding 5

The department's reported profits should be independently scrutinized.	Y
The reported profit should be recalculated.	N
NL should be supervised by at least one other Board member with foreign exchange experience.	Y
Reviewing other bank's foreign exchange profits to see if they too are generally rising each year.	Y
Verifying that NL is a qualified accountant and able to produce financial statements.	N

Option 2 – Recalculating the reported profits probably wouldn't help since simply adding up the profits would not ensure that the profit was actually realised.

Option 5 – NL is a qualified accountant and NL has worked for B Bank for three years. NL is probably quite capable of producing accurate financial statements, and also capable of manipulating them if NL wanted to. This activity would not help to control the potential problem.

Test your understanding 6

1   Window dressing is a type of false accounting. Management may occasionally wish to 'window dress' their statement of financial position (i.e. present either a better or worse picture than that which can be fairly presented) by a variety of devices such as keeping the cashbook open for some days after the year end so that money received after the year end is included in the cashbook balance or entering cheques paid before the year end but not sending them to payables until after the year end. This gives an incorrect impression of the company's creditworthiness to any stakeholders reading the accounts.

2   Examples of false accounting include:

- Obtaining external financing by falsely improving the results.

- Raising the share price by false means to aid acquisitions or to help a new issue of shares.

- Obtaining performance bonuses for managers by inflating profits.

- Covering up internal theft by falsifying or deleting records. A fictitious customer can be created. Orders can be sent, goods despatched on credit and the 'customer' can neglect to pay their bill. The debt is written off.

- Hiding losses in the hopes that fortunes may reverse.

3   Collusion is a common element in frauds whereby individuals pool their resources to achieve their aims – specialist skills might not be available to the individual acting independently. Employees can collude with customers, with other employees or with friends.

Examples are:

- The price, quantity or quality of goods sold to a customer can be manipulated to defraud the company.

- An employee could write off a debt or issue a credit note and get something in return.

- An employee could arrange for a supplier to falsify their invoice and show more goods or services than were received. Fictitious supply of goods or services.

4   Computer frauds include:

- Hacking/unauthorised access to bank accounts to transfer funds or to steal or manipulate information.

- Setting up as a legitimate Internet business and obtaining payment for goods that are either never delivered or are of lower quality than advertised.

- Theft of intellectual property.

- Publishing malicious claims about the company on anonymous bulletin boards, thus affecting the company's reputation.

- Disguising the true nature of a transaction by manipulation of date records and programs held on a computer.

5   Uncovering fraud means performing regular control checks, e.g. inventory and cash counts, being aware that fraud might be occurring and looking out for signs that there may be a problem e.g. late payments, work backlogs, incomplete audit trails.

6   Risks can be handled in a number of different ways. You can ignore the risks and do nothing, so accept the risk – appropriate where the effect of the risk is small and the chances of it occurring remote. You can purchase insurance against the risk, effectively transferring the risk. If the impact and probability are both high you could, and possibly should, avoid the risk, perhaps by withdrawing. Where the potential impact is low, but the probability is high, steps should be taken to either limit exposure or decrease the potential adverse effects.

7   There are three prerequisites for fraud to occur: rationalisation/dishonesty, opportunity and motivation.

8   The areas covered in a fraud policy statement could include an allocation of responsibilities for the overall management of fraud, such that all those concerned are fully aware of their individual responsibilities, and so that accountability can be ensured. It could also include a manual of formal procedures to which staff must adhere to if a fraud is discovered. This is required so that continuity of action results, and so that the actions of staff in such a situation are planned and well thought out, rather than ad hoc and ill conceived. It necessarily follows that where a manual of formal procedures exists, staff must be adequately trained to identify fraud or, better still, work to prevent it.

Performance indicators

7

Introduction

Within your previous AAT studies you have considered the use of performance indicators to assess performance.

Within this module you may be required to do exactly the same thing – assess performance. However, in addition to this there will also be tasks that ask you to analyse accounting ratios in order to identify problems in the system of internal control.

The logic behind this is that poor controls can lead to poor decisions or mistakes, which then affect one or more of the performance indicators.

In this chapter we revise specific key ratios and consider the link to internal controls.

PERFORMANCE CRITERIA	CONTENTS
1.3 Changes to management information	1 Profitability ratios
	2 Liquidity ratios
	3 Financial position ratio
	4 Interpreting financial ratios
	5 Question styles
	6 The link between ratios and internal controls

1 Profitability ratios

1.1 Introduction

Ratios calculated from financial statements help to interpret the information they present. We can break down the ratios into categories to make our discussion more structured. To begin with we look at ratios relating to profitability.

1.2 Return on capital employed (ROCE) %

$$\text{Return on capital employed} = \frac{\text{Profit from operations}}{\text{Total equity + Non-current liabilities}} \times 100\%$$

Return on capital employed is frequently regarded as the best measure of profitability, indicating how successful a business is in utilising the funding it has received.

The profit figure used is the operating profit, so the profit before interest and taxation.

The capital employed represents the value of assets used in the business and is calculated by adding the long-term funding, or non-current liabilities, to the total equity figure (share capital plus all reserves). This figure could also be calculated as total assets less current liabilities.

A low return on capital employed is caused by either a low profit margin or a low asset turnover or both.

1.3 Gross profit margin %

$$\text{Gross profit percentage} = \frac{\text{Gross profit}}{\text{Revenue}} \times 100\%$$

The gross profit percentage focuses on the trading account. A low margin could indicate selling prices are too low or cost of sales is too high.

1.4 Operating profit margin %

$$\text{Operating profit percentage} = \frac{\text{Profit from operations}}{\text{Revenue}} \times 100\%$$

The operating profit margin will be affected by the gross profit margin, so a low operating margin could indicate poor gross profit margin or high overhead costs or both. Comparative analysis could then reveal the level of prices and costs in relation to competitors.

KAPLAN PUBLISHING

1.5 Asset turnover

$$\text{Asset turnover} = \frac{\text{Revenue}}{\text{Total assets} - \text{Current liabilities}}$$

This is a measure of how fully a company is utilising its assets. Note that the denominator represents the capital employed figure and could be calculated as total equity plus non-current liabilities.

A low asset turnover shows that a company is not generating a sufficient volume of business for the size of its asset base.

This may be remedied by increasing sales or by disposing of some of the assets or both.

2 Liquidity ratios

2.1 Current ratio

$$\text{Current ratio} = \frac{\text{Current assets}}{\text{Current liabilities}}$$

This is a common method of analysing working capital (current assets less current liabilities) and is generally accepted as a good measure of short-term solvency. It indicates the extent to which the claims of short-term payables are covered by assets that are expected to be converted to cash in a period roughly corresponding to the maturity of the claims.

The current ratio should ideally fall between 1:1 and 2:1. A ratio below 1:1 would indicate insufficient assets to meet liabilities, whereas if the ratio was too high this may indicate excess current assets, such as inventory or trade receivables.

2.2 Quick ratio (acid test ratio)

$$\text{Acid test ratio} = \frac{\text{Current assets} - \text{Inventories}}{\text{Current liabilities}}$$

This is calculated in the same way as the current ratio except that inventories are excluded from current assets.

This ratio is a much better test of the immediate solvency of a business because often inventories are not quickly convertible into cash.

Contrary to what might be expected, this ratio may fall in a time of prosperity since increased activity may lead to larger inventories but less cash. Conversely, when trade slows down inventories may be disposed of without renewal and the ratio will rise.

Although increased liquid resources more usually indicate favourable trading, it could be that funds are not being used to their best advantage (e.g. large surplus cash balances).

2.3 Inventory turnover

$$\frac{\text{Cost of sales}}{\text{Inventory}}$$

Inventory turnover is a similar measure to asset turnover above, in that it measures how efficiently the inventory has been used to generate revenue. Note that it is the cost of sales rather than revenue that is divided by the inventory, because inventory is measured at cost. The higher the figure, the more efficiently inventory is being used.

2.4 Inventory holding period in days

$$\frac{\text{Inventories}}{\text{Cost of sales}} \times 365 \text{ days}$$

Inventory turnover can also be calculated in terms of days. This represents how many days' worth of inventory is being held.

2.5 Trade receivables collection period

$$\frac{\text{Trade receivables}}{\text{Revenue}} \times 365 \text{ days}$$

This is computed by dividing the trade receivables by the average daily sales to determine the number of days sales held in receivables.

A long average collection period probably indicates poor credit control, but it may be due to other factors such as overseas sales where the collection period will be much longer, or a deliberate decision to extend the credit period to attract new customers.

2.6 Trade payables payment period

$$\frac{\text{Trade payables}}{\text{Cost of sales}} \times 365 \text{ days}$$

This is computed by dividing the trade payables by the average daily purchases to determine the number of days purchases held in payables.

Note that if only cost of sales (rather than purchases) is available in the information given this can be used as an approximation to purchases.

If the payables period is very low, then the business might not be making the best use of its cash by paying suppliers early.

If the period is very long then this is a free source of credit but the business must be careful not to harm relations with suppliers.

2.7 Working capital cycle

Inventory days + Receivable days – Payable days

This is the length of time between paying out cash for inventory and receiving the cash for goods or services supplied, in other words the period of time for which inventory is funded.

The longer the period of time that cash is tied up in working capital the more cost that is incurred by companies either directly, by virtue of bank interest, or indirectly, as a result of the inability to invest cash surpluses into higher interest yielding accounts.

3 Financial position ratio

3.1 Gearing

$$\frac{\text{Non-current liabilities}}{\text{Total equity + Non-current liabilities}} \times 100\%$$

Gearing measures the extent to which a business is dependent on non-equity funds, as opposed to equity funding. A high gearing ratio means that the business has a high proportion of borrowed funds in its total capital.

Gearing gives an indication of long-term liquidity and the financial risk inherent within the business. Highly geared companies have to meet large interest commitments before paying dividends and may have problems raising further finance if expansion is necessary.

4 Interpreting financial ratios

There are some more general points on ratio analysis which should be particularly noted.

4.1 Caution in interpretation

Avoid forming conclusions without considering the situation. For example, a reduction in the inventory holding period may be a good thing, but if it is likely to cause loss of customer goodwill or production disruption due to inventory shortages, it may not be such an advantage.

Ratios rarely answer questions but they can highlight areas where questions might usefully be asked.

4.2 Statement of financial position figures

Many of the ratios considered in this chapter involve the use of figures from the statement of financial position. These ratios should be interpreted with caution since the statement of financial position shows the position at a specific moment only and this may not be typical of the general position.

This point is particularly important where the ratio is derived from a statement of financial position figure in conjunction with a figure from the statement of profit or loss and other comprehensive income.

This is because the first figure relates to a moment in time whereas the second represents the total for a period.

A sensible way to try to avoid possible distortions here is to use the average figure for the statement of financial position figure. So, for example, the receivables collection period would relate credit sales to the average of the trade receivables figures at the beginning and at the end of the year.

However in many industries the existence of recurrent seasonal factors may mean that averaging beginning and end of year figures will not solve the problem.

It may be for example, that the date up to which a business draws its final accounts has been selected because it is a time when inventory levels are always low, so that inventory is relatively easy to value.

In such cases, averaging the inventory figures for two consecutive year-end dates would simply mean averaging two figures which were both untypical of inventory levels throughout the rest of the year. Averaging monthly figures would usually be the solution to this problem. However, external stakeholders would not typically have access to such information.

4.3 Other financial ratios

There are a large number of ratios which can be calculated from a set of financial statements. The ones shown above are those most commonly used in practice and include those which have been specifically included within this module. It should be noted, however, that there are many other ratios which could be useful in particular contexts.

4.4 Additional performance indicators

It is usually unwise to limit analysis and interpretation to information revealed by ratios.

For example, revenue for a business could double from one year to the next. This would be a dramatic and important development, yet none of the ratios would reveal this, at least not directly.

However, this significant increase in performance would be fairly obvious from even a superficial glance at the financial statements.

5 Question styles

As well as being required to calculate ratios, you may be given a range of statements and asked to identify which

- reflect what the ratios are showing, or

- explain why ratios are different, from one period to another or between companies, or

- summarise cause and effect correctly.

When explaining why ratios have changed, try to refer to the underlying drivers of business performance where possible.

For example:

A higher gross profit margin could be due to a rise in sale prices and/or a drop in production costs per unit, but why might they have happened?

- Higher prices could be due to the introduction of new products or greater brand awareness or improvements in quality or greater market power over customers.

- Lower costs could be due to new machinery or improvements in efficiency or economies of scale or a more motivated workforce or fewer quality problems.

Test your understanding 1

The Return on Capital Employed (ROCE) for DF has increased from 12.3% to 17.8% in the year to 31 March 20X5.

Which one of the following independent options would be a valid reason for this increase?

Significant investment in property, plant and equipment shortly before the year end.	
Revaluation of land and buildings following a change of policy from cost model to revaluation model.	
Property, plant and equipment acquired in the previous period now operating at full capacity.	
An issue of equity shares with the proceeds being used to repay long-term borrowings.	

 Test your understanding 2

The following information is available for 2 potential acquisition targets that are situated in the same country and operate in the same industry.

	A	B
Revenue	£375m	£380m
Gross profit margin	28%	19%
Profit for the year/revenue margin	11%	11%

Which one of the following statements is NOT a valid conclusion that could be drawn from comparing the above information?

A's gross profit margin is better than B's as it is able to benefit from economies of scale.	
The difference between the gross profit margin of A and B may be due to how they classify their expenses between cost of sales and operating costs.	
A may have improved their gross profit margin by significant investment in new and efficient machinery, but could be suffering from high finance costs as a result of financing the investment with long-term borrowings.	
B may be selling a significantly higher volume of products than A, but at a lower price.	

KAPLAN PUBLISHING

Test your understanding 3

ABC is a small private entity looking for investment. It has been trading for more than 10 years manufacturing and selling its own branded perfumes, lotions and candles to the public in its 15 retail stores and to other larger retailing entities. Revenue and profits have been steady over the last 10 years. However, about 15 months ago ABC set up an online shop and also secured a lucrative deal with a boutique hotel chain to supply products carrying the hotel name and logo.

Extracts from the statement of profit or loss of ABC are provided below:

	20X2	20X1
	£000	£000
Revenue	6,000	3,700
Gross profit	1,917	1,095
Profit before tax	540	307

The revenue and profits of the three business segments for the year ended 31 December 20X2 were:

	Retail operations	Online store	Hotel contract
	£000	£000	£000
Revenue	4,004	1,096	900
Gross profit	1,200	330	387
Profit before tax	320	138	82

The online store and hotel contract earned a negligible amount of revenue and profit in the year ended 31 December 20X1.

Which THREE of the following statements could be realistically concluded from the extracts provided above?

The revenue growth is principally due to the online store and hotel contract.	
The gross profit margin would have fallen in 20X2 if the new operations had not been introduced.	
The online store should have a better gross profit margin than retail operations as it does not have the shop overheads.	
The hotel contract attracts a higher gross profit margin than the other operations.	
The hotel contract appears to require significant overheads in comparison to revenue when compared with other segments.	
The increase in profit before tax margin is principally due to the hotel contract.	

Test your understanding 4

LW, a listed entity, operates in the manufacturing sector. LW operates in a mature market and has not experienced growth in volume for the past five years. It is currently considering ways that it can increase revenue by diversifying its product range but has yet to implement any new strategy.

The following ratios have been calculated based on LW's most recent financial statements for the year ended 31 December 20X3.

	20X3	20X2
Gross profit margin	39.4%	36.6%
Operating profit margin	12.6%	14.4%
Quick ratio	0.5	1.1
Inventories holding period	141 days	112 days
Payables payment period	154 days	98 days

LW was involved in a major dispute with one of its key customers in 20X3 regarding the non-settlement of amounts owed by the customer. The dispute was eventually settled close to the reporting date and the majority of the cash has since been received, however LW incurred significant legal fees in the process and had to stop supplying the customer for a period of time.

Which THREE of the following statements could be realistically concluded from the extracts provided above?

Stopping supplies to the significant customer will have contributed to the increase in inventory holding period.	
The impact of the cost of the dispute can be seen in the operating profit margin, which has fallen despite an increase in gross profit margin for the year.	
The increase in gross profit margin is likely to have been achieved by increasing selling prices.	
The increase in payables payment period will have resulted in a reduction in cash and cash equivalents.	
The reduction in quick ratio is principally due to the significant increase in inventory holding period.	
The reduction in quick ratio is principally due to the significant increase in payables payment period.	

KAPLAN PUBLISHING

6 The link between ratios and internal controls

An important aspect of this module is the link between a ratio change (often a deterioration) and the business's internal control system.

Ideally you can follow the line of possible cause and effect from both directions.

From control issue to ratios

Suppose there is an error in the annual inventory stock-take that results in closing inventory being **undervalued** – which ratios could be affected?

- If closing inventory is undervalued, then cost of sales will be overstated and gross profit understated.

- An obvious result is that ratios involving profit will be affected:

    - Gross profit margin will be lower

    - Return on Capital Employed (ROCE) will most likely be lower (note: the impact on ROCE is not clear cut as profit will be lower, but so will capital employed)

- There will also be an impact on working capital ratios

    - The current ratio will be lower (note that the quick ratio does not contain inventory so will be unaffected)

    - Inventory days will be lower as we have lower inventory and higher cost of sales.

Alternatively, suppose a cut-off error at the end of an accounting period means that a sales invoice has been recognised for the period when it should be deferred to the next period.

- The error means that both sales (and hence, profit) and receivables are overstated.

- Profitability ratios will improve

    - Gross profit margin will be higher

    - Return on Capital Employed will be higher.

    - Liquidity ratios will be larger

    - Both current and quick ratios will get larger

    - Receivables days (and the length of the operating cycle) will be longer.

Test your understanding 5

It has been discovered that a dishonest credit controller has been writing off debts owed to their employer by their friends.

Identify the impact of the fraud on the following ratios

	Higher	Lower	No change
Gross profit margin			
Payables days			
Quick ratio			

From ratio to potential causes

If, for example, the receivable days ratio has worsened from one year to the next then this might be tracked back to poor control over the collection of cash from receivables. It would then be possible to suggest improvements to rectify the situation.

 Test your understanding 6

The quick ratio has declined from last year to this. During the year-end audit a number of errors were detected.

Identify which of the following errors would have contributed to the quick ratio being lower.

Year-end inventory over-valued during the inventory stock take	
A sales invoice was posted twice to the sales day book	
A purchase of a non-current asset was mistakenly posted to purchases	
A purchase invoice received after the year end had been posted to this year by mistake	

7 Additional Test your understanding questions

 Test your understanding 7

Data

Magnus Carter has recently inherited a majority shareholding in a company, Baron Ltd. The company supplies camping equipment to retail outlets. Magnus wishes to get involved in the management of the business, but until now NL has only worked in not-for-profit organisations.

Magnus would like to understand how the company has performed over the past two years and how efficient it is in using its resources. Magnus has asked you to help him to interpret the financial statements of the company which are set out below.

Baron Ltd – Summary statement of profit or loss for the year ended 31 March		
	20X1	**20X0**
	£000	£000
Revenue	1,852	1,691
Cost of sales	(648)	(575)
Gross profit	1,204	1,116
Expenses	(685)	(524)
Profit from operations	519	592
Tax	(125)	(147)
Profit for the period	394	445

Baron Ltd – Summary statement of financial positions as at 31 March		
	20X1	**20X0**
Assets	£000	£000
Non-current assets	1,431	1,393
Current assets		
Inventories	217	159
Trade receivables	319	236
Cash	36	147
Total assets	2,003	1,935
Equity and liabilities		
Equity		
Share capital	500	500
Retained earnings	1,330	1,261
	1,830	1,761
Current liabilities		
Trade payables	48	44
Taxation	125	130
	173	174
Total equity and liabilities	2,003	1,935

Task

Prepare a report for Magnus Carter that includes:

(a) A calculation of the following ratios for the two years:

(i) gross profit percentage

(ii) operating profit percentage

(iii) receivable collection period in days

(iv) payables payment period in days (based on cost of sales)

(v) inventory holding period in days (based on cost of sales).

(b) For each ratio calculated:

  (i) a brief explanation in general terms of the meaning of the ratio

  (ii) comments on how the performance or efficiency in the use of resources has changed over the two years.

(c) Outline three areas where the ratios might indicate potential for control weakness.

 Test your understanding 8

Data

Jonathan Fisher is intending to invest a substantial sum of money in a company. A colleague has suggested an investment to Jonathan in a private company called Carp Ltd which supplies pond equipment to retail outlets. You have been asked to assist Jonathan in interpreting the financial statements of the company which are set out below.

Carp Ltd – Summary statement of profit or loss for the year ended 30 September 20X9		
	20X9	**20X8**
	£000	£000
Revenue	3,183	2,756
Cost of sales	(1,337)	(1,020)
Gross profit	1,846	1,736
Expenses	(1,178)	(1,047)
Profit from operations	668	689
Finance costs	(225)	(92)
Profit before tax	443	597
Taxation	(87)	(126)
Profit for the period	356	471

Carp Ltd – Summary statement of financial positions at 30 September

	20X9 £000	20X8 £000
Assets		
Non-current assets	4,214	2,030
Current assets		
Inventories	795	689
Trade receivables	531	459
Cash	15	136
Total assets	5,555	3,314
Equity and liabilities		
Equity		
Share capital	700	500
Retained earnings	1,517	1,203
Total equity	2,217	1,703
Non-current liabilities		
Long term loan	2,500	1,000
Current liabilities		
Trade payables	751	485
Taxation	87	126
Total liabilities	3,338	1,611
Total equity and liabilities	5,555	3,314

Task

(a) Calculate the following ratios for the two years:

    (i)   gearing

    (ii)   operating profit percentage

    (iii) current ratio

(b) Using the ratios calculated, comment on the company's profitability, liquidity and financial position and consider how these have changed over the two years.

(c) Identify and explain two areas where the ratios might indicate poor internal controls.

8 Summary

By comparing the ratios of different companies, or of one company year-on-year, users of the financial statements will develop a more thorough understanding of a particular company and will therefore be able to make better decisions.

In this chapter we have covered profitability and liquidity ratios, together with gearing.

We have also considered the important link between deterioration in performance indicators and weak internal control.

Test your understanding answers

Test your understanding 1

Significant investment in property, plant and equipment shortly before the year end.	
Revaluation of land and buildings following a change of policy from cost model to revaluation model.	
Property, plant and equipment acquired in the previous period now operating at full capacity.	✓
An issue of equity shares with the proceeds being used to repay long-term borrowings.	

Notes

Statement 1 is incorrect.

A significant investment in PPE shortly before the year end would result in a large increase in capital employed with little effect in profit.

Statement 2 is incorrect.

A revaluation of land and buildings will increase capital employed (revaluation reserve is part of equity) but will have no positive effect on profit.

Statement 3 is correct.

The impact on capital employed would be in the previous period and therefore in the current year's ratio the improvement in profitability would be reflected.

Statement 4 is incorrect.

An issue of shares to repay long-term borrowings would have no effect on capital employed (as both equity and debt are included in the calculation). There would be a saving in finance costs, however the profit used in the ROCE calculation does not include finance costs and therefore the ratio would not be affected.

Test your understanding 2

A's gross profit margin is better than B's as it is able to benefit from economies of scale.	✓
The difference between the gross profit margin of A and B may be due to how they classify their expenses between cost of sales and operating costs.	
A may have improved their gross profit margin by significant investment in new and efficient machinery, but could be suffering from high finance costs as a result of financing the investment with long-term borrowings.	
B may be selling a significantly higher volume of products than A, but at a lower price.	

Notes

A's revenue is similar, and slightly lower, than B's so economies of scale is not a valid explanation of the difference in gross profit margins.

Test your understanding 3

The revenue growth is principally due to the online store and hotel contract.	✓
The gross profit margin would have fallen in 20X2 if the new operations had not been introduced.	
The online store should have a better gross profit margin than retail operations as it does not have the shop overheads.	
The hotel contract attracts a higher gross profit margin than the other operations.	✓
The hotel contract appears to require significant overheads in comparison to revenue when compared with other segments.	✓
The increase in profit before tax margin is principally due to the hotel contract.	

Notes

Statement 2 is incorrect.

The gross profit margin for retail operations in 20X2 is 30.0% (£1,200/£4,004) compared with 29.6% (£1,095/£3,700) last year.

Statement 3 is incorrect.

The shop overheads would affect operating profit and profit before tax margins, but not the gross profit margin.

Statement 6 is incorrect.

The online store has a higher profit before tax margin (£138/£1,096 = 12.6%) than the hotel contract (£82/£900 = 9.1%).

Test your understanding 4

Stopping supplies to the significant customer will have contributed to the increase in inventory holding period.	✓
The impact of the cost of the dispute can be seen in the operating profit margin, which has fallen despite an increase in gross profit margin for the year.	✓
The increase in gross profit margin is likely to have been achieved by increasing selling prices.	
The increase in payables payment period will have resulted in a reduction in cash and cash equivalents.	
The reduction in quick ratio is principally due to the significant increase in inventory holding period.	
The reduction in quick ratio is principally due to the significant increase in payables payment period.	✓

Notes

LW are unlikely to have increased selling prices when there has been no growth in sales volume for the past five years, therefore statement 3 is not a realistic conclusion.

An increase in payables payment period would improve rather than worsen the cash position therefore statement 4 is not a realistic conclusion.

The quick ratio does not include inventory and therefore statement 5 is not a realistic conclusion.

Test your understanding 5

	Higher	Lower	No change
Gross profit margin			✓
Payables days			✓
Quick ratio		✓	

Writing off debts unnecessarily means that both receivables and profit are too low. However, the irrecoverable debt expense account normally gets accounted for as part of administration or operating expenses, below the gross profit line. Payables days will be unaffected.

Test your understanding 6

Year-end inventory over-valued during the inventory stock take	
A sales invoice was posted twice to the sales day book	
A purchase of a non-current asset was mistakenly posted to purchases	
A purchase invoice received after the year end had been posted to this year by mistake	✓

The first and third errors would not have affected the quick ratio and the second would have made it higher.

Test your understanding 7

REPORT

To: Magnus Carter

From: A Student

Subject: Interpretation of financial statements

Date: 23 June 20X1

This report has been prepared to support the interpretation of the financial statements of Baron Ltd and to compare and contrast the company performance over the two year period.

(a) **Calculation of the ratios**

		20X1		20X0
Gross profit percentage	$\dfrac{1{,}204}{1{,}852}$	= 65%	$\dfrac{1{,}116}{1{,}691}$	= 66%
Operating profit percentage	$\dfrac{519}{1{,}852}$	= 28%	$\dfrac{592}{1{,}691}$	= 35%
Receivables collection period	$\dfrac{319}{1{,}852} \times 365$	= 63 days	$\dfrac{236}{1{,}691} \times 365$	= 51 days
Payables payment period	$\dfrac{48}{648} \times 365$	= 27 days	$\dfrac{44}{575} \times 365$	= 28 days
Inventory holding period	$\dfrac{217}{648} \times 365$	= 122 days	$\dfrac{159}{575} \times 365$	= 101 days

(b) **Explanation and comment**

- Gross profit percentage

  This measure of profitability shows the percentage of gross profit in relation to revenue, it is often termed the gross margin.

  The ratio has remained fairly constant over the two year period with only a marginal decrease from 66% to 65%. It is expressed as:

  $$\frac{\text{Gross profit}}{\text{Revenues}} \times 100\%$$

  The company has achieved a greater volume of business without having to significantly reduce its margins.

- Operating profit percentage

  This measure of profitability shows the percentage of operating profit in relation to revenue. It is influenced by the gross margin and the level of other costs in relation to revenue. There has been a significant fall in the net return over the period. The gross margin has only fallen marginally, however the expenses in relation to revenue have increased from 31% to 37% over the period and this has had an adverse effect on the performance.

  This indicates that the company is generating less operating profit per '£' of revenue than previously achieved.

- Receivables collection period

  This is a measure of management control as it relates to the effectiveness of the credit control policy.

  The ratio shows the average number of days it takes to collect debts. It is expressed as:

  $$\frac{\text{Receivables}}{\text{Revenues}} \times 365 \text{ days}$$

  The collection period has increased over the two years and it is taking 12 days longer to collect debts than previously. This may be due to either customer cash flow problems or poor and less effective credit control.

- Payables payment period

  This ratio shows the average days it takes for the company to pay its suppliers. This period has remained similar over the two years. It indicates that the company can meet its demands from trade payables on a timely and regular basis.

- Inventory holding period

  The inventory holding period, representing the period of time for which inventory is held before being sold, has risen by 21 days. This increase has been driven by a 36% uplift in inventory from £159,000 to £217,000, with only a 10% increase in revenue.

  The increase in holding period would appear to be due to poor inventory management, but may reflect a deliberate increase in inventory levels by management to cope with anticipated continued sales growth. It is important that inventory levels are monitored closely.

(c) **Control issues**

Gross profit

Gross profit has declined slightly from 66% to 65%. This could have many causes of course but it is possible that there is a control issue surrounding sales pricing. A reducing GP% could be due to reducing prices perhaps due to increased competitive pressure or increased discounts being given by sales people.

It is possible, therefore, that discount levels are not being properly authorised or controlled by the sales manager.

Receivable days

Receivable days are considerably up on the previous year. This could easily be linked to poor control.

Specifically, it is possible that existing credit terms are not being properly enforced and procedures that are normally used to collect debts (warning letters for example) are not being followed.

It is also possible that the vetting of new customers is not taking place, allowing less creditworthy customers to take excessive amounts of credit.

Inventory days

Inventory days are also up considerably. Purchase authorisation procedures may not be being followed allowing unnecessary or excessive quantities of inventory to be bought.

Test your understanding 8

Notes to Jonathan Fisher

(a) **Calculation of ratios**

The following ratios for the company have been computed:

		20X9		20X8	
(i)	Gearing	$\frac{2,500}{4,717}$	× 100 = 53%	$\frac{1,000}{2,703}$	× 100 = 37%
(ii)	Operating profit percentage	$\frac{668}{3,183}$	× 100 = 21%	$\frac{689}{2,756}$	× 100 = 25%
(iii)	Current ratio	$\frac{1,341}{838}$	= 1.6:1	$\frac{1,284}{611}$	= 2.1:1

(b) **Gearing ratio:** This measure represents the company's reliance on debt in relation to total equity. Although equity has increased between the two years, the gearing has increased due to the significant increase in long term loans. The company is now a 'highly geared' organisation, meaning that there is a greater reliance on borrowed funds in the second year. This increases shareholder risk as when profits reduce, interest payments must still be met.

Operating profit percentage: The operating margin has fallen over the period, showing the business to be less profitable. This reduction in profitability will be due to either lower gross margins or lack of control over expenses.

Revenue has increased by 15.5%, and operating expenses have only increased by 12.5%, suggesting that operating expenses are under control. The lack of profitability must therefore be due to lower gross margin. We could confirm this by calculating the gross profit margin, and see that this margin has reduced from 63% to 58%.

Lower gross margins could be due to lower sale prices, perhaps as a deliberate policy to increase sales or as a reaction to competition. Alternatively there may have been increases in costs, maybe due to new suppliers.

Current ratio: There has been a reduction in this measure of liquidity over the period, and when we analyse the components of the calculation we can see the reason.

Inventory and receivables have both increased, which would cause the current ratio to rise if it were not for the significant increase in trade payables of 55%. This increase could be caused by a policy decision to delay payments (which would need to have been pre-agreed), or possibly a backlog due to processing problems. The increased levels of payables at the year end may also be due to one-off asset purchases.

The decrease in cash levels will also have had a negative impact on the current ratio, but to a lesser degree.

(c) The operating profit percentage is down significantly on the previous year. Although this can have many causes, one possibility is poor control over expenses. Invoices may not be properly checked against orders or not authorised.

Gearing has increased significantly and this may well have been deliberate. However, management controls are common in this area. Raising debt finance should have been properly discussed and authorised at board level. This may well have been the case, but it is also possible that the FD acted independently.

Changes to the accounting system

Introduction

This chapter will cover all of the areas within an organisation that you might investigate when looking for ways to improve the effectiveness of an accounting system.

We have already made recommendations to deal with control weaknesses in Chapter 3. Here we address the change process in more detail.

There are three main issues in the syllabus:

1   What changes are needed and why

2   What are the implications of a change

3   What might be the effect on users of a change.

New methods might involve a new department structure, changes in planning and internal control systems, recommending computerisation of some activities, changing the equipment or changing the methods of working and documentation used.

PERFORMANCE CRITERIA	CONTENTS
5.1 Changes to the accounting system	1 Identifying changes
5.2 Cost and benefit of changes to the accounting system	2 General reasons for change
5.3 The effects of changes on the users of the system	3 Cost benefit analysis and cost control
	4 Implementing changes – dealing with resistance
	5 Implementing changes – approaches
	6 Training

1 Identifying changes

1.1 Methods for identifying the need for change

In order to identify the need for change, we should start by recording and reviewing the existing system.

A useful tool for this process is a flow of information diagram. The diagram below is an overview of an accounts department and the typical information flows involved:

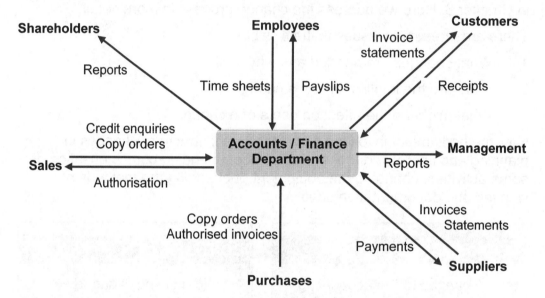

This can then be reviewed for potential change issues.

Another analysis tool is a review of the office procedures manual. Any changes implemented should then be used to update this manual.

Standard procedures are useful for organisations:

- they prescribe the most efficient way of getting a job done.

- there is no need to exercise judgement when conducting routine tasks.

- staff find jobs easier when they are familiar with established procedures.

- prescribed procedures ensure that certain types of task will be performed consistently throughout the organisation.

- the work will be performed consistently even when a new person joins or takes over from the previous holder.

- a written record can be maintained so that people can learn quickly and easily by referring to it.

- procedures reduce the likelihood of departmental friction because they should avoid disputes between departments about responsibilities.

- they can be reviewed for weaknesses and areas for improvement.

 Test your understanding 1

X Ltd is a small retailer that has seen considerable growth. Having suffered various problems with the purchasing function, the Chief Accountant has decided to introduce new internal controls.

Which TWO of the following controls in a purchase cycle could be implemented to reduce the risk of payment of goods not received?

Sequentially pre-numbered purchase requisitions and sequence check.	
Matching of goods received note with purchase invoice.	
Goods are inspected for condition and quantity and agreed to purchase order before acceptance.	
Daily update of inventory system.	

Which TWO of the following controls in the purchase cycle could be implemented to reduce the risk of procurement of unnecessary goods and services?

Centralised purchasing department.	
Sequentially pre-numbered purchase requisitions and sequence check.	
Orders can only be placed with suppliers from the approved suppliers list.	
All purchase requisitions are signed as authorised by an appropriate manager.	

2 General reasons for change

2.1 General reasons for change

There are many reasons for an accounting system to have to change:

Reason for change	Example
Regulation: Standards and regulations often change – the accounting system must be compliant with the latest rules.	If the VAT rules change, rendering a new product VAT exempt, then the accounting system would need to ensure that any invoice raised for it would not add VAT. This may require changes to computer software and staff training.
Growth: Some systems work well on the existing volume of transactions. However, if the business grows then the existing system can become cumbersome or unworkable.	A system where each sales invoice is independently reviewed by a supervisor will become too time-consuming if the volume of sales significantly increases.
New information flow: The diagram in section 1.1 above shows typical information flows. If another flow emerges then the accounting system would need to reflect it.	Many companies are now choosing to report on sustainability and environmental issues. This will require the retention and reporting of a whole range of additional information flows such as CO_2 emissions.
Resources: All systems require resources such as people and machines. Short-term capacity issues can result in a need to change the accounting system.	A PC failure might mean that in the short term a different system might be necessary to record transactions.

Reason for change	Example
Identified weakness: Past errors can reveal weaknesses in the accounting systems (see Chapter 3). It is the duty of the directors to maintain effective control by addressing weaknesses by changing and improving the accounting system.	A sales invoice might have contained a pricing error. As a result management decide to introduce an authorisation requirement for all sales invoices. This changes both the information recorder (the authorisation) and the document flow (documents must now be reviewed by management before issuing to customers).
Changes in the environment The business environment influences the design and structure of the accounting system. A **PESTLE** model could be used as a checklist – this considers political, economic, social, technological, legal and environmental drivers of change.	Increasingly consumers consider the environmental impact of an organisation as important. As a result, a company may choose to address this by reporting on environmental issues (as mentioned above) requiring additional data to be recorded.
New products: If a business introduced a new product this would require the creation of new general ledger accounts and a change to the allocation of overheads.	A car manufacturer introduces a new model. All costs and revenues for this new model need to be correctly allocated.

Understanding the need for change provides the **justification** for that change.

3 Cost-benefit analysis and cost control

3.1 Financial evaluation of information systems change projects

Changes to an accounting system should be 'cost-beneficial'. This means that the benefits of the changes outweigh their expected costs.

Cost-benefit analysis focuses on the balance between expected costs and benefits. Although non-financial benefits can be considered, costs and benefits are usually assessed in purely financial terms.

3.2 Costs of information system changes

Tangible costs associated with developing and running information systems can be classified into one-off costs (e.g. development, buying new equipment) and ongoing costs (e.g. maintenance, consumables). Tangible costs are easy to quantify and can be related directly to development and operation of a system.

However, information systems often incur intangible costs that are much harder to quantify or to relate back to specific systems. Examples of intangible costs include:

- staff dissatisfaction if systems are poorly specified or implemented

- the cost of increased staff mistakes and reduced performance during the learning period after a new system is implemented

- opportunity costs: whenever money is invested in one area of the company, the opportunity to invest in another area is foregone

- lock-in costs: purchasing a particular solution can bind a company to a particular supplier, reducing its ability to take advantage of future developments from other providers.

KAPLAN PUBLISHING

3.3 Benefits of information system changes

Benefits can also be classified into tangible and intangible benefits. Examples of these benefits are given below:

Tangible benefits:

- savings in staff salaries, maintenance costs and consumables
- greater efficiency: a new system should process data more efficiently and reduce response times
- benefits gained through improved management information, e.g. reduced inventory levels due to improved inventory control
- gaining competitive advantage: a fully integrated ordering and delivery system could reduce costs, generating the ability to price competitively.

Intangible benefits:

- better informed and/or quicker decision-making
- improved customer service, resulting in increased customer satisfaction
- automation of routine activities resulting in more time for strategic planning and innovation
- better understanding of customer needs through improved analysis of data.

Test your understanding 2

CHO Limited is considering converting its sales system from a manual system to a simple on-line computer system. This has been prompted by a growth in the number of transactions to be processed each month.

Which one of the following is a probable result associated with conversion to the computer system that can be incorporated into a cost-benefit analysis?

Increased number of processing errors	
Fraud risk is reduced	
Processing time is increased	
Less segregation of duty	

3.4 Cost-benefit analysis

Once information on project costs and benefits is available it becomes possible to carry out a cost-benefit analysis. Results should be interpreted with care, as analysis is based on estimates of future cash flows, and on assumptions regarding likely costs and benefits. Two possible methods of performing such an analysis should be familiar to you from previous studies: payback, and net present value.

3.5 Payback

Payback calculates the time taken for project cash inflows to equal project cash outflows. The decision rule is to accept the project with the shortest payback. Whilst projects that pay back quickly may be inherently less risky, the overall return on a project is not considered, as cash flows occurring after payback are ignored.

Payback is often used as an initial project filtering tool, to exclude projects that pay back too slowly to be acceptable. The remaining projects are then appraised using more sophisticated tools.

Payback example

	Project 1	Project 2
	£	£
Cost	(100,000)	(100,000)
Net savings in year		
1	50,000	30,000
2	50,000	38,000
3	25,000	45,000
4	0	37,000
5	0	29,000

Project 1 has recovered its cost by the end of year two.

Project 2, however, does not recover its cost until towards the end of year 3.

Using payback, Project 1 would be selected, even though total return is greater for Project 2.

3.6 Net present value (NPV)

This method calculates the net present value of all the project cash flows. If NPV is equal to, or greater than, zero the project should be considered, as its return is at least equal to the discount rate used.

To perform an NPV calculation we do the following:

Step 1: Identify future incremental cash flows.

Step 2: Discount the cash flows so they are in today's terms (present values).

Step 3: The present values are then added up and netted off to give a net present value or NPV.

Step 4: If the NPV is positive, then it means that the cash inflows are worth more than the outflows and the project should be accepted.

Example

(using cash flows from project 2 above, and a 10% discount rate):

Time	Cash flow £000	Discount factor @ 10%	Present Value £000
t = 0	(100)	1	(100.0)
t = 1	30	0.909	27.3
t = 2	38	0.826	31.4
t = 3	45	0.751	33.8
t = 4	37	0.683	25.3
t = 5	29	0.621	18.0
	Net Present Value		35.8

3.7 Cost estimation

Some costs might be difficult to calculate and some estimation will be needed.

Cost estimation invariably involves some judgement. For example, an estimation of labour time relies on the individuals in each section to give an opinion as to the time it would take to do a job. Depending on the individuals, these estimates may be understated or overstated and the lack of consistency can cause problems.

The accuracy of estimates can be improved by:

• learning from previous mistakes

• having sufficient design information

• obtaining a detailed specification, and

• breaking the project down into smaller jobs, detailing each constituent part.

There are different classifications to measure the accuracy of cost estimates:

• **definitive estimates** aim to be accurate to within 5% and are produced after the design work is done.

• **feasibility estimates** are accurate to within 10%. These are made in the early design stage.

• **comparative estimates** are made when the project under review is similar to a previous one. The accuracy of this estimate depends on the similarity and the prevailing economic conditions.

• **ball-park estimates** are a rough guide to the project costs and are often made before a project starts. They may be accurate to within 25%.

3.8 The supervisor's contribution to cost control

When a supervisor is controlling costs, staff will be more efficient and properly supervised, and working procedures will be carried out as they should. Good supervision ensures that costs are kept under control.

As a supervisor your role in cost control derives from your responsibility for resources – people or machines for example. You are in charge of activities that incur costs and therefore have a cost responsibility. You have the job of controlling costs within specified parameters or against clear cost standards. You may even be charged with reducing or eliminating costs. This is true of all systems including the accounting system. Accounting departments can easily become overstaffed or inefficient.

The typical costs in an accounts department include payroll, the costs of equipment and software, stationery and other overheads.

However, you will only be able to control costs if you are given realistic standards to work to and reliable information about performance, especially about any variance or deviation that occurs. The standards should be derived from a thorough analysis of the job, the methods used and the efficiency of performance.

KAPLAN PUBLISHING

3.9 Cost reduction

Cost reduction means reducing the current or planned unit cost of goods or services without impairing their suitability for the use intended. As far as an accounting system is concerned cost reduction will mean a lower cost per transaction or report. The main areas that will be considered will be reducing staff levels, reducing expenditure on new equipment, changing operations to make them cheaper and using cheaper suppliers.

3.10 SWOT analysis

Another method of assessing a new system is to carry out a SWOT analysis.

This is a structured approach which considers:

Strengths: Does the new system add to the strengths of the business and its reporting? For example will the new system produce better or quicker information?

Weaknesses: Will the new system reduce the existing weaknesses in the business? For example if could be that the existing system was prone to invoicing errors or costing inconsistencies and the new system might reduce those errors.

Opportunities: The new system may have external implications giving the business opportunities to succeed. For example the new system may mean that tender pricing is more reliable or accurate, leading to more successful tenders.

Threats: New systems can be temperamental. Breakdowns can be costly and give competitors an edge.

3.11 PESTLE analysis

PESTLE is an acronym used to help organise the analysis of the business environment into broad categories. PESTLE analysis divides the business drivers into political, economic, social (and cultural), technical, legal and ecological/environmental factors. You will sometimes see PEST analysis which just looks at the first four factors, and you may see PESTLE referred to as PESTEL.

Analysing these factors can help organisations understand the opportunities and threats within their environment and this understanding is crucial in shaping the organisation's current and future strategic decisions. Examples are shown in the table below:

PESTLE factor	Explanation
Political	Political influences and events – legislation, government policies, changes to competition policy or import duties, etc.
Economic	These will vary according to the type of business. A multinational company will be concerned about the international situation, while an organisation trading exclusively in one country might be more concerned with the level and timing of domestic development. Items of information might include changes in the gross domestic product, changes in consumers' income and expenditure, and population growth.
Social	Social influences include social, cultural or demographic factors (e.g. population shifts, age profiles, etc.) and refers to attitudes, value and beliefs held by people, as well as changes in lifestyles, education and health and so on.
Technological	This is an area in which change takes place very rapidly and the organisation needs to be constantly aware of what is going on, for example changes in material supply, processing methods and new product development.
Legal	Laws and regulations governing businesses are widespread. These include laws on health and safety, information disclosure, the dismissal of employees, vehicle emissions, the use of pesticides and many more.
Environmental/ Ecological	These have become increasingly important in recent years and include the impact the organisation has on its external environment in terms of pollution etc.

3.12 Sustainability

It is important when considering changes to the accounting system that recommendations are reviewed against ethical and sustainability principles.

You will have seen in your previous studies that sustainability is about meeting the needs of the present without compromising the ability of future generations to meet their own needs.

It is the practice of doing business in a way that balances social, environmental and corporate needs, and as such is often referred to as 'The Three Ps' – People, Planet, Profit.

Corporate social responsibility (CSR) is a business approach that contributes to sustainable development by delivering economic, social and environmental benefits for all stakeholders.

As a result many companies now consider how their operations affect the environment and future generations. This will also apply to any changes to the systems within those operations.

Ways in which this may be manifested include:

- introduction of a paper recycling policy within an office building

- adoption of 'paperless' office procedures

- reduction of business-related travel, perhaps by use of 'virtual' meetings

- introduction of schemes to encourage employees to use public transport, cycle or even walk to work – such as a 'bike to work' scheme where the company provides a bicycle to the employee at low cost and provides space to keep it at work during the day

- introduction of energy saving schemes – turning off lights and heating when not required

This list is clearly not exhaustive and you may well be able to think of other ways in which companies can operate more sustainably.

There may be initial sustainability costs when implementing CSR policies. This may explain why some organisations choose not to adopt CSR policies.

However, over time, as the values of society have changed, many organisations recognise that they can reap economic benefits by following a sustainable path. This includes the recognition, by customers and potential customers, of the ethical stance being taken, now acknowledged by many to be a key driver to increase sales and business activity over time.

For instance, when changing accounting systems an organisation may decide to select the most environmentally friendly options, e.g. shared energy-efficient printers, maximising the use of recycled materials, etc. There will probably be an additional cost to the organisation in selecting these options, potentially paying more for being environmentally-friendly. However, this should be offset by the positive effect their actions will have on the environment, and the resulting improved image projected to their customers and potential customers, who may well switch from a competitor.

4 Implementing changes – dealing with resistance

4.1 Introduction

The existing system will be embedded and so the introduction of any new system may be disruptive. Change is time-consuming and some delay is almost inevitable. This can be minimised through proper planning.

4.2 Identifying resistance to proposed changes

Resistance is 'any attitude or behaviour that reflects a person's unwillingness to make or support a desired change'.

Resistance to change is an action taken by individuals and groups when they perceive that a change is a threat to them.

Resistance may take many forms, including active or passive, overt or covert, individual or organised, aggressive or timid. For each source of resistance, management need to provide an appropriate response (see later). Resistance can be classified into three general categories:

Job factors

These generally revolve around fear – fear of new technology, fear of change or fear of demotion or reduction in pay.

Social factors

The people affected may dislike the potential new social dynamic (or like the existing social dynamic).

Equally there could be a dislike of the person driving the change.

Another factor is that people prefer to be consulted about change, so a lack of consultation is likely to make them disinclined to support any proposal.

Personal factors

These, by definition, are more varied as each person may react differently to a particular change.

There could be an individual that feels undervalued as a result of the change or may refuse to relocate due to personal circumstances.

4.3 Dealing with resistance to change

Various factors might cause resistance to a change of accounting (or other) systems. It is important to respond to these threats to ensure a successful changeover.

Source of resistance	Possible responses
• the need for security and the familiar	• provide information and encouragement, invite involvement
• having the opinion that no change is needed	• clarify the purpose of the change and how it will be made
• trying to protect vested interests	• demonstrate the problem or the opportunity that makes changes desirable
• dislike the social upheaval.	• organise social team building events.

4.4 Increase the forces for change

Lewin identified that in most situations there will be some forces for change. Stronger forces will make it more difficult to resist the change.

Drivers for change were covered at the start of this chapter.

To increase the force for change, various tactics can be used:

- allow participation in the decisions surrounding the change. Staff will be much more accepting if they have been involved in the change decisions.

- educate and communicate the reason for the change. Staff are much more likely to accept change if they understand the reasons for it.

- negotiate with the staff. The new system might involve more work for the staff. It is sometimes justifiable to consider rewarding staff in some way in order to achieve the objective.

- remove the support infrastructure for the old system, making it impossible to use.

- adopt a zero tolerance policy regarding the use of the old system.

4.5 Change agents

Many organisations employ 'change agents' to encourage and facilitate change. They can play a major role in helping deal with resistance to change.

Usually change agents are figures who are familiar and non-threatening to other people.

The quality of the relationship between the change agent and key decision makers is very important, so the choice of change agent is critical.

 Test your understanding 3

M publishes several major magazines in Country A. M's best-selling title is a fashion magazine – Mean – although it also produces magazines on other topics, such as sport and technology.

The majority of M's shares are held by members of the founding Alves family, who have traditionally occupied all of the senior management positions, although most key decisions are made in consultation with the staff.

M currently employs around 2,500 staff in one large office building in Country A's capital city.

The Alves family has always been concerned with maintaining the family name and have focused on the quality of the magazines. Unfortunately, in recent years this has not prevented a significant reduction in M's profitability leading to M's first ever loss being recorded in the most recent financial year.

This has led M to hire a Finance Director, Francesca Dybala, who is not a member of the owning family for the first time in its history. After a careful review she has discovered a large amount of unnecessary expenditure.

Francesca has proposed centralising a number of key functions, such as accounting, printing and proof-reading which are currently duplicated in each magazine. This will lead to around 300 job losses.

In addition Francesca has suggested that the magazines should be produced using cheaper paper and inks, that the large expense accounts offered to senior managers should be cut and that M should start making use of intranets and groupware to allow staff to share ideas quickly and easily.

Francesca's proposals have been met with significant resistance from M's employees, as well as a number of members of the owning family. She is unsure as to why this is the case and has asked for your help.

Task

Write an email to Francesca discussing the reasons that her proposals are likely to have met with resistance.

5 Implementing changes – approaches

5.1 Introduction

Changes to accounting procedures can be fraught with difficulty. Transactions or records can be lost or duplicated and so it is essential to apply an organised process.

5.2 Testing

There are various forms of testing to be carried out before implementation can begin. This is to ensure that bugs or inefficiencies are removed in advance of implementation.

Testing methods include the following:

- **Realistic data testing** – the new system is tested against normal transactions to ensure it operates as expected.

- **Contrived testing** – the new system is presented with unusual data to see how it reacts e.g. negative sales invoices.

- **Volume testing** – a common problem with systems is that they fail to cope when volumes increase, so this is tested in advance. Systems may crash or slow down excessively.

- **User acceptance testing** – systems are often designed by IT experts but then used by people with limited IT skills. The system may be difficult to use and so it is important to make sure that the users are able to test it before full implementation.

5.3 Changeover method

If new systems are being introduced, then it is critically important that the changeover is managed effectively.

There are four options here, although sometimes only one of these methods will realistically work.

Direct

The old system ceases and the new system starts on the same day. This may be risky if the new system fails, as there will not be the option to rely on the old system.

As mentioned above, in some circumstances this can be the only option.

For example a real-time airline booking system is a system that cannot be run in combination with a second system. It would not make sense to issue two tickets to every passenger.

Parallel

In this system both the old and new systems are operated at the same time. This enables a comparison of results between the systems and so increases confidence in the results from the new system.

However, parallel running will increase the workload as processing is duplicated, and this can cause stress amongst the staff. A valid criticism of this method is that it can be expensive, as more resources are needed.

Pilot

The new system is introduced in a particular location. In this way operational bugs can be identified and removed before wider implementation takes place.

Phased

This is similar to a pilot, but the system is introduced in stages or in one sub-system at a time.

For example an accounting system is made up of different sub-systems (payroll, accounts receivable and so on), so a phased introduction might implement payroll first, followed by the other sub-systems.

Introducing new systems is very disruptive so phasing is sometimes a less stressful approach. Clearly, it takes more time to achieve full implementation and the interaction between old and new sub-systems can be problematic.

📝 Test your understanding 4

Which of the following statements relating to parallel systems changeover is correct?

It is cheaper than the direct changeover method	
It is mainly used for critical systems	
It is less likely to identify errors in the new system than the direct changeover method	
It involves gradual implementation of the new system, one sub-system at a time	

---

6 Training

6.1 Introduction

New systems affect the operating users in many ways. It is important that these users are provided with appropriate levels of support in order for the introduction of the new system to be successful.

6.2 Training

Training is necessary to ensure an adequate supply of staff that are technically and socially competent and capable of career advancement into specialist departments or management positions. It increases the level of individual and organisational competence and helps to close the gap between desired targets and actual levels of work performance (i.e. what should happen versus what is actually happening).

In particular, when an accounting system changes it is vital that accounting staff are given the training they need for the new system.

6.3 Training model

The training model below takes account of all the major steps:

Stage 1 – Identification of training needs: identifying the skills and attributes necessary for the job, the skills and attributes of the job-holder, and the extent of the gap.

Stage 2 – Design, preparation and delivery of training.

Stage 3 – Assessing the trainee's attitude to training (reaction) and whether the training has been learnt (learning). Reaction involves the participant's feelings towards the training content, the trainer and the training methods used. Learning is the extent to which the trainee has actually absorbed the content of the training.

Stage 4 – Assessing whether the lessons learned during training are being used effectively in doing the job. Once training needs have been met, work activities could be rescheduled, for example, to optimise the use and time of the available accounts department personnel.

Stage 5 – Evaluating the effects of the training on the organisation. This is the area in which there is perhaps most confusion, and subsequently little real action in the workplace.

Stage 6 – Reinforcement of positive behaviour. It is important that any positive outcomes are maintained for as long as possible. It is not unusual for changes in behaviour to be temporary, followed by a reversion to previous ways of working.

6.4   Identifying training needs

Job training analysis is the 'process of identifying the purpose of a job and its component parts and specifying what must be learnt in order for there to be effective work performance'.

A training 'gap' or need is any shortfall in terms of employee knowledge, understanding, skill or attitudes compared to what is required by the job or the demands of organisational change.

There are four main methods for determining the training needs of individuals.

(1)   **Performance appraisal** – each employee's work is measured against the performance standards or objectives established for their job. Current performance is assessed in terms of specific and measurable parts of the employee's job and potential performance is also considered.

(2)   **Analysis of job requirements** – uses data concerning jobs and activities e.g. job descriptions, personnel specifications. The skills and knowledge specified in the appropriate job description are examined. Those employees without the necessary skills or knowledge become candidates for training.

(3)   **Organisational analysis** – uses data about the organisation as a whole e.g. its structure, markets, products or services, human resources requirements, etc. The key success factors are identified and analysed into Human Resources (HR) activities.

(4)   **Departments and/or individuals not performing up to standard will require additional training.**

HR surveys use data about individuals e.g. appraisal records, personal training records, test results, etc. Individuals are surveyed to establish any problems they are experiencing in their work and what actions they believe need to be taken to solve them.

6.5   Who gets trained?

This covers the whole spectrum of employees:

- new starters who require induction training
- operatives who require skills training on a new system
- supervisors who require supervisory training.

KAPLAN PUBLISHING

7 Additional 'Test your understanding' questions

 Test your understanding 5

1   In a training business consider one example of a technological factor that could cause a change in the accounting function of the business.

2   A person is upset that a change to the accounting function organisation will mean that they will not be able to sit near to one of their friends. Outline which type of resistance this is and suggest one way of overcoming that resistance.

3   A debit entry was attempted when a credit entry is more normal. Which type of testing is this?

4   Briefly explain what you understand as intangible benefits of a system change.

8 Summary

In this chapter we have considered the need for a change to an accounting system. Systems need constant monitoring to ensure they meet the business need. If a system does change then it is important that you recognise and can respond to the implications of that change.

Test your understanding answers

Test your understanding 1

Which TWO of the following controls in a purchase cycle could be implemented to reduce the risk of payment of goods not received?

Sequentially pre-numbered purchase requisitions and sequence check.	
Matching of goods received note with purchase invoice.	✓
Goods are inspected for condition and quantity and agreed to purchase order before acceptance.	✓
Daily update of inventory system.	

Note:

1 ensures that all purchase requisitions have been recorded allowing checks to be performed to ensure that a purchase order has subsequently been raised. 4 prevents unnecessary goods being ordered.

Which TWO of the following controls in the purchase cycle could be implemented to reduce the risk of procurement of unnecessary goods and services?

Centralised purchasing department.	✓
Sequentially pre-numbered purchase requisitions and sequence check.	
Orders can only be placed with suppliers from the approved suppliers list.	
All purchase requisitions are signed as authorised by an appropriate manager.	✓

Note:

2 ensures that all purchase requisitions have been recorded allowing checks to be performed to ensure that a purchase order has subsequently been raised.

3 gives assurance about the quality of goods and reliability of supply.

Test your understanding 2

Increased number of processing errors.	
Fraud risk is reduced.	
Processing time is increased.	
Less segregation of duty.	✓

If the system is simple there shouldn't be an increased number of processing errors. Processing time is usually faster by a computer.

Fraud risk can be increased when using a computerised system with many transactions viewed by only a few employees.

When computerised tasks are automated fewer staff are usually needed and segregation of duties becomes more difficult.

Test your understanding 3

EMAIL

To: Francesca Dybala, Finance Director

Re: Resistance to change

Job factors

Many employees may be resisting due to concerns about their jobs. For 300 employees, your proposals will mean unemployment, which means they are likely to be strongly resistant to them.

Many other employees will be affected by the plans to centralise key functions. Those members of staff who remain may be forced to take on a heavier workload to cover the roles of employees made redundant. This may also cause resistance.

Senior managers will be unhappy due to the reduction in their expense accounts as this will be perceived as a loss of their status within the business.

In addition, you are proposing increased use of intranets and groupware. Staff may well be unfamiliar with these systems and dislike the idea of having to learn how to use them. They may also have concerns over the impact they will have on their jobs.

Personal factors

The changes you have suggested may well be seen as an implied criticism of the long-standing methods of the business. This may well cause resistance from not only the staff, but also the owners who have been heavily involved in running the business.

Senior managers may feel less valued under the proposals due to the cuts to their expense accounts, leading to further resistance.

The owners of the company have traditionally focused on the quality of the magazines as they feel this reflects on their family name. The proposal to reduce the quality of the paper and ink is therefore likely to be poorly received by them.

Social factors

The family has normally made key decisions within the company in full consultation with the employees. This does not seem to have been the case with your proposals, reducing the likelihood that employees will accept the changes.

You are also new to the role, a position that has previously only been held by a member of the owning family. This may reduce your perceived authority, making it more likely that employees, managers and owners may feel that they do not have to follow your suggestions.

I hope you have found the above useful, please get in touch if you need any more information about this.

Test your understanding 4

It is cheaper than the direct changeover method	
It is mainly used for critical systems	✓
It is less likely to identify errors in the new system than the direct changeover method	
It involves gradual implementation of the new system, one sub-system at a time	

Parallel changeover involves running the new and old system simultaneously. This is more expensive than a direct changeover, but provides assurance that the new system works properly – which is crucial for critical systems. Gradual implementation of sub-systems is part of a phased changeover.

Test your understanding 5

1   On-line booking for courses and programmes are increasingly common and indeed expected in the market. The accounting function will need to be capable of capturing the order and taking payment. Note: many other answers are possible here.

2   This is an example of social factors resistance. Overcoming this is possible by the organisation of social events for the new team where new friendships can be formed.

3   This is an example of contrived testing.

4   An intangible benefit is a benefit that is difficult to quantify. Any of the items below are good examples of intangible benefits.

- More informed or quicker decision-making

- Improved customer service, resulting in increased customer satisfaction.

- Freedom from routine decisions and activities, resulting in more time being available for strategic planning and innovation

- Better understanding of customer needs through improved analysis of data.

Ethics and sustainability

Introduction

The accounting systems and control syllabus includes ethics and sustainability.

At first glance this might not seem significant but, amongst other aspects, honesty of recording of transactions, freedom from bias are integral to the proper functioning of the accounting systems.

PERFORMANCE CRITERIA	
1.1	The accounting function
1.2	Financial information used by stakeholders
2.1	Internal controls
3.1	An organisation's accounting system and its effectiveness
3.3	Operating practice
5.2	Cost and benefit of changes to the accounting system

CONTENTS	
1	Ethical considerations
2	Sustainability

1 Ethical considerations

1.1 Introduction

Business ethics is the application of ethical values to business behaviour.

Whether an action is considered to be right or wrong normally depends on a number of different factors, including:

*   the consequences – does the end justify the means?
*   the motivation behind the action
*   guiding principles – e.g. 'treat others as you would be treated'
*   key values – such as the importance of human rights.

These principles must be applied to the accounting system as well as general business actions.

 Example – Ethical considerations

You discover that a colleague at work has been stealing from the company. What do you do?

Do you report them to management which might lead to their dismissal and the loss of a friend?

Do you keep quiet and risk being punished yourself if your knowledge of the situation later becomes clear?

Do you urge the colleague to confess what they've done?

Does it depend on the size of the theft, e.g. a £1 pad of paper, or a £1,000 piece of machinery?

Does it depend on how friendly you are with the colleague?

You can see that ethical problems require moral judgements that can be extremely difficult and depend on many different factors.

1.2 Fundamental principles

You will be familiar with the following fundamental ethical principles from your other studies.

Professional Competence and Due Care – The individual should possess the necessary professional knowledge and skills required to carry out the task.

Objectivity – Business or professional judgement should not be compromised because of bias or conflict of interest.

Professional Behaviour – The individual should comply with all relevant laws and regulations and avoid any actions that would bring the profession into disrepute.

Integrity – This implies fair dealing and truthfulness.

Confidentiality – Information obtained in a business relationship is not to be disclosed to third parties without specific authority to do so, unless there is a legal or professional reason for disclosure.

 Test your understanding 1

For each of the fundamental principles identify two ways that an organisation can adhere to them.

1.3 Why business ethics are important

Businesses are part of society. Society expects its individuals to behave properly and similarly expects companies to operate to certain standards. Business ethics is important to both the organisation and the individual.

For the organisation	For the individual
• Good ethics should be seen as a driver of profitability rather than a burden on business.	• Consumer and employee expectations have evolved over recent years.
• An ethical framework is part of good corporate governance and suggests a well-run business.	• Consumers may choose to purchase ethical items (e.g. Fairtrade coffee and bananas), even if they are not the cheapest.
• Investors are reassured about the company's approach to risk management.	• Employees will not blindly accept orders to act in a manner that they personally believe to be unethical.
• Employees will be motivated in the knowledge that they operate in an environment of good ethical corporate behaviour.	

1.4 Practical examples

Understanding the fundamental principles will enable you to see where the business may face issues which are not clear cut. There might not be a definitive right or wrong response. An ethical dilemma may be present.

An ethical dilemma involves a situation where a decision maker has to decide what is the 'right' or 'wrong' thing to do. Examples of ethical dilemmas can be found throughout all aspects of business operations, but we will focus on accounting issues within this chapter.

Accounting issues

- **Creative accounting** to boost or suppress reported profits. This can manifest itself in various ways. Transactions could be supressed if undesirable. The accounting treatment of a transaction could be manipulated (e.g. understate a provision) or transactions could be deliberately recorded in the wrong period. This would affect the performance and position shown by the key financial reports and therefore influence the stakeholders' understanding of that performance and position. This is all unethical.

- **Directors' pay** arrangements may come under scrutiny if the company is underperforming, and we may need to consider whether levels of directors' pay are justifiable.

- **Bribes** may be commonplace in certain countries in order to facilitate contracts, but bribes are generally forbidden in the UK. The view is that a bribe is used to benefit an individual at the expense of their organisation, which must be viewed as unethical. Clearly the accounting department has a role in this as all cash transactions must be accounted for.

- **Insider trading** concerns situations where, for example, directors are aware of sensitive information, which may affect the company's share price. They may be tempted to buy shares in the company knowing that the price is about to rise. The accounting system contains price sensitive information, and it is important that this is kept confidential from those who might benefit from it.

In Chapter 3 of this text, the area of internal controls was discussed. The prevention of the above ethical issues is encouraged by a robust system of internal control.

Production issues

We may need to consider whether the company should:

- produce certain products at all, e.g. guns, pornography, tobacco

- be concerned about the effects on the environment of its production processes

- test its products on animals.

Sales and marketing issues

We may need to consider whether the company should:

- engage in price-fixing or other anticompetitive behaviour, whether it is overtly illegal or subtler.

- target advertising at children, e.g. for fast food or for expensive toys at Christmas?

- advertise products by junk mail or spam email?

Personnel (HRM) issues

- Employees should not be favoured or discriminated against on the basis of gender, race, religion, age, disability, etc.

- The contract of employment must offer a fair balance of power between employee and employer.

- The workplace must be a safe and healthy place in which to work.

1.5   Corporate code of ethics

Most companies (especially if they are large) have approached the concept of business ethics by creating a set of internal policies and instructing employees to follow them. These policies can either be broad generalisations (a corporate ethics statement) or can contain specific rules (a corporate ethics code).

There is no standard list of content – it will vary between different organisations. Typically, however, it may contain guidelines on issues such as honesty, integrity and customer focus.

Many organisations appoint Ethics Officers (also known as Compliance Officers) to monitor the application of the policies and to be available to discuss ethical dilemmas with employees where needed.

 Example – Tesco plc

Tesco states that it is committed to conducting its business in an ethical manner, treating employees, customers, suppliers and shareholders in a fair and honest manner and ensuring that there are constant and open channels of communication.

Tesco has a code of ethics for its employees, including a policy on the receipt of gifts and a grievance procedure to cover employment issues.

Employees are able to ring a confidential telephone helpline to raise concerns about any failure to comply with legal obligations, health and safety issues, damage to the environment, etc.

1.6 Safeguards

Business organisations can also help to reduce the threat of ethical breaches by their employees by, amongst other things, having an effective internal complaints procedure that enables the reporting of unprofessional and unethical behaviour.

They can also create a culture that makes it as easy as possible for employees to follow their professional codes and behave ethically.

There are six values that organisations can apply in order to accomplish this. They can be easily remembered using the acronym HOTTER.

If these principles are part of an organisation's values, it will foster an ethical culture which will make breaches of the IFAC and AAT codes far less likely.

Honesty – employees should be encouraged to be honest at all times, even when this may be seen as detrimental to the organisation itself.

A salesperson should never overstate the benefits or features of the product they are selling.

Openness – this means that the organisation should be willing to freely provide information, as needed, to stakeholders.

This should make it easier for shareholders, for example, to decide whether to invest in the business or not.

Transparency – this is similar to openness in many ways and indicates that a company makes it easy for key stakeholders to review its activities.

This can be helped by regular audits and the production of detailed reports on business activities.

Trust – organisations need to be trustworthy in their dealings with others and attempt to work in the best interests of as many stakeholders as possible.

This could involve, for instance, not overcharging customers.

Empowerment – this involves giving employees and other stakeholders more ability to make their own decisions.

This will improve their self-image and their motivation.

Respect – all employees and stakeholders should be treated with dignity by the organisation regardless of their age, gender, ethnicity, religion or sexuality.

This could be embedded into the organisation by having a diversity policy in place.

KAPLAN PUBLISHING

2   Sustainability

2.1   What do we mean by 'sustainability'?

 Definitions of sustainability

There are a number of different definitions of sustainability:

- Sustainable development is development that meets the needs of the **present** without compromising the ability of **future** generations to meet their own needs.   *(The UN's Bruntland Report)*

- A sustainable business is a business that offers products and services that fulfil society's needs while placing an equal emphasis on people, planet and profits. *(The Sustainable Business Network)*

- Sustainable trading is a trading system that does not harm the environment or deteriorate social conditions while promoting economic growth.   *(European Union (EU) website)*

Sustainability can thus be thought of as an attempt to provide the best outcomes for the human and natural environments both now and into the indefinite future.

One aspect of this is the ability of the business to continue to exist and conduct operations with no effects on the environment that cannot be offset or made good in some other way.

Importantly, it refers to both the inputs and outputs of any organisational process.

- Inputs (resources) must only be consumed at a rate at which they can be reproduced, offset or in some other way not irreplaceably depleted.

- Outputs (such as waste and products) must not pollute the environment at a rate greater than can be cleared or offset.

Recycling is one way to reduce the net impact of product impact on the environment.

Firms should use strategies to neutralise these impacts by engaging in environmental practices that will replenish the used resources and eliminate harmful effects of pollution.

Example – Firms acting sustainably

- Some logging companies plant a tree for every one they fell.

- Coca Cola is one of the companies that have taken a stand in writing a corporate water strategy where they aim to return as much water to nature and communities as they use in their drinks.

- Apple tries to make its products easy to recycle, helping to ensure that materials are reused rather than wasted.

However, it is important to note that sustainability is more than just looking at environmental concerns. It relates to environmental ('planet'), social ('people') and economic ('profit') aspects of human society.

 Example – Unsustainable practices

Environmental

- deforestation

- the use of non-renewable resources including oil, gas and coal

- long-term damage from carbon dioxide and other greenhouse gases.

Social

- anything contributing to social injustice

- rich companies exploiting labour in developing countries for cheap manufacturing.

Economic

- strategies for short-term gain (e.g. cutting staff costs to increase reported profits)

- paying bribes (also unethical and often illegal)

- underpayment of taxes.

 Test your understanding 2

Why do you think the under-payment of taxes (by large businesses in particular) is considered to be an unsustainable practice?

2.2 Why businesses should act in a sustainable manner

Business sustainability is about ensuring that organisations implement strategies that contribute to long-term success.

Organisations that act in a sustainable manner not only help to maintain the well-being of the planet and people, they also create businesses that will survive and thrive in the long run.

In addition, it may be in the firm's **financial** interest to act sustainably.

 Example – How sustainability can boost profits

- Sustainability may help directly **increase sales** of products and services.

  For example, some customers may buy your product because a label on it says it has been manufactured using extra-safe working conditions for the labour force, or because it is Fairtrade.

- It may result in **cost savings**.

  For example, lower energy usage may reduce costs and increase profit.

- It may create **positive Public Relations (PR)** and thus contribute to business in the long run.

  While sustainability may not enhance product sales right away, if it enhances the image of a company which in turn contributes to better business in the long-term, then it's worth it.

- **Avoiding fines** for pollution.

  The Deepwater Horizon oil spill in 2006 resulted in BP being fined $4.5 billion by the US Department of Justice. However, it is estimated that the total cost to date is in excess of $42 billion in terms of criminal and civil settlements and payments to a trust fund.

Directors have a duty to try to increase the wealth of their shareholders and some would see sustainability as conflicting with this objective.

However, many would argue that sustainability should result in better business performance in the long run.

Example – Sustainability and business success

A 2012 working paper from Harvard Business School, '*The Impact Of A Corporate Culture Of Sustainability On Corporate Behaviour And Performance*', compared a sample of 180 US-based companies.

Over an 18-year period, those classified as high-sustainability companies dramatically outperformed the low-sustainability ones in terms of both stock market (i.e. share prices) and accounting measures, such as profit.

2.3 Sustainability and the accounting system

In this particular module we are looking at the accounting system. Sustainability considerations in this area would include within the accountancy department:

- The paperless office – how much of the paper used in the accounting department is justified?

- The energy usage for lights, the machines and for heating

- The use of sustainable materials for the office furniture

- The carbon footprint of the business

- Only travelling when necessary – holding meetings online as an alternative whenever possible.

'What gets measured gets done'

- The accountancy function can help champion sustainability by suggesting environmental key performance indicators and measuring these KPIs.

 Test your understanding 3

List three different actions an accounting department in a manufacturing company could do to improve the effect it has on society.

Test your understanding 4

Ravinder is a professional accountant working for Hoggs Furniture Ltd ('Hoggs'), a furniture manufacturer that supplies many high street retailers.

At the last management meeting it was announced that a major client of the company was threatening to terminate their contract with Hoggs unless Hoggs could demonstrate a clear commitment to sustainability.

The team were unclear what this meant for Hoggs and asked Ravinder to investigate further.

Required:

Explain FOUR areas that Hoggs should appraise in order to answer the client's concerns.

List THREE other ways Ravinder can contribute to sustainability through their role as an accountant.

2.4 The future

At the moment, there are no laws as to the level of sustainability an organisation should achieve. However, there are plans afoot to make it a compulsory requirement. Any organisation therefore that adopts a sound policy ahead of this legislation will find themselves ahead of the competition and be able to implement measures at their own speed.

It will not be easy to implement so it is important that senior management show that they embrace the ethos and lead by example. There is much to be done if we, of this generation, are to leave a bountiful legacy for the next.

Human beings, whether as individuals or organisations, cannot afford to use up all of the earth's resources and leave nothing for future generations but, by the same token, we must exist, prosper and consume. The key is balance.

Resources should be renewed in at least the same proportion as they are being consumed. Quality of life, for everyone, should be the goal while renewing the environment and resources, raising the standards of living in a community where all elements of resource, whether human, natural or economic, live in harmony.

Test your understanding 5

You work in the finance team of a well-known chain of fast food restaurants. There has been a lot of negative press recently about the responsibilities of such companies towards society.

Name five things you could suggest which would help to improve their image.

3 Summary

In this chapter we have explored the ethical and sustainability issues surrounding the accounting function of businesses.

Test your understanding answers

Test your understanding 1

The following are suggestions rather than an exhaustive list:

Professional competence and due care

- realistic targets, goals and deadlines
- training for all staff, relevant to their job role
- refresher courses for production personnel or those in Health and Safety (H&S)
- Continuing Professional Development (CPD) for all members of professional bodies
- quality supervision

Objectivity

- transparent tender/order process
- open-door promotions
- the Board of Directors not being under the control of one forceful character

Professional behaviour

- staff uniforms
- Health and Safety, Data Protection Act and accounting standards all complied with and up to date
- management lead by example and foster a professional attitude
- no gifts, bribes or other incentives allowed

Integrity

- equal pay for men and women
- evidence of a diversity policy
- transparent discount schemes for customers based on order quantities

Confidentiality

- confidential footer on emails
- restricted access to sensitive information

- passwords for every computer with a requirement to change it every so often.

- door codes and locks.

- bag searches.

- use of removable discs is prohibited.

- whistle-blowing policy with anonymous phone line.

- confidential information is dealt with on a 'need to know' basis.

- files and customer information is not allowed off the premises.

- privacy screens on computers where payroll information is being processed.

Please note that only two examples were required for each principle.

Test your understanding 2

Underpayment of tax is considered to be unsustainable as the organisations concerned are not contributing to maintaining the country's infrastructure (schools, roads, etc.).

Test your understanding 3

Manufacturing company accounting department

- set measurements to assist reducing its inputs and waste to more acceptable levels. This should be monitored year-on-year.

- authorise only the use of recyclable packaging wherever possible.

- assist in sourcing raw materials to more environmentally friendly ones where possible.

- implement Total Quality Management (TQM) policies.

- review machinery and equipment regularly to ensure efficiency.

- monitor pollution and emissions and aim to reduce them year-on-year.

Test your understanding 4

(a) Areas that Hoggs should appraise in order to answer the client's concerns include the following:

- Whether non-renewable hard woods are used in manufacture.

  The client would want reassurance that all materials are form renewable sources.

- The energy efficiency and level of emission of greenhouse gases due to the operation of the factory.

  While these cannot be eliminated altogether, the client would want to see evidence that Hoggs has taken steps to improve energy efficiency (e.g. thermal insulation, double glazing, installation of solar panels, etc.) or uses carbon offset schemes.

- Treatment of staff

  Sustainability is not just about environmental issues but also incorporates social (people) aspects. The client may want to know what Hoggs' record is concerning accidents, staff development, diversity, etc.

- Tax

  Economic sustainability includes factors such as whether the company is paying tax and so contributing to the local and national community.

(b) Other ways Ravinder can contribute to sustainability through their role as an accountant include the following:

- Helping create an ethics-based culture in Hoggs.

- By championing and promoting sustainability.

- By highlighting the risks of not acting sustainably and draw attention to reputational and other ethical risks.

- By incorporating targets and performance measures consistent with a sustainability approach.

Test your understanding 5

The fast food restaurant could:

- use fresh, wholesome ingredients which are sourced ethically

- eliminate the use of single-use plastic in straws

- stop including plastic toys in children's meals

- introduce healthier food onto the menu.

- publicise the dietary information to allow consumers to make their own choice

- fully train and develop staff so that they understand the significance of the product's, and the company's, impact on society

- develop strong ties with the community by holding fund-raising days, donating to local charities, etc.

- monitor waste and reduce levels year on year

- ensure that the supply chain is vetted and transparent

- review the logistics policy and see whether more efficient delivery methods could be used

MOCK ASSESSMENT

Mock Assessment Questions

DejaBrew Limited

Scenario

The tasks in this assessment are all based on the scenario of DejaBrew Ltd.

DejaBrew Ltd started life as an independent drinks manufacturer and retailer. DejaBrew has grown significantly since it started operating as a business.

Following this period of rapid expansion, DejaBrew Ltd have asked you, Michael Johnstone, an Accounting Technician, to review the processes of the company and identify weaknesses in the internal controls that may have occurred due to the recent growth of the company.

Company background

History

DejaBrew Ltd is a private limited company based in Aberdeen which produces and distributes a range of independent tea-based drinks.

The business began ten years ago when Elaine Thompson started a tea shop to support her through her time at University studying Chemistry. Elaine was so successful that she decided to expand the business by obtaining premises and manufacturing tea-based drinks.

Elaine was joined by her wife, Sally-Anne Fraser, who had recently completed a degree in Economics and Law and took over the day-to-day administration of the business while Elaine began to develop and produce her own range of new drinks and products.

Elaine and Sally-Anne decided to form DejaBrew Ltd. They bought a large warehouse on an industrial estate in Aberdeen and turned part of it into a production line for its variety of drinks and other tea-based merchandise.

Recent developments

DejaBrew Ltd has expanded rapidly over the last four years, through intense marketing activities and a successful online presence on popular social media sites. The company now employs several staff. DejaBrew focussed on expanding into other countries, starting with factories and warehouses in England. It has successfully opened manufacturing plants and distribution centres in Widnes, Grimsby and Reading.

In the last few months, the company has opened a second factory on its site in Reading and each site develops a range of bespoke products tailored towards its regional customers. The sites also produce limited special edition products linked to current affairs and events.

The company has also signed supply contracts with various high street retailers and supermarkets in addition to many existing deals with independent stores. Retail customers are also able to purchase directly from the company's website.

DejaBrew also opening a number of teashops, branded as DejaLing, in city centres and popular tourist towns in Britain and overseas, that only stock DejaBrew's own ranges of drinks and merchandise.

Sally-Anne had been researching recent developments in the industry and felt that the company would be able to expand more quickly if it raised finance by offering the ability to its customers to buy DejaBrew Ltd shares through Crowdfunding sources online. A launch of shares called 'Slice of the Cake' occurred two years ago, which was very successful, and new campaigns are now scheduled on an annual basis.

Resources

On 30 June 20X9, DejaBrew Ltd had 300 employees.

Department	Number of staff
Production, storage and distribution	168
Sales	32
Administration	48
Marketing	32
Design and development	20

Currently, the majority of employees are based at the Aberdeen site, which is where most of the production is carried out. However, this site is now operating at capacity, so production also occurs at the regional sites, focusing on the regional, bespoke products.

This has led to significant costs for the company and they are considering alternative ways of operating including researching the ways in which they could outsource production as a means to reduce costs.

Staff

Some of DejaBrew's key personnel are listed below:

Managing Director	Elaine Thompson
Operations Director	Sally-Anne Fraser
Finance Director	Linford Jackson
Production Director	Abdul Azad
Sales Director	Karsten Warholm
Financial Controller	Alison Dos Santos
Purchasing Manager	Xijing Tang
Aberdeen Warehouse Manager	Alan Wells
Transport Manager	Keely Hodgkinson
Credit Controller	Hattie Canny
Accounts Payable Clerk	Agnieszka Silvana
Accounts Receivable Clerk	Serena Serene
General Accounts Clerk and Cashier	Marcel Bruno
Payroll Clerk	Florence Joyner

Sustainability

DejaBrew Ltd recently faced some controversy due to social media groups and posts from anonymous workers that criticised working conditions and expectations across the company as well as claiming that working processes caused unnecessary wastage and damage to the environment.

In response to this, DejaBrew Ltd has published its commitment to sustainable development and improvements with regard to the economic, social and environmental aspects of its business.

The company has launched a comprehensive training programme for all employees which allows it to advance in workplace safety, productivity and satisfaction. It is also looking to develop by taking advantage of emerging new technologies. This training is especially important given the large influx of new members of staff.

In relation to the environment, DejaBrew Ltd is keen to make financial savings in water, waste and energy. DejaBrew Ltd has made a 'zero-carbon' pledge to reduce carbon emissions (with an aim to become 'carbon negative').

Task 1 (25 marks)

This task is about the purpose, structure and organisation of the accounting function.

You have been asked to review and develop a policy on ethics and sustainability for implementation over the next few years.

(a) (i) Identify whether each of the following would be a way to improve ethics and sustainability.

Statement	Would improve ✓	Would not improve ✓
Replace current bottled products with easier to recycle aluminium cans.		
For any new purchase of plant and equipment within the business, 3 tenders must be received to ensure a competitive price is achieved		
Adopting a new policy of a maximum numbers of hours that individual front-line staff can work per week		

(3 marks)

You are training Angus, a new junior accountant who is joining your team. You feel that in order to provide the best training to Angus, it is important that Angus understands the purpose of both internal and external accounting information. Angus has told you that he has recently studied stakeholders and the use of financial information.

(a) (ii) Identify which ONE of the following is an internal stakeholder.

Elaine Thompson ☐

Potential 'Slice of the Cake' investors ☐

Customers ☐

Suppliers ☐

(1 mark)

(a) **(iii)** **Complete the following statements about stakeholders and the use of financial information.**

The financial statements produced at the end of the year are for ___**GAP1**___ use. They can be used by the ___**GAP2**___ to enable them to make an informed decision regarding ___**GAP3**___ that will influence the continued employment of the directors.

Gap 1	✓
internal	
external	
the board of directors'	

Gap 2	✓
bank	
general public	
shareholders	

Gap 3	✓
a loan application	
continuing to sell on credit	
the stewardship of the company	

___**GAP 1**___ financial reports need to comply with the conceptual framework for financial reporting. If the business is looking to raise finance by applying for a loan, ___**GAP 2**___ will use the ___**GAP 3**___ to assess the business's liquidity before making the decision to lend.

Gap 1	✓
All	
Internal	
External	

Gap 2	✓
shareholders	
the bank	
directors	

Gap 3	✓
budgeted production report	
statement of cash flows	
the monthly analysis of expenses per department	

(6 marks)

A new working from home policy for non-production staff has been introduced to improve staff morale and as a way to save employees both time and money in respect of travel to work. Staff will need to ensure that appropriate data is kept securely and that data security regulations are not breached. To facilitate this process, DejaBrew will use cloud accounting.

(b) **(i)** **Identify whether the following statements relating to the software and hardware needed for the move to remote working are true or false.**

Statement	True ✓	False ✓
Remote working will create irreparable problems regarding document access and accessibility		
The use of cloud accounting will lead to savings in hardware costs.		
The use of cloud accounting will mean that businesses are more likely to lose data.		
There will no longer be a need for physical and password controls relating to laptop access as laptops will only ever be stored at the home of staff members.		

(4 marks)

As part of a review on data security, you have been working with Angus to review the data and operational security policy. Angus is unsure which type of risk the following circumstances demonstrate.

(b) (ii) Identify the correct risk for each statement below.

Statement	Risk
You have heard that Alison, who now works remotely, will often work all day out of a local coffee shop for a 'change of scenery'. When approached on this, Alison said 'It's a really nice atmosphere and very quiet. I only leave my laptop for a toilet or cigarette break. There are only ever 3 or 4 other people in the shop, so it's very safe'.	
Angus received an unusual email from a colleague's personal email address saying 'You won't believe what happened!' Angus needed to click on a link to find out what had occurred. Angus rarely works with the emailing staff member.	
Barry, your office cleaner, has unplugged the main server in order to plug in his phone charger.	
Agnieszka has decided to deactivate her antivirus software as it makes her PC too slow.	
Linford wanted to send the details of production worker salaries to a board member but accidentally sent it to a mailbox containing all employees of DejaBrew.	

Options
Unauthorised remote access
Phishing
Loss of data
Physical loss of equipment
Data breach

(5 marks)

The volume of data processed by DejaBrew has significantly increased as the levels of business have grown over the years. The approach to using the data at DejaBrew's disposal is complicated. Different levels of management need different levels of data. Angus is unsure about these management levels and the type of data relevant to each level. To assist Angus, you have produced a training document which includes a brief statement to describe the different types of management level and the information that each level will use.

(c)   (i)   Identify the corresponding information level to the described management roles within DejaBrew.

Management role	
Elaine Thompson chairs any board meetings where discussions regarding long-terms plans of DejaBrew occur. The Sales, Production and Operations Directors report their issues and findings to Elaine periodically at these meetings.	Gap 1
Alan Wells is responsible for the day-to-day running of the Aberdeen warehouse.	Gap 2
Abdul Azad is responsible for the assessment of performance and allocation of production resources to all locations.	Gap 3

Gap options	No.
Tactical level	
Strategic level	
Operational level	

(3 marks)

(c) (ii) **Identify the correct information option that corresponds with the described information available within DejaBrew**

Data available	
Weekly budget production outputs and staff shift pattern planner reports.	Gap 1
Annual budget versus actual production outputs per unit and canning machine utilisation percentage reports.	Gap 2
Profit or loss and cash flow forecasts spanning a 5 year period used to help plan the timing of investments in machinery and new locations for factories and teashops.	Gap 3

(3 marks)

Gap options	No.
Tactical information	
Strategic information	
Operational information	

Task 2   **(25 marks)**

This task is about the types of fraud in the workplace combined with ways in which it can be detected and prevented.

In addition to the manufacturing locations, DejaBrew Ltd has many teashops across the country. Due to the number of locations it is not possible for the Senior Management team to attend all the inventory counts but local management have clear counting instructions and report back to head office.

DejaBrew Ltd's warehouses are operational 24 hours a day, receiving raw materials from suppliers and despatching them to their factories, as well as receiving finished goods from the factories before despatching them to customers and teashops. The company uses a courier service for all its outward deliveries. Due to the volume of business involved, when the courier driver arrives for a collection, the warehouse receptionist passes them the Goods Delivery Notes (GDNs) and directs them to the appropriate area of the warehouse, where they are expected to load the inventory onto their vehicles themselves.

In order to give customers time to sort any issues arising such as missing or damaged items, all customers are allowed a 30 day credit period. In order to ensure that inventory records are kept up-to-date, inventory counts are completed by the local staff, who then make any necessary adjustments to the inventory records.

(a) Complete the following statements.

The above may result in the occurrence of ___GAP 1___ fraud, that occurs as a result of ___GAP 2__

In order to address this risk DejaBrew need to implement ___GAP 3___ as soon as possible. This will ensure that the impact on ___GAP 4___ is minimised.

Gap 1	✓	Gap 2	✓
e-crime		lack of controls	
misappropriation of assets		lack of interest	
misstatement of financial statements		lack of a risk matrix	
Gap 3	**✓**	**Gap 4**	**✓**
a series of physical controls		liabilities	
segregation of duties		income	
authorisation and approval processes		assets	

(4 marks)

Sally-Anne Fraser, Operations Director, has noted that unfavourable discrepancies between budgeted and actual income, cash and inventory levels have been reported in recent management reports from the DejaLing section of the business.

She has ordered a review into the processes within the DejaLing sites.

The following issues have been reported back to Sally-Anne:

(1) Customers can order cases of drinks (via the DejaBrew website) for 'click and collect' at their local DejaLing teashop. Teashops store these deliveries in a small, unlocked stockroom at the back of the teashop. Once customers have provided staff with a reference number for their order, the customers are left to collect their order from the stockroom themselves.

(2) DejaLing customers pay with cash or card when buying drinks or food. Orders are placed via an app for table service or at the counter. Each teashop has two online till systems to place orders, payments and issue refunds and a number of PDQ machines to take card payments. Each staff member has a unique access code for the till log in, which must be entered before transactions can be posted. In busy times, staff are known to share their codes and will process transactions using the code of other staff members.

(3) Nightly reconciliations of the till records compared to the cash takings and card receipts from PDQ machines are performed by the branch managers once the teashops have shut. Branch managers often serve customers during the shifts when the teashops are busy. As teashops often close late, branch managers will take cash takings home before banking the next day.

(4) Deliveries are signed for by the branch managers. Inventory counts for each branch should occur on the last Saturday before month-end, prior to opening. They are performed by the branch managers, who provide a monthly inventory report to operational regional managers. It has been reported that a number of branch managers actually perform the counts once the teashop has opened on a Saturday to avoid coming in early.

(b) (i) Identify FOUR weaknesses in the system that may result in fraud occurring.

(4 marks)

(b) (ii) Recommend an internal control for EACH weakness, giving a reason why it would help to prevent fraud.

(8 marks)

Weakness that may result in fraud	Internal control to help prevent fraud	Reason it will help prevent fraud

You work within the Accounts department. During your AAT studies, you learned about recording fraud risk on a fraud matrix. A number of areas where you feel that fraud may be possible are described below and you need to complete the fraud matrix.

(c) Identify the appropriate rating for each of the situations given below.

Rating	Situation
Option 1	When the business first opened the accounts were prepared by a local accountancy firm in Aberdeen. However, due to the speed of growth of the business, DejaBrew soon required an internal accounts department. This has been operating for a number of years and staff turnover is low. The business uses a well-established accounting software package across all the different functions of the business. The performance of the accountancy package is regularly reviewed and the system regularly updated.
Option 2	DejaBrew Ltd are reviewing the payroll system and discover that there is a high turnover of staff, particularly in the DejaLing sites and the warehouses. DejaLing's staffing levels fluctuate during peak and off-peak seasons. As a result, lots of temporary staff are hired during peak times such as Christmas and during summer. Temporary staff are sometimes paid in cash.
Option 3	DejaBrew Ltd acknowledge the need for staff within each department to be well-trained for their role. Initially, training was provided to ensure that at least two people within each department were trained for each role, to provide cover for holidays and sickness. As the business has become more cost-conscious, this has been felt to be extravagant, so it has now been decided to only train one person for each role.

Options

5 – Very high
3 – Medium
1 – Very low

(3 marks)

You have discussed the system of ordering and accepting goods into the warehouse with Alan Wells, the Warehouse Manager. You have identified the following risk with this system:

- Goods delivered are unloaded by couriers at the entrance to the warehouse, where they are later checked for quantity and damage, before being transferred into the warehouse. Alan admits that deliveries often appear to be short or damaged.

(d) **Outline how you can MONITOR, REVIEW and REPORT on the risk described.** **(6 marks)**

Task 3 **(10 marks)**

This task is about the effectiveness of internal controls.

Having recently completed your studies, you know that you have an extensive knowledge of internal controls and the benefits of a robust system. Having reviewed the current system, you have been asked a number of questions by Marcel Bruno, General Accounts Clerk and Cashier. Marcel wants to check that he fully understands what internal controls are and how they work. Marcel has asked you to check that the internal controls suggested are suitable for the identified purpose.

(a) Identify whether the following internal controls are suitable for the purpose given.

Internal control	Purpose	Is the internal control suitable? ✓
Ensuring all new staff members must complete pre-employment checks before employment and payments can only occur via the official monthly payroll (therefore forbidding cash payments)	Compliance	Yes ☐ No ☐
All deliveries received checked to supplier delivery note, then entered onto Goods Received Note (GRN), signed as checked by recipient. Sample of GRNs checked to confirm.	Safeguard assets	Yes ☐ No ☐
Complete regular cash and bank reconciliations, reviewed and signed by responsible person.	Ensure quality internal and external reporting	Yes ☐ No ☐
Fire safety systems are installed in each location – e.g. automatic heat and smoke triggered sprinkler systems	Prevent and detect fraud	Yes ☐ No ☐

(4 marks)

Due to the negative press arising from the ex-employee's social media campaign, DejaBrew Ltd is keen to develop and maintain a reputation for ethical behaviour. Following a review of the finance department, it has been identified that some of the systems in place do not promote ethical behaviours.

You have been presented with the following improvements to the system to address this.

(b)   Identify which of the following would promote ethical behaviours within an organisation.

Improvement	Promote ✓	Would not promote ✓
Staff bonus scheme to be introduced that rewards staff for increasing revenue on their customer accounts.		
Ensure that ethical codes are included in corporate objectives and shared as company policy.		
Ensure that all new starters sign a non-disclosure agreement that prevents staff from posting negative comments about DejaBrew online.		
Every staff member has the ability to utilise fully-paid volunteer days (e.g. at local charities).		
When recruiting for vacant positions within the department, managers should ensure that recruitment and promotion is restricted to those above the age of 25 and below the age of 60.		
Ensure that all new starters are given a copy of the disciplinary process as part of their induction.		

(6 marks)

Task 4 **(15 marks)**

This task is about the monitoring of accounting systems and how they work in practice.

The current systems for retail customers (other than DejaLing customers) to place orders and for sales to be recorded are:

- orders are placed using DejaBrew's website (using customer log-ins).

- all orders are processed by the sales department who do not require an order number.

- all customers are given a 30 day credit account to ensure that they place repeat orders.

- sales orders are passed to the warehouse where they are packed ready for collection, either by the courier or by local customers.

- deliveries are made by a national courier.

- on collection, couriers sign a goods despatched note (GDN) which is retained by Alan Wells (Warehouse Manager) to enable him to resolve any customer queries in respect of damage or shortage.

- proofs of delivery (including mobile device photos where necessary) are provided by the courier to Alan Wells. Alan stores them at the warehouse for reference. Any returned goods are placed back into the warehouse.

- no GDN or proof of delivery is obtained for those local customers who collect in person.

- invoices are prepared by the accounts department and issued by the sales department once the goods are despatched. Serena Serene, the Accounts Receivable Clerk, enters the invoices into the accounting system.

- at the end of each month Serena sends out customer statements.

- Serena opens the post each morning and banks any cheques received. She also reviews the online banking system for any direct credits from customers. Serena then enters the receipts into the accounting system, and to the relevant customer accounts.

(a) Analyse the potential deficiencies in the system outlined above, together with their cause AND impact.

(10 marks)

Linford Jackson decided that a thorough review of cash controls across the business is needed. The last time a similar review occurred was 24 months ago. One of the staff recently queried why this was needed, and said 'I don't see the point in having to do all this work again. We've done it once. The controls were perfectly adequate then, and there's no chance mistakes or fraud can occur with those control procedures in place.'

(b) Identify the correct response to complete the gaps below.

The control systems need to be reviewed to ensure that the controls…	Gap 1	which may have occurred because…	Gap 2

Gap 1	✓
have not become obsolete	
prevent and detect every incidence of fraud and error	

Gap 2	✓
of the low turnover of staff.	
of the rapid growth of the business.	

(2 marks)

(c) Identify whether the following statements are true or false.

Statement	True ✓	False ✓
Management override of controls shows a strong control environment		
As DejaBrew has its own accounts department, it cannot outsource any of its accounting activities to third parties e.g. payroll, control reviews.		
To work in an accounting department, staff must be fully qualified accountants		

(3 marks)

Task 5 (25 marks)

This task is about the analysis of internal controls with recommendations to improve whilst considering the impact on users.

You are Marcel Bruno, the General Accounts Clerk.

DejaBrew is looking to continue with the recent rapid expansion and Elaine Thompson (Managing Director) believes that the way to achieve this will be through expansion of its existing regional products.

The current system for costing a new regional product requires the costing to be produced manually, causing significant delay in the production of these popular products. Linford Jackson, the Finance Director, believes that there are increased risks of inaccuracy when using manual costings.

Research seems to indicate that the most suitable tailored costing system is one called BAGZ. The cost of this research was £12,000.

You would need to attend a two-day training course charged at £900 per day. The Production Manager and Warehouse Manager would also need to attend the course. As the Production Manager is not currently very IT literate, the Production Manager needs one additional day of training.

The BAGZ system would require new hardware to run it, so Elaine has decided to upgrade all DejaBrew Ltd's hardware will be updated to ensure maximum capacity and integration. This will result in a cost of £165,000 per annum for the hardware. The software will have a total annual licence fee of £52,000.

On reviewing the potential benefits of the new system you have identified that:

- a permanent decrease in inventory holding of raw materials of £32,000 will be possible

- less overtime will be needed by both production and finance staff, with monthly management reports produced more quickly

- a customer focus group with total orders of the standard beverage product totalling £620,000 were shown the new system and have decided to switch their orders to regional bespoke products at a value of £880,000.

(a) (i) Complete a financial cost-benefit analysis for the above proposal.

Costs	£
Benefits	**£**
(Net Cost)/Benefit (£)	

(6 marks)

(a) (ii) Identify SIX non-financial factors that should be taken into account as part of the cost-benefit analysis.

(6 marks)

(a) (iii) Recommend, with TWO reasons, whether or not the proposed investment should be made.

As an additional task, and in preparation for the potential changes needed if the new system is introduced, you have also been looking at benefits of implementing new systems.

(b) (i) Identify which FOUR of the following would be considered to be tangible benefits of changing the information system.

Benefit	✓
Improved customer service	
Quicker decision-making	
Savings in maintenance costs	
More time for strategic planning	
Reduced inventory levels	
Competitive advantage though lower costs	
Reduced staff overtime	
Better understanding of customer needs	

(4 marks)

(b) (ii) Identify whether the following characteristics are associated with running a new system in parallel with the old system.

Characteristic	Associated ✓	Not associated ✓
More expensive than alternative methods of implementation		
The business must ensure that the new system is working perfectly before commencing parallel running		
Increases confidence in results from the new system		
Eases the processing workload		
Increases risk for the main roll out		
Can cause increased stress amongst staff		

(6 marks)

Mock Assessment Answers

Task 1 **(25 marks)**

(a) **(i)** **Identify whether each of the following would be a way to improve ethics and sustainability.**

Statement	Would improve ✓	Would not improve ✓
Replace current bottled products with easier to recycle aluminium cans.	✓	
For any new purchase of plant and equipment within the business, 3 tenders must be received to ensure a competitive price is achieved		✓
Adopting a new policy of a maximum numbers of hours that individual front-line staff can work per week	✓	

(3 marks)

(a) **(ii)** **Identify which ONE of the following is an internal stakeholder.**

Elaine Thompson (who is a director) ☑

Potential 'Slice of the Cake' investors ☐

Customers ☐

Suppliers ☐

(1 mark)

(a) (iii) **Complete the following statements about stakeholders and the use of financial information.**

The financial statements produced at the end of the year are for ___GAP 1___ use. They can be used by the ___GAP 2___ to enable them to make an informed decision regarding ___GAP 3___ that will influence the continued employment of the directors.

Gap 1	✓
internal	
external	✓
the board of directors'	

Gap 3	✓
a loan application	
continuing to sell on credit	
the stewardship of the company	✓

Gap 2	✓
bank	
general public	
shareholders	✓

___GAP 1___ financial reports need to comply with the conceptual framework for financial reporting. If the business is looking to raise finance by applying for a loan, ___GAP 2___ will use the ___GAP 3___ to assess the business' liquidity before making the decision to lend.

Gap 1	✓
All	
Internal	
External	✓

Gap 3	✓
budgeted production report	
statement of cash flows	✓
the monthly analysis of expenses per department	

Gap 2	✓
shareholders	
the bank	✓
directors	

(6 marks)

(b) (i) Identify whether the following statements relating to the software and hardware needed for the move to remote working are true or false.

Statement	True ✓	False ✓
Remote working will create irreparable problems regarding document access and accessibility		✓
The use of cloud accounting will lead to savings in hardware costs.	✓	
The use of cloud accounting will mean that businesses are more likely to lose data.		✓
There will no longer be a need for physical and password controls relating to laptop access as laptops will only ever be stored at the home of staff members.		✓

Cloud accounting should enable the staff to access documents even at home.

(4 marks)

(b) (ii) Identify the correct risk for each statement below.

Statement	Risk
You have heard that Alison, who now works remotely, will often work all day out of a local coffee shop for a 'change of scenery'. When approached on this, Alison said 'It's a really nice atmosphere and very quiet. I only leave my laptop for a toilet or cigarette break. There are only ever 3 or 4 other people in the shop, so it's very safe'.	Physical loss of equipment (1)
Angus received an unusual email from a colleague's personal email address saying 'You won't believe what happened!' Angus needed to click on a link to find out what had occurred. Angus rarely works with the emailing staff member.	Phishing (1)
Barry, your office cleaner, has unplugged the main server in order to plug in his phone charger.	Loss of data (1)
Agnieszka has decided to deactivate her antivirus software as it makes her PC too slow.	Unauthorised remote access (1)
Linford wanted to send the details of production worker salaries to a board member but accidentally sent it to a mailbox containing all employees of DejaBrew.	Data breach (1)

(5 marks)

(c) (i) Identify the corresponding information level to the described management roles within DejaBrew

Elaine Thompson chairs any board meetings where discussions regarding long-terms plans of DejaBrew occur. The Sales, Production and Operations Directors report their issues and findings to Elaine periodically at these meetings	Strategic level (1)
Alan Wells is responsible for the day to day running of the Aberdeen warehouse	Operational level (1)
Abdul Azad is responsible for the assessment of performance and allocation of production resources to all locations	Tactical level (1)

(3 marks)

(c) (ii) Identify the correct information option that corresponds with the described information available within DejaBrew

Data available	
Weekly budget production outputs and staff shift pattern planner reports.	Operational information (1)
Annual budget versus actual production outputs per unit and canning machine utilisation percentage reports.	Tactical information (1)
Profit or loss and cash flow forecasts spanning a 5 year period used to help plan the timing of investments in machinery and new locations for factories and teashops.	Strategic information (1)

(3 marks)

Task 2 (25 marks)

(a) **Complete the following statement by selecting the correct options to complete the gaps below.**

The above may result in the occurrence of ___GAP 1___ fraud, that occurs as a result of ___GAP 2__

In order to address this risk DejaBrew need to implement ___GAP 3___ as soon as possible. This will ensure that the impact on ___GAP 4___ is minimised.

Gap 1	✓
e-crime	
misappropriation of assets	✓
misstatement of financial statement	

Gap 2	✓
lack of controls.	✓
lack of interest.	
lack of a risk matrix.	

Gap 3	✓
a series of physical controls	✓
segregation of duties	
authorisation and approval processes	

Gap 4	✓
liabilities	
income	
assets	✓

(4 marks)

(b) (i) **Identify FOUR weaknesses in the system that may result in fraud occurring.**

(4 marks)

(b) (ii) **Recommend an internal control for EACH weakness, giving a reason why it will help prevent fraud.**

(8 marks)

Weakness: 1 mark per weakness, max 4 marks Marks will not be given for generic responses, must link to the given scenario	Internal control: 1 mark for internal control. Max 4 marks Marks will not be given for generic responses, must link to the weakness given	Reason: 1 mark for the reason it will help prevent fraud. Max 4 marks
Customers collect their own orders from the stock room. (1)	Physical security over inventory/stock. (1) OR Always have a member of staff in the stockroom to supervise/collect the order. (1) OR Ensure customers are not left unattended (1) OR Stock room should be locked with a key pad on the door(s). (1)	Prevents theft or damage to inventory. (1) OR Ensures that items are secure and will remain undamaged. (1) OR Ensures access is restricted only to authorised individuals. (1)
Staff sharing access codes will make errors/ fraud more difficult to trace (1). OR Sharing codes increases the risk of: – theft from the till – inappropriate refunds – errors being unnoticed or untraceable. (1)	Branch managers should review the outputs per access code at the end of each shift. (1) OR Have a published policy stating how sharing codes is not authorised and staff will be disciplined. (1) OR Appoint managers to monitor staff procedures and ensure at least one manager is working on each shift. (1)	This will identify if certain staff have unusually high/low orders during a shift which would indicate that staff are involved in code sharing. (1) OR Disciplining staff who are caught sharing codes will act as a deterrent. (1) OR Management supervision can help prevent inaccurate till log ins. (1)

Lack of segregation of duties within the role of a branch manager (1) OR Branch managers are responsible for: – serving and taking customer payments – reconciling the tills each night – banking the cash takings – reconciling inventory (1) OR This increases the risk of branch managers being able to cover their tracks after committing fraud through theft of inventory or cash (1)	Segregation of duties required: – having different staff members on the till, branch managers on the till reconciliations and on the bank runs (1) – ensuring that inventory counts are performed in teams of pairs. (1)	This should ensure that the person involved in the till reconciliations has not been working on the till. (1) Inventory counting in teams of pairs prevents the risk of deliberate miscounting (1)
Cash is taken home by branch managers before banking. (1)	All cash must be kept in a safe within the store premises. (1) Banking runs must take place in pairs. (1)	This reduces the risk of theft and fraud by branch managers or third parties (1)
Inventory counts should be made at off-peak times or when the teashops are closed. (1) OR Performing inventory counts during opening hours increases the risk of theft/fraud of goods, as counts will be inaccurate and theft may be unnoticed. (1)	Retrain branch managers to ensure all staff know that inventory counts must be performed prior to opening (1). Regional management should perform random spot checks on days when the inventory counts are due. (1).	Staff understanding of why it is required will be enhanced. (1) Regional management checks ensure the counts are performed before opening. (1)

(12 marks)

KAPLAN PUBLISHING

(c) **Identify the appropriate rating for each of the situations given below.**

Rating	Situation
Low (1)	When the business first opened the accounts were prepared by a local accountancy firm in Aberdeen. However, due to the speed of growth of the business, DejaBrew soon required an internal accounts department. This has been operating for a number of years and staff turnover is low. The business uses a well-established accounting software package across all the different functions of the business. The performance of the accountancy package is regularly reviewed and the system regularly updated.
High (1)	DejaBrew Ltd are reviewing the payroll system and discover that there is a high turnover of staff, particularly in the DejaLing sites and the warehouses. DejaLing's staffing levels fluctuate during peak and off-peak seasons. As a result, lots of temporary staff are hired during peak times such as Christmas and during summer. Temporary staff are sometimes paid in cash.
Medium (1)	DejaBrew Ltd acknowledge the need for staff within each department to be well-trained for their role. Initially, training was provided to ensure that at least two people within each department were trained for each role, to provide cover for holidays and sickness. As the business has become more cost-conscious, this has been felt to be extravagant, so it has now been decided to only train one person for each role.

(3 marks)

(d) Outline how you can MONITOR, REVIEW and REPORT on the risk described.

Risk	Monitor	Review	Report
No system to check and record items delivered. Deliveries may: – include incorrect items/quantity of items – be damaged, – be stolen prior to being transferred into the warehouse.	Volume of goods damaged on delivery (1) Volume of theft of goods that are awaiting transfer to storage (using delivery note matching) (1) Compare how much have Dejabrew ordered and how much have been recorded (1)	Check order against delivery note, invoice, PDB, PL, remittance and payment details (1) Perform internal audit /walk through test to identify weaknesses where additional controls are necessary(1) Purchase order matched to invoice in accounts department (1) Inconsistencies checked with supplier (1)	Produce table/chart that shows potential shortages, loss of inventory (1) Report of under/over inventory discovered on the count (1) Produce table/chart that shows inventory written off due to damage (1)

(6 marks)

Task 3   **(10 marks)**

(a) Identify whether the following internal controls are suitable for the purpose given.

Internal control	Purpose	Is the internal control suitable? ✓	
Ensuring all new staff members must complete pre-employment checks before employment and payments can only occur via the official monthly payroll (therefore forbidding cash payments)	Compliance	Yes	✓
		No	
All deliveries received checked to supplier delivery note, then entered onto Goods Received Note (GRN), signed as checked by recipient. Sample of GRNs checked to confirm.	Safeguard assets	Yes	✓
		No	
Complete regular cash and bank reconciliations, reviewed and signed by responsible person.	Ensure quality internal and external reporting	Yes	✓
		No	
Fire safety systems are installed in each location – e.g. automatic heat and smoke triggered sprinkler systems	Prevent and detect fraud	Yes	
		No	✓

(4 marks)

(b) **Identify which of the following would promote ethical behaviours within an organisation.**

Improvement	Promote ✓	Would not promote ✓
Staff bonus scheme to be introduced that rewards staff for increasing revenue on their customer accounts.		✓
Ensure that ethical codes are included in corporate objectives and shared as company policy.	✓	
Ensure that all new starters sign a non-disclosure agreement that prevents staff from posting negative comments about DejaBrew online.		✓
Every staff member has the ability to utilise fully-paid volunteer days (e.g. at local charities).	✓	
When recruiting for vacant positions within the department, managers should ensure that recruitment and promotion is restricted to those above the age of 25 and below the age of 60.		✓
Ensure that all new starters are given a copy of the disciplinary process as part of their induction.	✓	

(6 marks)

Task 4 (15 marks)

(a) **Analyse the potential deficiencies in the system outlined above, together with their cause AND impact.**

Indicative content

Deficiencies

- No order numbers

- Orders are not matched to delivery notes, which are not matched to invoices

- No credit checks done by accounts department before allowing credit

- Warehouse do not receive signed delivery notes as proof of collection by local customers

- Signed delivery notes are not passed to the accounts department

- Accounts department is not informed about returns or damaged goods

- Serena has full responsibility for recording of invoices, payments and statements

Causes

- No formal ordering system – should use order numbers

- No formal procedure for granting of credit

- No formal system for recording shortages or damaged goods

- No segregation of duties, notably within sales ledger

- No formal procedure to ensure that all orders result in an invoice

Impact

- Incorrect orders may be delivered

- Invoices may be for the incorrect goods or amount

- Potential manipulation of sales ledger accounts by accounts receivable clerk, could create fake accounts

- Poor relationship with or loss of customers due to delivery disputes

- Unrecorded sales – no integrated system for orders, deliveries and invoices. All completed separately, so potential for omissions

Other relevant points may be considered.

Descriptors
0 marks – No response worthy of credit.
1 – 3 marks Attempts one of the three sections (deficiency/cause/impact) OR limited detail on deficiency and cause with no meaningful evaluation. Identifies deficiencies in current system with some explanation.
4 – 7 marks Attempts two out of three sections. Causes and/or impact must link to deficiency identified, some reference to the scenario included in response. Demonstrates a reasonable understanding of potential issues as a result of poor internal controls.
8 – 10 marks Attempts all three sections. Deficiency, cause and impact must link to each other and have strong links to the scenario. Demonstrates a good understanding of potential issues as a result of poor internal controls. To achieve top marks for this band, the response will include a thorough evaluation, linked to the scenario. Overall demonstration of excellent understanding of the potential issues and the impact of poor internal controls.

(10 marks)

(b) Identify the correct options to complete the gaps below.

The control systems need to be reviewed to ensure that the controls…	Gap 1	which may have occurred because…	Gap 2

Gap 1	✓
have not become obsolete	✓
prevent and detect every incidence of fraud and error	

Gap 2	✓
of the low turnover of staff.	
of the rapid growth of the business.	✓

(2 marks)

 KAPLAN PUBLISHING

(c)   Identify whether the following statements are true or false.

Statement	True ✓	False ✓
Management override of controls shows a strong control environment		✓
As DejaBrew has its own accounts department, it cannot outsource any of its accounting activities to third parties e.g. payroll, control reviews.		✓
To work in an accounting department, staff must be fully qualified accountants		✓

(3 marks)

Task 5 (25 marks)

(a) (i) Complete a financial cost-benefit analysis for the above proposal.

Costs	£	Marking
Training course 2 days × 3 people × £900 plus one extra day £900	6,300	1 × mark for correct cost identified and correct figure
IT equipment	165,000	1 × mark for correct cost identified and correct figure
Licence fee	52,000	1 × mark for correct cost identified and correct figure
Benefits	**£**	
Inventory holding	32,000	1 × mark for correct cost identified and correct figure
Increase in sales (880 – 620)	260,000	1 × mark for correct cost identified and correct figure
(Net Cost)/Benefit (£)	68,700 (benefit)	1 × mark for correct figure AND specifying whether cost or benefit (OFR applies unless alien items included)

(6 marks)

KAPLAN PUBLISHING

(a) (ii) Identify SIX non-financial factors that should be taken into account as part of the cost-benefit analysis.

1 x mark for reference to any points below: max 6 marks

- Improved speed of costing (1)
- Impact of additional IT training? (1)
- Will existing staff be able to use the new system? (1)
- Will staff be happy with less overtime? (1)
- Will reduced overtime improve DejaBrew's reputation as an ethical employer (work-life balance) (1)
- How quickly will new system get up to speed (learning curve)? (1)
- How will we switch from the current system to the new one? (1)
- Better information for informed management decisions (1)

Other relevant points may attract marks

(6 marks)

(a) (iii) Recommend, with TWO reasons, whether or not the proposed investment should be made.

1 x mark for recommendation: 2 marks for supporting explanation – max 3 marks

Recommendation:

Yes, the proposed investment should be made (OFR based on own calculations) and fits with reasons below (1)

Reasons:

Increased sales (1)

Reduced costs (1)

Cost-benefit analysis shows net benefit (1)

Improved speed of costing (1)

Improved reporting (1)

Improved ethical reputation due to reduced working hours (1)

OR

Recommendation:

No, the proposed investment should not be made (OFR based on own calculations) and fits with reasons below (1)

Reasons:

Staff unrest – reduced overtime (1)

Staff unrest – fear of change (1)

Difficulty implementing (1)

Staff may not be able to use the new system (1)

(3 marks)

As an additional task, and in preparation for the potential changes needed if the new system is introduced, you have also been looking at benefits of implementing new systems.

(b) (i) Identify which FOUR of the following would be considered to be tangible benefits of changing the information system.

Concern	✓
Improved customer service	
Quicker decision-making	
Savings in maintenance costs	✓
More time for strategic planning	
Reduced inventory levels	✓
Competitive advantage though lower costs	✓
Reduced staff overtime	✓
Better understanding of customer needs	

(4 marks)

KAPLAN PUBLISHING

(b) (ii) Identify whether the following characteristics are associated with running a new system in parallel with the old system.

Characteristic	Associated ✓	Not associated ✓
More expensive than alternative methods of implementation	✓	
The business must ensure that the new system is working perfectly before commencing parallel running		✓
Increases confidence in results from the new system	✓	
Eases the processing workload		✓
Increases risk for the main roll out		✓
Can cause increased stress amongst staff	✓	

(6 marks)

INDEX